THE BICYCLE AND CITY TRAFFIC

The Bicycle and City Traffic

Principles and Practice

Edited by
Hugh McClintock

Belhaven Press
London
Copublished in the Americas by Halsted Press,
an imprint of John Wiley & Sons, Inc., New York

Belhaven Press
(a division of Pinter Publishers)
25 Floral Street, London, WC2E 9DS, United Kingdom

First published in 1992

Copublished in the Americas by Halsted Press, an imprint of
John Wiley & Sons, Inc., 605 Third Avenue, New York, NY 10158–0012, USA

British Library Cataloguing in Publication Data

A CIP catalogue record for this book is available from the British Library.

ISBN 1 85293 198 1 (UK)

Library of Congress Cataloging in Publication Data

The Bicycle and city traffic: principles and practice/edited by Hugh McClintock.
  p. cm.
  Includes bibliographical references and index.
  ISBN 0–470–21928–9
  1. Bicycles – Cross-cultural studies. 2. City traffic – Cross-cultural studies. I.
McClintock, Hugh.
HE5736.B52 1992
388.3'472–dc20   92–20664
                                                                       CIP

ISBN 0470–21928–9 (in the Americas only)

Typeset by Mayhew Typesetting, Rhayader, Powys
Printed and bound in Great Britain by Biddles Ltd., Guildford and King's Lynn

Contents

List of figures

List of tables

Notes on contributors

Tilman Bracher studied economics and transportation in Freiburg (Germany) and London. He has worked with the Berlin IVU (Gesellschaft für Informationsverarbeitung und Verkehrsberatung und angewandte Unternehmensforschung mbH) Consultancy since 1985 and is the author of a basic book on *Concepts for Bicycle Transportation (Konzepte für den Radverkehr)*, which was published in 1987. He works as an expert on transportation planning and research in the fields of cycling, public transport, freight transport and integrated planning. This work has included studies on bicycle transportation for the European Commission (*Comparative Policies and Provision for Cyclists in Europe*, published in 1987) and the German Federal Ministry of Transport, published in 1991 (see Bracher et al., 1991, at end of Chapter 1). Since 1982 he has been involved in the Germany Cycling Campaign, ADFC (Allgemeiner Deutscher Fahrradclub), and is the editor of the ADFC's twice-monthly *Bicycle Research Report*.

Ian Chatfield trained as a civil engineer and since 1978 has been responsible for traffic management, including the development of the Nottingham Cycleway Route network, in the Nottingham city area. He is also the Executive Director of the International Velo City '93 Conference.

Andrew Clarke is a Project Manager with the Bicycle Federation of America, where he has worked since 1990. Prior to this he worked for the League of American Wheelmen, a national membership group, Friends of the Earth in England, and the European Cyclists' Federation. He manages the National Bicycle Program Campaign and National Bicycle Policy Project for the BFA.

Johanna Cleary is a Research Assistant at the Institute of Planning Studies, Nottingham University, where she has been working since 1990 on an evaluation of cyclists' safety and cycle planning in Greater Nottingham. This has been funded by the Nottinghamshire County Council University Research Fund, the Rees Jeffreys Road Fund and the Cycle Touring and Countryside Trust. From 1988–90 she was National Rights and Planning Officer for the Cyclists' Touring Club and is still a member of the CTC's Transport and Road Safety Advisory Committee. She is also a former member of the Management Committee of the European Cyclists' Federation, and a member of the Labour Party's Advisory Group on Transport Policy (1990–92).

Hans Jul Jacobsen graduated in Civil Engineering at the Technical University of Denmark and worked on road projects at the Danish Road Department in Copenhagen and abroad. Since 1978 he has been City Chief Engineer at the City Council of Odense (population 180,000). In this period a new traffic plan, including cycle routes, has been carried out in the city centre.

Nick Lester is London Parking Manager and was until 1992 the Planning and Transport Officer for the Association of London Authorities. Although originally trained as an architect, he is a qualified transport planner. For some years he was Executive Director of Transport 2000, the transport and environment group, and before working for the ALA, he worked for the former Greater London Council as a policy advisor in both transport and industrial development. He was a founder member and the first chair of the London Cycling Campaign and also a founder member of the European Cyclists' Federation.

Hugh McClintock is a Lecturer at the Institute of Planning Studies at Nottingham University. He has been extensively involved, in association with the Nottingham Cycling Campaign, 'Pedals', in the planning and implementation of local cycling schemes, and has been responsible for several studies of these. He is maintaining a national and international database for the Local Authorities Cycle Planning Group in the UK. From 1990–92 he was a member of the Cycle Safety Steering Group of the British Medical Association which produced the report *Cycling: Towards Health and Safety*.

Leif Siboni studied Civil Engineering at the Technical University of Denmark and has worked on road design and construction and traffic planning in several municipalities. Since 1983 he has been Coordinator of the comprehensive plan for traffic in Odense city centre, and Technical Manager for the implementation of the plan. He has worked on cycle planning and traffic schemes at Odense City Council since 1978.

Gerrit van Werven studied urban planning, economics and literature at the universities of Groningen and Delft. He worked in the transport sector for a Dutch contracting firm, the Greater London Council, and the city of Groningen. Since 1988 he has been a policy advisor for urban planning, transport and culture for the city of Groningen. In his work he has always stressed the importance of a more environmental transport policy, including cycling. He was the organiser of the third Velo City Conference in 1987.

Andrew Wallace is Team Leader (Traffic Signals, Systems and Special Projects) with Cambridgeshire County Council which involves general traffic management in Cambridgeshire. He has worked with the Council since 1976, having previously worked with Cambridge City Council since 1973 where he was a member of the team which produced the Cambridge Cycleways Report in 1975. More recently, his County Council work has included involvement with the implementation of the cycle route through south-east Cambridge, especially the traffic signal installations.

Preface and acknowledgements

The person who, at least indirectly, first inspired me to write this book was Henry Odinga of Kisumu, Kenya in East Africa. While I was working as a town planner in Kisumu in the early 1970s Henry, a colleague in the Town Engineer's Department, was knocked off his bike at a roundabout just up the road from the Town Hall where we both worked. I had borrowed his bike on several occasions and the incident really brought home to me the vulnerability of cyclists and the need for commitment to improve cyclists' safety and promote cycling.

I would like to pay particular tribute to numerous people in Nottingham, especially in 'Pedals' and in Nottinghamshire County Council, with whom I have worked over the years and with whom I have developed ideas on how to encourage cycling. These include John Abbiss, Lawrence Geary, Eve Parker, Susan Young, Robin Schoolar, Steve Parry, Ian Chatfield, Ian Drummond, Chris Charnley, Pat Armstrong, Neil Hodgson, Chris Randall, Sean Shiels, Steve Jones, and Steve Brazier. Several of these people also took the trouble to make very helpful comments on draft chapters. Other very valuable contributions to my thinking have been made by Johanna Cleary, Don Mathew and John Franklin, especially. Many others have contributed indirectly. On more specific matters, I am grateful to Peter Whitehouse for help in preparing the drawings. I must also thank several people, in addition to the chapter contributors, for lending me photographs: Pete Chapman, Chris Randall, Tim Hughes/Cyclographics and Groningen City Council. Lastly, I would like to express my appreciation to Alan Odell of the Nottingham University's Cripps Computing Centre who helped in transferring contents of different contributors' disks.

Hugh McClintock
February 1992

PART I

PRINCIPLES

1 The significance of the bicycle in urban transport

Hugh McClintock

The bicycle is the vehicle of a new mentality. It quietly challenges a system of values which condones dependency, wastage, inequality of mobility, and daily carnage. There is every reason why cycling should be helped to enjoy another Golden Age.
James McGurn, *An Illustrated History of Cycling*,
John Murray, 1987.

Introduction

The total number of cars in the world grew from 50 to 400 million between 1950 and 1989 (Rose, 1989). It has been estimated that this total could reach half a billion by the end of the century. The car has come to be such a dominant part of the urban scene in industrialised countries that it is easy for us to forget that, in the world as a whole, the total number of bicycles, around 800 million, outnumbers the number of cars owned by two to one. Moreover, as Marcia Lowe from the Worldwatch Institute has pointed out (Lowe, 1990) global production of bikes each year exceeds car manufacturing by about three to one. Bicycles in Asia alone transport more people than do all of the world's cars.

We should also not overlook the role of the bicycle in developed countries, the focus of this book. In recent years a growing awareness of the benefits of the bicycle in terms of cheapness, health, the environment, and convenience in busy urban conditions has resulted in a major revival of bicycle usage.

This book aims to examine this revival of cycling more closely, to assess both current patterns of bicycle usage in towns and cities, and the potential for increasing this. Part I discusses the principles of cycling policy. In this chapter the current significance of the bicycle in city traffic is assessed. Chapter 2 examines the development of special measures to promote bicycle traffic in relation to wider trends in traffic policy and town planning since 1945.

Chapter 3 examines current trends in highway planning, traffic management and town planning, both in older and newer towns and cities and the opportunities presented by these to encourage cycling. In Chapter 4 there is an assessment of the relationship between cycling and planning for public transport, while the concluding chapter of Part I, Chapter 5, discusses the appropriate balance in cycle policy between planning or engineering measures on the one hand, and, on the other, policies on road safety education and training and traffic law provision and enforcement.

Part II contains seven case studies of actual experience in a variety of places which have given some special attention to encouraging cycling. This includes three cities in Great Britain (Nottingham, Cambridge and London), and two cities on the European mainland (Groningen in the Netherlands, Odense in Denmark). There are also two chapters analysing general cycle planning experience in Germany and the USA.

The costs of car dependence

Awareness of the advantages of the bicycle in urban traffic has been greatly encouraged by the recent greater awareness of the damaging effects of motor traffic in general and the private motor car in particular. Forecasts of further major growth in traffic levels in developed countries have only served to strengthen this concern.

Since the late 1980s the greenhouse effect has moved up the environmental and political agenda, with consequent pressure to reduce the present major contribution to the greenhouse effect from traffic-generated carbon dioxide emissions. According to a British report from Earth Resources Research, (ERR) (Cyclists' Touring Club, 1991):

Car traffic is one of the major sources of atmospheric and noise pollution, causing adverse effects to the built environment, plants and human health. In addition, atmospheric emissions from motor vehicles are contributing increasingly to global climate change.

The same report emphasised the particularly damaging effects of car use in the urban environment where air quality is at its worst, since journeys are typically short and in congested conditions. One result, increasingly recognised, has been the growth of respiratory diseases, especially asthma (Greenpeace, 1991).

The general trend in Western countries is for motor traffic to continue to increase. Some official forecasts, such as those from the UK Department of Transport in 1989, seem very complacent in accepting this as inevitable, and even desirable. The assumption has been that the use of unleaded petrol, the development of catalytic converters and much more economical cars will prevent any serious problems arising. On the other hand, the ERR report emphasises the view of an increasing number of environmentalists that current and planned measures to reduce vehicle emissions will have a limited effect, particularly if car use continues to increase in line with official forecasts. Even now, it pointed out, air quality standards in cities are increasingly being breached and, in the majority of cases, this is the fault of motor vehicles as the largest single source of air pollution.

Although there have been many suggestions for alternative fuels it is questionable how far our apparently limitless demand for energy can be fully satisfied without creating very costly and enormous projects. Electric cars still require considerable power to be produced to fuel their batteries, and the growth of any sort of motor vehicles will still produce major parking and congestion problems.

It has become increasingly clear that the use of private cars, while bringing many benefits to their users, have a large number of hidden costs. These include roadbuilding costs, noise, policing, the provision of accident services, congestion and loss of amenity and safety to pedestrians and cyclists, as well as the costs to the natural environment from exhaust gases, oil pollution, and resource wastage (Greenpeace, 1991). In the UK road travel alone causes about 5,000 deaths and 300,000 injuries each year (Cyclists' Touring Club, 1991, p. 8). Most accidents involve a car, and cars and lorries are far more likely to cause injury to other road users than are cyclists or pedestrians (Hillman, 1991).

The increased use of the private car, together with higher incomes, has had a profound influence on settlement structure and lifestyles. Again, many of these effects appear at first glance to be wholly beneficial, offering more people in society freedom of choice on where they live, work and spend their leisure, and more space in which to conduct these activities.

However, again, the disadvantages have become much more evident. As urban areas have become more spread out, with much longer average distances from homes to workplaces, so have energy consumption, congestion and pollution increased. The relatively low costs of running cars in relation to their purchase price, in most Western countries, has encouraged car owners to make more, and longer, journeys. One effect of this spreading out has been that social contacts have often become much weaker, especially among those away all day in full-time jobs. This has tended to make conditions less pleasant and safe for those who are at home during the day, especially the elderly and women, and contributed to increased anxiety about personal safety in different parts of cities, for example in residential areas during the day and in city centres at night. Those who drive cars, or are passengers in cars for their journeys to work, tend to take less exercise than those who use other means of transport, contributing to the level of unfitness in society (Public Health Alliance, 1991).

There is a special responsibility on richer industrialised countries to make major reductions in energy use. A report from the Organisation for Economic Cooperation and Development stated that OECD nations own 78 per cent of all road vehicles and consume 58 per cent of the world's energy (OECD, 1991).

Advantages of bicycle use

These disadvantages of dependence on a high level of car use can be contrasted with the many advantages of encouraging use of bicycles.

Firstly, the bicycle is the most efficient means of transport in terms of energy use. In contrast to the private motor vehicle with its inefficient use of finite fuels, the bicycle maximises use of human energy. Bicycles consume less energy per passenger mile than any other form of transport, including walking, as pointed out by Lowe (1990). Cycling consumes 35 calories per passenger mile, compared with 100 for walking, and 1,860 for a car with one occupant.

Many car journeys to work in cities in developed countries are still less than 8km (5 miles) and average speeds on these are often now less than 20km/h (12 mph). It is therefore often the case, especially for journeys of less than 3km (2 miles), that the bicycle can be the fastest means of transport in busy urban traffic.

There are also enormous potential advantages from cycling in terms of health, both to the individual user and also to public health generally. People who exercise regularly are much fitter, enjoy improved strength and endurance, and the ability to perform everyday tasks with less fatigue (Hillman, 1991).

Exercise lowers blood pressure and weight, and promotes bone formation. As a consequence it is associated with lower rates of cardiovascular disease and cancer. There is also a growing body of evidence that exercise contributes to mental well-being, being beneficial for depressive and anxiety states. (Morris, 1990; Hillman, 1991; British Medical Association, 1992).

As Hillman argues, cycling is particularly well suited to help most people attain these fitness benefits. Even in countries with lower than average cycle use such as Great Britain, a majority of the population can ride a bike. This means that cycling has wide scope for take-up across all sections of the population. It also has the great advantage, unlike most other forms of exercise, that it can be incorporated into the daily routine of travel to work, to education, or to the shops. Morris (1990) has stated that cycling is, among common physical activities, one that comes nearest to an ideal form of exercise, making regular cyclists feel younger and likely to live longer.

In contrast to the car again, the bicycle is a much more efficient user of space. A travelling car needs about eight times more space than a travelling bicycle whereas a parked car can require about twenty times as much as a parked bicycle. With average car occupancy in cities often only about 1.3 people per vehicle, a car requiring 18 sq m of space uses about 14 sq m per person, in contrast to the 4 sq m per person for a cyclist to move freely and 2 sq m for a pedestrian. In a study of the environmental and economic effects of car use and bicycle use in Groningen, where 50 per cent of trips are by bike, it was found that a decline in cycling to a typical European city average of 5 per cent would mean that an extra 22 hectares for car parking would need to be found in the central area (Krommendijk, 1988). This would result in much greater expense as well as worse air quality and more noise and energy consumption.

Cycle use

There are great variations in the level of cycle use in different developed countries, with the Netherlands and Denmark being those where the bicycle is the most important part of the urban transport scene. Twenty-nine per cent of all trips in the Netherlands are made by bicycle, as compared with 18 per cent in Denmark, 11 per cent in Western Germany and only 4 per cent in Great Britain (Bracher, 1989). In terms of total distance, the figures are lower: 1 per cent in Great Britain, 2.5 per cent in Western Germany, 7 per cent in Denmark and 8 per cent in the Netherlands (Bracher et al., 1991, p. 32). This confirms that, on average, cycle trips are clearly shorter than average trip distances.

In the Netherlands an average of 30 per cent of trips to work are made by bike but in medium-sized cities this is often as high as 50 per cent. For Delft the figure is 43 per cent (Bracher, 1989). For trips to school the average is as much as 60 per cent. One-third of all trips to the shops are made by bike and these represent the largest number of bicycle trips in absolute terms (Welleman, 1991). The average Dutch person is likely to make 14 times as many trips per day by bike as the average Briton (Tight and Carsten, 1989). Furthermore, in the Netherlands the amount of cycling is in general higher for women than men, almost one-third of all their trips, compared with 1.5 per cent in Great Britain (British Medical Association, 1992, Table 7.3, p. 73). The same report also noted that cycling in the Netherlands remains very common for the older age groups, especially older women; 23.1 per cent of all journeys, as compared with 0.5 per cent in the UK.

Most of Western Germany has a much weaker cycling tradition than
the Netherlands, but there has been a big revival in recent years with
cycle ownership now almost at Dutch levels (Bracher et al., 1991). In
1982, 11 per cent of all journeys made by Germans over 10 years old
were made by bike (Monheim, 1990, pp. 134–5). Most trips are for work
and education (36 per cent) rather than shopping (34 per cent) or leisure
(30 per cent), contrary to popular belief. There is slightly more cycling
among women than men. As in the Netherlands, cycling is more common
in medium-sized and smaller towns than in large cities. There are,
however, exceptions, such as Bremen, but the towns and cities with the
highest levels of cycling, about 30 per cent of traffic, are all smaller than
this. Apart from Münster near the Dutch border, with a population of
269,000, these are all places with populations of 50,000–100,000, such as
Dessau in Eastern Germany, Erlangen, Rosenheim and Landshut.

The revival of cycle use in Great Britain has been far less pronounced
than in Western Germany, with cycling on average accounting for only
2.5 per cent of all personal journeys (Morgan, 1991). For trips to work
by bike the proportion was a little higher, 4.6 per cent. This is still the
lowest level in the European Community (Bracher, 1989). This is despite
the fact that about 90 per cent of the population can cycle (Hillman,
1990, p. 3) and that cycle sales increased by 80 per cent in the 1980s,
often now exceeding yearly car sales (Cyclists' Touring Club, 1991, p.
10). It seems that there has been a very marked and growing disparity
between cycle ownership and cycle use, a very different pattern from car
ownership and car use. Whereas 94 per cent of cars owned in Britain are
used daily, only one bike in three is actually likely to be used each week.
In most of Britain women are much less likely to cycle than men
(Morgan, 1991), although the reverse is often true in places, with more
women cycling (Banister, 1990).

Again, it is mainly younger people who cycle, especially those aged
between 12 and 15, who make 6 per cent of journeys by bike (Hillman,
Adams and Whitelegg, 1991, p. 95). However, this is only about one-
tenth of the Dutch level and much lower, too, than Germany. The same
report found a large decline in Britain in the proportion of children cycling to school compared with a similar survey in 1970, largely, it seems,
because of worse traffic conditions making parents more reluctant to
allow their children to ride bikes to school. The average proportion of
trips to education made by bike is only 3.6 per cent (Banister, 1990)
which reflects an even greater disparity between cycle use and cycle
ownership than for adults, especially among primary schoolchildren.
Ownership among primary schoolchildren has increased steadily
(Hillman, Adams and Whitelegg, 1991), ranging from 79–95 per cent
(ibid., Table 49, p. 164) whereas, even among 10-year-olds, only 2 per
cent cycled to school (Table 4, p. 133).

It should also be mentioned that there are particularly wide variations in the levels of cycle use within Britain. In terms of trips to work the proportion was highest in Cambridge, at the time of the 1981 census, i.e. 26.7 per cent. There were 23 other districts with a level of more than 10 per cent of work trips by cycle (Banister, 1990, p. 6).

The total number of bikes in the UK has been estimated at 13 million (Morgan, 1991) and 11 million people use bikes at least once a year. In an average week 3.6 million people cycle. Although this total is much lower than in some Continental countries it is still true, as Morgan points out, that more journeys are made by bike than by British Rail and London Underground railways combined. For young people the bike is the only private vehicle available, providing them with mobility and independence. It seems that official figures have tended easily to underestimate the total amount of cycling, with the Department of Transport refusing to record journeys of less than one mile (1.6 km) (Hillman, 1990) and traffic counts taking place mostly on main roads that cyclists are less likely to use. As a result, Morgan says that the official figure for cycling in the UK was suddenly revised from 4.36 to 5.74 billion km (Morgan, 1991).

In terms of journey purpose, work-related trips predominate (34.0 per cent), whereas for education trips the proportion by bike (14.4 per cent) is much lower than the Netherlands or Germany. Next most important purposes of cycle trips are social/entertainment (19.1 per cent) and for shopping trips (15.4 per cent). Although cycle ownership has traditionally been associated with people on low incomes, it is now clear that it is households owning cars, and especially those owning two or more cars, which are more likely to own at least one bicycle in the household.

From all these European examples the predominance of the bicycle in short trips should be noted. Bearing in mind the continuing, although less marked, predominance of short trips in many car journeys also (Banister, 1990; Cyclists' Touring Club, 1991), this suggests a potential for increasing cycle use in urban areas in Europe that is probably greater than North American cities with their lower densities and greater physical extent, itself in part the product of a long-standing, much higher level of car ownership. In Germany it has been estimated that cycling could account for 15 per cent of trips to work, 25 per cent of shopping trips and 50 per cent of school journeys (Herz, 1985), while another survey suggested that 25–35 per cent of all car journeys could be transferred to bikes (Otto, 1985). The ERR report in the UK called for a major effort to increase the amount of cycling, as part of a wider strategy to reduce the harmful effects of vehicle emissions (Cyclists' Touring Club, 1991). It suggested that 40–50 per cent of all non-walking journeys could be undertaken by bike without greatly increasing the average length of bike trips. This increase, it argued, could displace up to one-sixth of all car mileage, and up to half of all car trips, given the introduction of suitable policies.

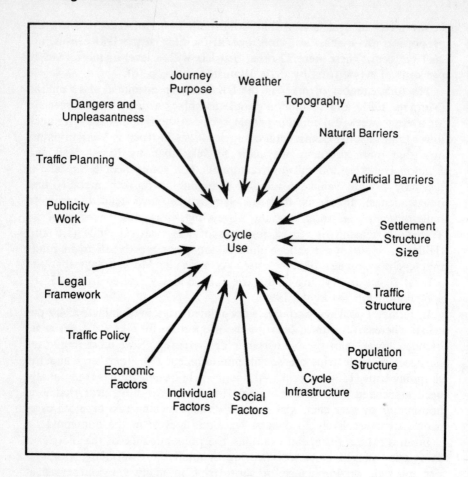

Figure 1.1   Summary of influences on cycle use.

Source: BENDIAS 1987

Factors influencing cycle use

There are many factors influencing cycle use in different countries, among men and women, young and old cyclists. These are summarised in Fig. 1.1, adapted from a Research Report on Urban Cycling from the German Ministry of Transport (Bracher et al., 1991, p. 27).

Topography

In general, towns and cities with flatter terrain will have a higher level of cycling. In Great Britain the level of cycling in Cambridge is 13 per cent, as against less than 1 per cent in Glamorgan in Wales (Banister, 1990). In Western Germany the incidence of cycling is 50 per cent above average in flat terrain and 20 per cent below average in mountain areas (Herz, 1985). The relatively flat terrain is certainly one major explanation for the high level of cycling in the Netherlands and Denmark.

However, it should not be overstated because there are several parts of Denmark, for example Eastern Jutland, that are not flat but where cycling is still very popular! Winterthur in Switzerland is by no means flat but is still popular for cycling, with cycle routes making good use of the valleys and green spaces, with fairly gentle inclines. Furthermore, the significance of slopes as a deterrent to cycling has been at least to some extent eroded by the development of lighter weight and better-geared bikes.

It is still true, however, that the flatness or otherwise of the local terrain will have had an important influence on people's willingness to cycle. The amount of effort needed to ride a bike tends to be over-estimated by non-cyclists (Schmidt and Midden, 1988). Nevertheless, this perception remains an important explanation of variations in cycle use, and cycling is always likely to be more common in flatter areas.

Weather

Adverse weather, or perhaps more precisely, fear of adverse weather, clearly has an impact on levels of cycling, especially snow and ice, with the amount of cycling, in countries prone to such conditions, at its lowest in the months of January and February. Light rain or drizzle appear to have negligible effects on cycle use compared with heavy rain. On the other hand, it may well be that this factor is also one that is much more likely to be regarded as significant by non-cyclists than those who cycle at all regularly (Schmidt and Midden, 1988). It has been shown that, in a normal year in most parts of England, it is only on average on about 12 days a year that a cyclist riding to and from work will get really wet! The incidence of rain on a typical cycle journey is very low (British Medical Association, 1992, p. 36) and the improved quality of protective wind and rainproof clothing and gloves has helped to lessen the problem. The presence of icy patches is probably the greatest adverse weather deterrent to cyclists' safety.

Cycle theft

The fear of cycle theft can certainly be a significant deterrent (Bracher et al., 1991) and the number of bikes stolen or tampered with has tended to rise steadily in most European countries. It is hard to get accurate figures on this because of the common under-reporting to the police of bikes stolen (Wheeler, 1988). It is also common for a very low proportion of bikes owned to be returned to their owners. Plentiful provision of carefully sited and secure cycle parking, geared to the different needs of short- and long-term cycle parkers, can, however, help to mitigate this, although the fear of cycle theft can still be pervasive, especially for owners of the now common mountain bikes and other high-value bikes.

Settlement structure

Whereas the most efficient settlement structure for encouraging public transport is one with a strong radial pattern, and development concentrated along these radial routes, cycling (and walking) are encouraged by a more compact settlement structure. Many cities, especially in North America, have much more dispersed structures and lower densities, as Newman and Kenworthy (1990) have emphasised, and traffic levels tend to be higher. Such dispersal makes it harder to erode the habit of car use, once people are thoroughly used to it. Cycling tends therefore to be significantly more popular in medium-sized towns and cities, of not more than 300,000 population, than in large cities (Copenhagen, Bremen and Amsterdam being notable exceptions to this rule). In more compact cities, with relatively high densities, it is much more likely to be possible to reach most parts of the urban area on a bike in a maximum of 20–30 minutes, and a large proportion of likely destinations will come within the typical cycle trip distance of 2–3km. The land use pattern, as well as the size and shape of the urban area, also influences choice of transport mode. In larger cities there are often more distinct divisions between areas designated for housing, shopping and employment, with significant distances between these that militate against the use of bicycles, or certainly against the use of bicycles as the only means of completing a journey.

Traffic volumes and speed

Cyclists' safety, and the general willingness of local people to use bikes, is heavily influenced by both the levels of motor traffic and its speed (Apel et al., 1988). It is very important to remember that, in most urban areas most of the time, cyclists will be making most of their journeys on ordinary roads and streets. This is the case even in places with extensive special facilities for cyclists. The enormous growth in motor traffic levels has certainly tended to increase general fears about cycling, especially when accompanied by signs of more aggressive driving. On the other hand, cyclists, along with pedestrians, can benefit greatly from traffic-restraint measures. Area-wide speed reduction schemes, with lower speed limits, are especially important.

With increased urban traffic congestion, especially at peak periods, even journeys of as much as 10km are often faster than by alternative means of transport. This is particularly the case when relatively quiet routes exist, away from main roads, and not substantially less direct. Indeed, levels of pollution from traffic on main roads, as well as traffic volumes, can also be an incentive to use quieter back streets.

The total traffic situation influences decisions to use bikes as well as traffic volumes, speed and levels of congestion. One important part of this is the extent and quality of cycling provision. For example, in the Netherlands, with much greater proper cycling provision than in Great Britain, the cyclist casualty rate per km travelled is half to one-third of the British rate, and cyclists run only one-tenth the rate of being injured per km cycled (Tight and Carsten, 1989, p. 10). These differences underline the importance of official attitudes to cycling and cycling provision (Bracher, 1989; Bracher et al., 1991).

The extent of speed reduction measures, both through police enforcement and through traffic-calming measures, are also important in the cyclist's perception of the total traffic situation, as is the extent of pedestrianisation and other measures to restrain car use.

Also important in decisions on means of transport is of course the quality of public transport and there may be competition between this and cycling for some trips, influenced in part by its reliability, quality, comfort, quality of information and publicity, as well as pricing structure. However, it is not true that good public transport necessarily means less cycling, as is clear from the experience of places like Amsterdam, Freiburg and Karlsruhe where both cycling and public transport have been strongly promoted (see Chapter 4).

Population structure

It is clear that certain age groups, especially the young, are more likely to use bikes regularly than others. One reason for the less impressive growth in cycling in the Western German bicycle-friendly project town of Detmold than Rosenheim (described in Hulsmann, 1990) appears to have been Detmold's relatively large proportion of elderly people. On the other hand, towns and cities with a higher than average number of young people are likely to have fairly high levels of cycle use. This is particularly true for important centres of higher education.

Social and cultural factors

A variety of social and cultural factors seem to influence levels of cycle use. The fact, for example, that cycling is highly popular even in hillier parts of Denmark indicates how much cycling is part of the Danish way of life, a complete contrast to the USA in particular where, at least until recently, very few adult cyclists would dream of being seen riding a bike on their daily journeys, and where cars and cheap gasoline have been particularly freely available (see Chapter 12).

Levels of cycle use can be influenced by the local employment structure. In England, there are often fairly high levels of cycling in towns where the railways have been a major employer. Examples include Peterborough, Crewe and Swindon, reflecting the importance of shift patterns in employment, for which the bicycle, rather than public transport, was more suited for work journeys. Sometimes, as in Winterthur in Switzerland, a major local employer has encouraged its workforce to cycle, stimulating a wider local cycling tradition.

It has been suggested that one explanation for the relatively higher levels of cycling in places with a higher overall rate of cycle use may be because there is less social stigma associated with cycling in such areas (Banister, 1990).

Whereas more people in North America and Western Europe are now aware of the disadvantages of such a high degree of dependence on car use it would seem that attitudes in Eastern Europe are very different. Aspirations for car ownership have been long suppressed, making it all the harder to spread awareness of the dangers of 'automania' and the positive attributes of the bike.

Individual attitudes to cycling

Individual attitudes to the use of the bicycle overlap with social and cultural attitudes and like all individual attitudes are much influenced by earlier experiences, personal values, long-standing habits, and the adequacy of information available about alternatives. In decisions about travel alternatives, people evaluate perceived options in terms of their personal needs and goals (Schmidt and Midden, 1988). In terms of their attitude to cycle use this means their perception of the effort involved, what they need to carry on their bikes, and their own vulnerability to heavy traffic and cycle theft. These potential disadvantages have to be balanced against the factors that encourage people to cycle (Speed, 1988), that is, enjoyment, health, cheapness and independence.

In general, the more car-oriented a society, as in the USA, the more the bicycle is likely to be regarded as a means of transport most suitable for children, or, if at all for adults, then only for recreation and sport.

France has a very strong tradition of recreational and sporting cycling but, in most areas, a very low level of daily cycling, and the same is largely true in most parts of Spain and Italy.

In Britain a survey by Finch (1984) found that, for most people, the image of cycling discouraged cycle use. Cycling was associated with pleasurable experiences of childhood but not seriously regarded as a means of daily transport for adults. In other countries, especially the Netherlands and Denmark, the bicycle is much more likely to be used by all occupational groups as a matter of habit.

Individual attitudes to the use of the bicycle can change over a few years and it is possible, for example, that people attracted for health reasons to riding bicycles for recreation may then start to use bikes for other trips. With the rise of the environmental movement the bike has come to be seen by many as a symbol of environmental purity and righteousness, whereas the car has increasingly been portrayed as an environmental monster. Just as some people like to drive a large and powerful car as a statement of their status and attitudes, a growing minority of other people do so by riding a bicycle! It also seems quite likely that one reason for the attractions of the mountain bike in recent years has been that it has appealed to people who previously would not have been willing to have been seen at all riding a bike. Links to fashion and to health and fitness in marketing have helped to bring about this change in attitude.

The wider range of gears on modern bikes means less effort in cycling, a point of particular importance for women who tend to put greater emphasis on the amount of effort and discomfort.

Although Schmidt and Midden (1988) found that most drivers who changed to cycling said they had overestimated the extent of many negative factors this was rather less so in the case of 'luggage' and 'speed'. Poor load-carrying ability, poor weather protection, and, in rural areas in particular, long distances remain significant deterrents to cycle use, as well as fears about car drivers' behaviour, fumes and speed. This underlines the importance of subjective factors as well as the quality of provision in encouraging people to cycle. Individual attitudes will be improved by more attention to these factors and, in particular, the problems of comfort and suspension, weather protection, carrying luggage and theft prevention (Bracher et al., 1991).

Official attitudes to cycling

Official attitudes can also encourage a change in individual attitudes to regarding the bicycle as a serious means of transport, and help overcome its second-rate image in many countries. Bracher's comparative European survey in 1988 found that cyclists in the Netherlands, Denmark and

Western Germany felt generally respected whereas those in Austria, Sweden, France, Great Britain and Belgium felt that 'bicycling is being neglected or obstructed'. The Dutch Government has since made an even stronger commitment to cycling with the adoption of the Bicycle Master Plan (Welleman, 1991). Encouraging well-known local people to cycle regularly is important. In Germany the cycling commitment of Erlangen as early as the late 1970s was embodied in the lead given by its cycling mayor.

Even minor signs of official promotion of cycling, such as cycle stands outside offices and public facilities, and cycle route signs, may contribute to changing attitudes. It helps also to reinforce these effects when official commitment extends to encouraging employees to use bikes for official duties and giving financial incentives to use bikes, rather than cars, for these. Reluctance to use bikes for journeys to work may also arise from inadequate facilities at work and may be countered by the provision of storage facilities under cover, showers and changing rooms. Storage space needs to be adequate for accessories, clothing and helmets.

The extent of official commitment to cycling is very much bound up with the whole question of promotion and publicity for the use of the bike. This needs to be tackled at two levels, in terms of general promotion of cycling and with wide publicity of new cycle facilities. General promotion should include small guided rides, mass rides and other events. Publicity for the opening of new facilities should be extensive and include special opening events and publicity leaflets.

Conclusion

This chapter has shown that even the existing significance of the bicycle is often underrated. Even in a country like Britain it has a very great significance among certain groups, especially the young, and in some urban areas. Strong official commitment to cycling is very important in pursuing a wide range of measures to promote cycle use and overcome the understandable negative attitudes of many current non-users. The lessons from this analysis of its importance need to be clearly understood before going on to make recommendations for maximising its potential. First, however, it is important to understand how a combination of transport and planning policies have for many years eroded the position of the bicycle and constrained special facilities introduced to encourage it. This is the focus of the following chapter.

Key references

Banister, Chris, 1990, *Existing Travel Patterns: The Potential for Cycling*, report of proceedings of the Conference on 'Cycling and the Healthy City', organised by Friends of the Earth, Hammersmith Town Hall, London, 27 June.

Bracher, Tilman, 1989, *Policy and Provision for Cyclists in Europe*, Commission of the European Communities, Directorate-General for Transport, Brussels.

Bracher, Tilman, Luda, Helmut and Thiemann, H., 1991, *Zussamenfassende Auswertung von Forschungsergebnissen zum Radverkehr in der Stadt*, Forschung Stadtverkehr, Band A7, Bundesminister für Verkehr, Bergisch Gladbach/Berlin, Bonn.

British Medical Association, 1992, *Cycling: Towards Health and Safety*, Oxford University Press, Oxford and New York.

Brög, Werner, Erl, Erhard and Katteler, H., 1988, *Existing and Potential Bicycle Use – Key Factors*, report of proceedings, Velo City '87 Conference, (ed. T. de Wit), CROW, Ede, Netherlands.

Cyclists' Touring Club, 1991, *Bikes Not Fumes: The Emission and Health Benefits of a Modal Shift from Motor Vehicles to Cycling*, report produced for the CTC by Andy Rowell and Malcolm Fergusson of Earth Resources Research, CTC, Godalming, Surrey.

Herz, K., 1985, The use of the Bicycle, *Transport, Planning and Technology*, 9, 311–328.

Hillman, Mayer, 1990, *Cycling and Health: a Policy Context*, report of proceedings of the Conference on 'Cycling and the Healthy City', organised by Friends of the Earth, Hammersmith Town Hall, London, 27 June 1990.

Hillman, Mayer, 1991, *Educating Decision Makers about Health Benefits and Safety Aspects of Cycling in Current Traffic Environments*, paper given at the Velo City '91 Conference, Milan.

Hillman, Mayer, Adams, John and Whitelegg, John, 1991, *One False Move: a Study of Children's Independent Mobility*, Policy Studies Institute, London.

Lowe, Marcia, 1989, *The Bicycle: Vehicle for a Small Planet*, Worldwatch Paper 90, Worldwatch Institute, Washington DC, USA.

Lowe, Marcia, 1990, Cycling into the Future, Chapter 7 in Lester, R. et al. *State of the World*, W. W. Norton and Company, New York and London.

Monheim, Rolf, 1990, Policy issues in promoting the green modes, in Tolley, Rodney (ed.), *The Greening of Urban Transport: Planning for Walking and Cycling in Western Cities*, Belhaven Press, London.

Morris, Jerry, 1990, *Cycling and Health*, report of proceedings of the Conference on 'Cycling and the Healthy City', organised by Friends of the Earth, Hammersmith Town Hall, London, 27 June.

Welleman, A.G., 1991, *The Importance of the Bicycle in an Environmental Transport Policy*, paper presented to the meeting of the Local Authorities Cycle Planning Group, York, 17 May.

Other references

Apel, Dieter, Kolleck, Bernd and Lehmbrock, Michael, 1988, *Stadtverkehrsplanung Teil 4: Verkehrssicherheit in Städtevergleich*, Institut für Urbanistik, Berlin.

Finch, Helen, 1984, *Attitudes to Cycling*, Report 11/791, Social and Community Planning Research, London.

Greenpeace (UK), 1991, *Mad Car Disease*, Greenpeace, London.

Hülsmann, Wulf, 1990, The Bicycle-Friendly Towns Project in the Federal Republic of Germany, Ch 15 in Tolley, Rodney (ed.), *The Greening of Urban Transport: Planning for Walking and Cycling in Western Cities*, Belhaven Press, London.

Krommendijk, Erna, 1988, *The Bicycle and the Environment in the City: a quantification of a bicycle-oriented traffic policy in Groningen (Netherlands)*, Professor H. C. van Hall Institut, Rijks Agrarische Hogeschool, Groningen, Netherlands.

Morgan, J. M., 1991, *Cycling in Safety?*, proceedings and programme, Safety '91, Transport and Road Research Laboratory, Crowthorne, Berkshire.

Newman, Peter W. and Kenworthy, Jeffrey R., 1989, *Cities and Automobile Dependence; An International Sourcebook*, Gower, Aldershot.

Organisation for Economic Cooperation and Development, 1991, *Environmental Policies for the Cities in the 1990s*, OECD, Paris.

Otto, K., 1985, *Policies to Promote the Bicycle as a Means of Reducing Pollution*, German Federal Environment Office, Berlin.

Public Health Alliance, 1991, *Health on the Move*, Public Health Alliance, Birmingham.

Rose, Chris, 1989, *The Dirty Man of Europe: The Great British Pollution Scandal*, Simon and Schuster, London.

Schmidt J. & Midden. C.J.H., 1988, *Changing Modal Split by a Behavioral Science Approach*, report of proceedings, Velo-City '87 Conference, Groningen, Netherlands, Netherlands Centre for Research and Contract Standardisation in Civil and Traffic Engineering (CROW), Ede, The Netherlands.

Speed, Liz, 1988, Road User Attitudes and the Safety of Cyclists, *Bicycles Bulletin* No. 44, Friends of the Earth, London.

Tight, M.R & Carsten, O.M.J., 1989, *Problems for Vulnerable Road Users in Great Britain, the Netherlands and Sweden*, Institute of Transport Studies, University of Leeds.

Wheeler, A.H., 1988, *Cycle Theft Update*, Transport and Road Research Laboratory Working Paper WP/TS/3, Transport and Road Research Laboratory, Crowthorne, Berkshire.

2 Post-war traffic planning and special provision for the bicycle

Hugh McClintock

Trends in transport planning and traffic management since 1945

Any assessment of the experience of special measures to help cyclists can only be made with a full understanding of the wider context of transport, traffic management and town planning policies since 1945 and how these have in most areas in so many ways constrained the potential of the bicycle in urban traffic.

In the UK, for example, car traffic between 1951 and 1991 grew tenfold. Road mileage grew by only 18 per cent, but with extra lanes, widening and motorways, road capacity grew by more than 50 per cent (Transport Studies Unit, 1991). It is hard to appreciate just how great the transformation in our transport pattern has been. For example, the proportion of the total distance travelled by private vehicle grew from 57 per cent to 88 per cent between 1961 and 1991 (Social Trends, 1992). Travel by bus and coach fell from 25 per cent of total travel to 8 per cent. Just in the ten years from 1981–91 car ownership increased by 26 per cent, and it is clear both that people have been making more trips each week and that they are going further on each of these trips.

It is not surprising that the start of this great increase in car traffic was accompanied by a dramatic decrease in the 1950s and 1960s in cycle sales and cycle use, in Britain as in other Western European countries. Cycle sales declined to about half a million units a year in the late 1960s (Stores, 1980, p. 18, Fig. 2).

Traffic policies in most Western European cities became more and more focused on the need to cater above all for motor traffic, and the greatly increased projected future levels. This developed even more strongly in the 1960s and early 1970s, as more and more cities produced their comprehensive land use and transportation studies, on which were based plans for many new road schemes in urban areas, involving urban motorways and other new roads as well as substantial widening of existing roads. This concentration on catering for car traffic was particularly marked in the later plans for some new towns, as well as older urban areas. In Britain, for example, earlier post-war new town plans for places like Harlow and Stevenage included plans for cycleways alongside new roads (Dupree, 1987) but that for Milton Keynes, published in 1968, made no reference at all to cycling.

This emphasis in transport planning reflected a common attitude at that time that, in terms of transport, as in other spheres, the American way of life pointed to the future and that Europeans only had to examine current American trends to learn how things would and should go in their societies too. Los Angeles and Detroit pointed the way.

The obsession with catering for the car was encouraged by the big increase in real incomes in this period for many people, with car ownership becoming a reality for many rather than just for the privileged few, as before 1945. In addition, people felt that the car offered a sense of freedom, opening up new horizons, particularly for leisure, along with shorter working hours. Mobility was the imperative, along with speed and flow of motor traffic. This emphasis in traffic policy laid the basis for the car industry to develop an ever more prominent role in national economies and national transport decision-making (Monheim and Monheim-Dandorfer, 1991; Thomson, 1978).

It seemed that those who made the key decisions on transport experienced the world of traffic very largely from the perspective of drivers, rarely using public transport, seldom riding a bike and infrequently going on foot, at least in urban areas. Children, women and the elderly, on the other hand, were much less likely to be car-focused and much more likely to experience traffic problems in confrontation with the car. However, they had little say in traffic policy and planning.

In practical terms this private motor-vehicle focused traffic policy meant more roads, widening of existing roads, and the allocation of more and more space to other types of car-oriented infrastructure such as car parks, both surface level and multi-storey. Public authorities came to demand the provision of quotas of car parking spaces at workplaces and other new public facilities. The retailing sector also became more car-oriented, pressing for ever larger shopping centres, and increasingly at peripheral sites with good road access and plenty of free car parking.

The fact that these types of development, and larger educational and medical institutions, might be encouraging driving and increasing congestion was either not addressed, or, if so, was regarded as a pretext for more road-building to overcome bottlenecks and relieve congestion. This in turn came to encourage further car use, and, particularly significantly, longer, as well as more, journeys by car. This was particularly so in the case of journeys to work (May, 1991). In turn, this inevitably meant less

⤳ reliance on those modes which are more suitable for short journeys: walking, cycling and, to some extent, the bus.

Criticisms of post-war transport and traffic policy

It was not until the early 1970s that anything more than a small minority began to question the benefits that mass car ownership was claimed to have brought, and to consider its negative effects. Indeed, pedestrians, and especially perhaps cyclists, were often simply not counted in traffic surveys. On the contrary, conditions for those on foot and on bicycle were in most cases made far worse, by increasing volumes of traffic, wider roads and higher speeds. Crossing the road could increasingly be made only by long detours, often via awkward to use subways and bridge crossings. More complex arrangements were introduced at road junctions which also inhibited cyclists, whether in the form of multi-lane traffic-signal-controlled junctions or, as particularly common in the UK, large roundabouts.

The legacy of these subway and bridge facilities commonly provided for non-motorised users wishing to cross such fast roads and junctions continues to pose major problems for walkers and cyclists, especially for women and for those with children or shopping, and most of all at night when personal security of users, especially female, is most threatened (Atkins, 1989; Krause, 1991). These groups suffered also from the exodus of pedestrians from residential districts during working hours. With fewer people about on foot, those left with no alternative often came to feel more at risk of attack, especially in parks and other green areas, away from roads. Yet governments, at national and local level, by and large continued to favour the car in transport policy and indeed became heavily dependent on purchases of cars and fuel as a source of revenue.

By the 1970s increasing opposition to road-widening and road-building in some places, especially in densely built-up areas of older towns and cities, encouraged the adoption of more sophisticated traffic-management techniques to maximise capacity for motor traffic on existing streets. These included one-way systems (which often aggravated conditions for cyclists both by speeding up traffic and by forcing them to take much longer more circuitous routes to their destinations) and increasing use of traffic signals, with more complex timing and synchronised control systems. This partially slowed down the pressure for new road-building within some urban areas but this pressure continued to be very strong elsewhere.

Generally the bias in transport policies towards catering for the car, bad as it was, did not go as far in Western Europe as in the USA. As Untermann says (1990), the post-war years in the USA saw a rapid move away from a pattern of mixed land uses and relatively compact districts, often based around public transport links. With relatively weak planning controls the pattern of development soon became much more car-oriented and random, with business and retail centres being much less concentrated. Distances between residential and other areas became much longer, making car ownership and use increasingly a necessity for most sections of the population that could possibly afford it. Relatively cheap gasoline in the USA and a general police willingness to tolerate speed limit abuse further encouraged this, and car ownership in many American states soon rose to more than one car for every two people. America was by and large much less urban-oriented than Europe where cities have evolved more slowly, over many centuries, and in a more compact form, with higher average densities and greater mixed use patterns than in the US, making it easier to avoid the build-up of congestion. Generally European cities, despite the common major redevelopment to cater for motor traffic, remain more compact, with narrower streets and a more mixed and settled land use pattern.

However, there are of course within European cities often major differences between the older parts of the urban area and newer suburban development where densities are often lower and viable public transport harder to maintain. This is particularly the case in a country like Britain where much post-war development has taken the form of one-family houses at relatively low densities, rather than flats. As Susan Owen stated (1990):

The built environment has evolved (been planned) in ways which reflect diminishing energy constraints in the transport system, predominantly low-density dispersed residential development.

The Yom Kippur war of 1973 between Israel and Egypt, with its disruption to oil supplies from the Middle East, brought home very dramatically to many people in Western Europe the extent of their countries' dependence on imported sources of oil. This helped greatly to extend beyond a tiny minority the awareness of the many harmful effects of transport policies geared principally to private motor traffic and the journey times and time savings of its users. More people came to appreciate the way in which massive reliance on the car had begun to undermine the convenience it was meant to provide (Adams, 1981; Thomson, 1978; Renner, 1988). This way of thinking began to permeate some official opinions, especially in the Netherlands. In Britain the Government's 1977 Transport White Paper recognised the need to reduce energy consumption in transport, even if this appeared to mean mainly a focus on the development of cars requiring less petrol consumption. As Hillman and Whalley (1983) commented, it still did not question the continued growth in car ownership.

It proved much harder to gain official recognition that increasing road capacity tended more often than not to generate more traffic, by encouraging both relatively shorter journey times for cars than public transport and also, effectively, more trips and longer average distances for trips. It proved even harder for official thinking to accept both the idea of the social value of time and the idea that for individuals benefits other than time-saving, such as protecting the environment, could be important (Atkins, 1991).

Official moves towards assisting the revival of cycling

Following the 'energy crisis' of the early 1970s, questioning of the wisdom of such a high degree of dependence on motor traffic and fossil fuels started to infiltrate some government attitudes, as well as to become a main feature of the pronouncements of environmental groups.

The Dutch Government in 1975 announced two major cycle route demonstration projects, in The Hague and Tilburg (Hartman, 1990). In Western Germany the Federal Environment Office invited bids from local authorities to be considered for its bicycle-friendly towns project, started in 1976 (Hülsmann, 1990).

In Britain official recognition of the renewed importance of the bicycle came more slowly but can be traced back to the Transport White Paper of 1977. Until then, cycling provision in Britain was very rare, being largely confined to some of the post-war new towns such as Harlow and Stevenage, and a few stretches of cycle path, mostly dating from the 1930s, in a few older towns and cities (Perraton, 1968). Portsmouth, in 1975, was one of the few places to have introduced an experimental cycle scheme, but this was soon abandoned (Quenault and Head, 1977; Quenault, 1979).

The 1977 White Paper is important for cycling policy in Britain in that it announced the inauguration of the Innovatory Projects Budget under which the Department of Transport agreed to share the costs of experimental cycling schemes with interested local authorities. The first of these, in Peterborough and Middlesborough, were cycle routes linking their centres to other neighbourhoods and included the first sets of traffic lights for cyclists and among other special features. These were followed by other schemes in Chichester, Bedford, Cambridge, London, York, Chelmsford, Nottingham and Derby. An average of about four to five schemes a year were supported and a total of almost 80 such innovatory schemes had been introduced by early 1992. York, Cambridge and Nottingham have all made good use of this assistance to develop their considerable pro-cycling policies. York was in fact described as Britain's most cycle-friendly city in a survey of 150 towns and cities (Mathew, 1992).

Dissemination of the results of these schemes was fairly slow and most councils remained largely ignorant of their experience. However, the Department of Transport was sufficiently encouraged by the success of the early schemes to announce in its Cycling Consultation Paper (Department of Transport, 1981) that it would extend the scope of these experiments from single schemes or schemes involving a few facilities to experiments involving a network of routes. The object of these, confirmed in the Statement of Cycling Policy (Department of Transport, 1982), was to assess the impact of a network of facilities in encouraging more people to cycle and in helping existing cyclists to feel safer. In fact, when the selection of places for these schemes was finally announced in 1984, there was only one, Nottingham (see Chapter 6) that could really be considered a true network of cycle routes. The others, including Bedford, Stockton, Exeter, Canterbury (later dropped) and Cambridge (substituted for Canterbury in 1986) comprised essentially one route, with several facilities, and connecting spurs. The Cambridge scheme, completed in 1989, included by far the largest single special facility for cyclists completed anywhere in Britain: the cycle and pedestrian bridge near Cambridge Station (see Chapter 7).

It is important to remember that several other British local authorities embarked on significant cycling initiatives around this time. These included conversions of disused railways to cycleways in Derbyshire, Avon and the Lothian Region of Scotland. The major expansion of Peterborough, started in 1968, included plans to provide extensive cycleways, building on the town's distinct cycling tradition. The new city of Milton Keynes in Buckinghamshire also dated from the same period and made a belated attempt in the late 1970s to develop a network of cycle and pedestrian paths, known as the redways. The most notable example was London (see Chapter 8) where between 1981 and 1986 under the Greater London Council a special Cycling Project Team was set up, which planned and implemented more than 50 schemes in the capital. The GLC also took a leading role in 1984 in setting up the Local Authorities Cycle Planning Group which has met regularly since then to promote the exchange of cycle planning experience.

In general the Department of Transport-sponsored innovatory schemes have been modestly successful (Harland and Gercans, 1991) although not fulfilling some of the more optimistic hopes when introduced for encouraging large numbers of new cyclists. In terms of cyclist numbers the main impact has been a diversion of cyclists from less suitable routes rather than encouraging new cyclists. This is an important benefit, even if urban traffic conditions generally for cyclists remain dangerous. A similar effect was found in the evaluations of the major cycle schemes in the 1970s in The Hague and Tilburg (Ministry of Transport and Public Works, 1979) although the more ambitious cycle route network scheme in Delft in the early 1980s (Hartman, 1990) did manage to increase the already considerable share of cycling in traffic from 40 per cent to 42 per cent.

In Western Germany the experience with the bicycle-friendly towns project completed in 1987 (Hülsmann, 1990) showed in particular that promoting bicycle transport must not be confined to building cycle paths. As Hülsmann commented, 'Attempts must be made to dismantle the obstacles to the use of the bicycle with the help of a comprehensive package of aims and measures.'

This German project was notable for its recognition of the need to promote a 'bicycle-friendly climate' on a wider basis, including the formation of a working group with wide representation to plan and implement the project. There was a special attempt in the main centres of the project, Detmold and Rosenheim, to provide bicycle offices and a higher profile generally for cycling, including mass cycling events. Attempts were made to encourage local officials and well-known local personalities to be seen riding bikes. The aim was also to ensure that any improvement in the bicycle climate of a town kept pace with the extension of the bicycle infrastructure and vice versa (Hülsmann, 1990, p. 227). There was, moreover, an attempt to develop different cycle paths and bicycle streets to form cycle networks, as well as to take advantage of the opportunities for promoting safer cycling opened up by the new developments of traffic-calming and lower speed limits on residential streets with low traffic volumes.

Analysis of experience of cycle paths

In terms of achieving increased cycling numbers the results of the bicycle-friendly towns project were mixed, with more success in Rosenheim than Detmold. However, the project was still very helpful in highlighting a number of lessons of value in future cycle planning. Too often in Germany provision for cyclists has tended to be seen just in terms of providing cycle paths, regardless of their standard and, in particular, regardless of whether or not the common dangers where they crossed roads and accesses outweighed the advantages for cyclists' safety on the link sections between junctions. They also showed the importance of making paths as direct as possible without diversions, to help yield net reductions of journey times, and stressed the need for routes of adequate width, which were continuous as well as attractive to use in terms of their surroundings. Cycle parking and a good signing system were also shown to be essential.

Analysing this extensive experience in Germany (Alrutz et al., 1989; Bracher et al., 1991; Knoche et al., 1981; Wolf, 1988b) and the conclusions of a number of studies elsewhere, for example the Netherlands (Welleman and Dijkstra, 1988), Sweden (Lind and Wollin, 1986) and

Denmark (Bach et al., 1985) it is clear that it is far from guaranteed that cycle paths have a positive effect on cyclists' safety. Because they seem safer than cycling on the road and because they thus can attract people who would not otherwise cycle their users may behave more carelessly. Pedestrians may suffer if the space between them and cyclists is limited, and there is often a higher risk of collision with other cyclists, as some users come to take less care (Bracher, 1989, pp. 80–99). Evidence in Britain, from the shared cycle and pedestrian redways in Milton Keynes (Milton Keynes Cycle Users' Group, 1984) shows that there may be a particularly high level of under-reporting of such accidents.

It is however very important to analyse a number of detailed local factors before reaching conclusions about the net positive or negative contribution to cyclists' safety of cycle paths. For example, there is a need to look at the detailed widths and visibility standards, taking account of whether the path is designed and also used for two-way cycling. The detailed crossing arrangements are important, in terms of the distance from the parallel road at which the cycle path crosses a junction, and whether it crosses at a higher level than the road, or the same level, as well as how clearly it is marked and signed.

In general, experience suggests that cycle paths are more likely to be beneficial when the paths are wide enough to permit safe two-way riding, where they cross few roads or driveways, and when the detailed layout, routeing, marking and signing arrangements at any junctions are carefully thought out to promote intervisibility of cyclists and drivers. It is generally easier to provide good standard cycle paths in the more spacious outer suburban areas of towns. In the outer parts of most Continental cities there tends to be more space than on equivalent roads in the UK. In these outer areas road crossings are likely to be fewer in number, helping to reduce conflicts, and motor traffic speeds are generally higher, making the case for segregation stronger.

However, the value of even basically well-designed cycle paths can be marred by poor details. These include sharp corners or other features impeding visibility and unnecessarily restricting momentum, excessive gradients, and tortuous routes which are hard to follow. The layout of some paths make unrealistic expectations of cyclists' inclination to make long detours, or to wait for long periods at signals. Great care needs to be taken with details both in design and construction, to encourage usage. Particular attention needs to be paid to potential problem points such as bus stops by cycle paths, garage entrances and exits and pinch points where visibility is substandard and space not available for ideal widths.

Experience suggests that cycle paths will actually increase dangers for cyclists where they are too narrow, where they take space from pedestrians, where surfaces are worse than nearby carriageway surfaces and where intervisibility is poor. Account also has to be taken of the conditions on the roads they run alongside, with cycle paths more likely to be of benefit when such roads carry high volumes of traffic, especially a high proportion of heavy vehicles, with average speeds in excess of 50–60 km/h.

It is important to bear in mind the risk that by encouraging a subjectively greater feeling of safety cycle paths can sometimes encourage more careless riding behaviour. Cyclists may be more likely to collide with each other, for example, slow cyclists with fast cyclists, and adult cyclists with child cyclists. Cycle paths may well encourage people to cycle who otherwise do not do so, and these may not be very skilled or confident. Where cycle paths are shared with pedestrians with no form of segregation there can also be a higher risk of collision with them. This may, however, not be borne out by accident statistics, as the common phenomenon of under-reporting of cycle accidents tends to be particularly pronounced in the case of accidents with cyclists and pedestrians on cycle paths (Milton Keynes Cycle Users' Group, 1984).

There may also be particular safety problems with two-way cycling on cycle paths, particularly if the paths are not adequately built for two-way use. Having cycle paths that are two-way potentially offers important advantages in saving detours and permitting more direct cycle access. However, there is also the risk at junction crossings that drivers will not be expecting cyclists to come in the 'wrong' direction and will not be looking out for them. The extent of this risk partly depends on whether the two-way cycling facility is official or unofficial and, if official, whether it is long-standing or the result of a recent conversion of a one-way cycle path. It also depends on the signing and marking of the crossing, with the risk of collision much greater without clear markings. These include, in some countries, marking the surface of the cycle track at such vulnerable crossing points in a different colour, complete with clear and repeated white cycle logos. Keeping the cycle track at a higher level across the junction, as common in Denmark, for example, can also help safety.

Another potential problem with cycle paths is that posed by complex junctions where cyclists want to make turning manoeuvres across oncoming motor traffic, i.e. right turns in the UK and Ireland or left turns in other European countries and North America (Godefrooij, 1991). Without a cycle path the cyclist can signal and move across in good time to take up position ready to make the desired manoeuvre. With cycle paths other arrangements have to be made, such as provision for an indirect turn whereby the cyclist first goes ahead and then turns right (UK or Ireland) or left (rest of Europe and North America). This is a slower but safer manoeuvre and has in fact been the compulsory way in Denmark in recent years for cyclists to turn at signalled junctions.

In discussions about cycle paths the focus is normally on paths alongside main roads but it is important also to consider the scope for

hway cycle paths. These can avoid some of the problems of cycle
or shared paths) alongside main roads but may have some of their
own. Their major potential advantage is the opening up of more direct
links than when cyclists have to use the same routes as motor traffic,
saving both distance and time, if they also mean less need to wait at
junctions. This can offer great advantages compared with using roads.
Such routes often go through parks or other open spaces with more
attractive surroundings, and since they make it easier for cyclists to avoid
the noise and other unpleasantness of riding in traffic they may be
particularly likely to encourage people who would not otherwise cycle,
even on cycle paths alongside roads. Disused railways or canals, as in
Derby, can also offer valuable traffic-free routes, in urban as well as
rural areas.

However, such off-highway routes have some potential drawbacks.
Precisely because they appeal to more inexperienced riders and have
more attractive surroundings where riders' attention is easily diverted by
other sights away from the path they may prove hazardous to cyclists
who want to use them just as short cuts. Moreover, they can be hazardous in other ways when they are not busy because of fears about 'social
safety' or personal security, especially for women, and most of all after
dark (Krause, 1991).

Experience with other kinds of cycle facility

There is a danger in failing to distinguish between the effects of both
kinds of cycle paths, i.e. those running parallel to highways and off-
highway paths, and other special facilities for cyclists. In addition to
paths for cyclists alone, special provision can take the form of paths
shared with pedestrians, with or without segregation, and segregation in
the form of a white line, differential surfacing or colouring, or by level,
with the cycle path at a lower level than the footway. The detailed treatment given varies according to local circumstances such as the space
available, and the anticipated relative numbers of cyclists and
pedestrians.

In recent years the range of available facilities for cyclists has been
greatly expanded. The Netherlands and Denmark have often shown the
way, particularly with on-highway cycling provision. These innovations
have included a number of special measures at junctions, where cyclists
tend to be particularly vulnerable. Special junction measures have
included traffic lights for cyclists and cycle 'reservoirs' or advanced stop
lines (as they are generally known in Britain) to give cyclists priority over
motor traffic when waiting at traffic lights and preparing to make
difficult manoeuvres across oncoming traffic. Less ambitious facilities
can also be very valuable, such as cycle gaps in road closures, if kept free

from obstruction by parked cars. Exemptions for cyclists from turning bans can also help.

A number of criteria are important when assessing the value of special facilities for cyclists, which should not be seen as an end in themselves. As one Dutch cycle planner commented, 'The object of the cyclist is to have a comfortable trip, not to travel in a bicycle lane.' (Ploeger, 1991). The most important criteria are directness, comfort, safety, convenience, and attractiveness of routes, or 'trafficability, safety and comfort', as suggested by Ljungberg (1990). It is difficult for special facilities, especially in the often limited space available within older urban areas, to satisfy all of these criteria fully but schemes are likely to be poorly used by cyclists when they satisfy only a few of these. It is also of course often the case that there will be some conflict between them, and this will affect the likelihood of their use by different categories of cyclist (Jansen, 1988).

This diversity of attitudes makes defining ideal standards for cycle facilities very difficult. Even in the Netherlands, Ploeger comments (1991), there is no consenus of opinion on sizing, which can be very subtle. Substandard widths can encourage conflict but too generous dimensioning can encourage abuse by riders. Cycle lanes that are unnecessarily wide are more likely to be obstructed by parked cars or intruded into by moving cars. The wide-ranging analysis of German experience commented that

Cycle infrastructure has to serve very different groups . . . to provide a cycle system to enable quick cycling for experienced cyclists and as much protection as possible for unsafe cyclists (Bracher et al., 1991).

If lack of space and resources do not permit the construction of good standard facilities it is all the more important to see that the roads are fit for cyclists to use safely.

Reducing travelling time by bike is particularly important to encourage cycle use and, according to Kropman (1991) facilities that achieve this will be well used. This was an important aim of the Delft cycle network, and Fig. 2.1 shows two examples from that city, a bridge over a canal and a subway under a railway. Westerdijk's survey of cyclist route choice (1990) found that most cyclists are not prepared to divert from the shortest route, in terms of distance and time. It should not be forgotten, moreover, that habit is also important in influencing route choice, including the habits in terms of other activities that people have when making particular trips. These include stopping off to buy a paper or cigarettes at a shop that may well be located on a busy road rather than a cycle path or back-street route. A facility that diverts cyclists suddenly off a familiar route can in any case be less attractive than one which lures them at a gentler angle, giving the impression of being less likely

Figure 2.1   Cycle bridge over canal and cycle subway under railway, Delft, Netherlands.

to take them much further! Delays in construction of parts of a major cycle scheme can also affect the development of habits and people's willingness to use the whole scheme when completed. For example, use of a new cycle crossing may be affected by disruption to the cycle path approaching it which is the result of building work on an adjoining site. In any case it takes time for usage patterns to become established.

Special junction facilities like traffic lights may help cyclists to feel safer but tend to involve a time penalty, making overall journey times longer. This can be a disadvantage of cycle signals. The same can be true of routes, including quieter back streets and gaps in road closures, designed to take cyclists right away from busy junctions. Less confident cyclists may still find these attractive while more experienced cyclists, especially males, will tend to keep to the most direct and fastest route, with less regard for the dangers they may encounter there. This inclination will be stronger too in the case of cyclists on trips to work rather than shopping or leisure trips. It is clear that women in general more than men appreciate the safety effects of facilities (Harland and Gercans, 1991). However, it has been suggested by Tight and Carstens (1989) that the general use of a safe route can be encouraged by making routes more attractive even if they are a little longer.

A more attractive route meandering through a park or other green area, perhaps with a less smooth surface, may also often involve a time penalty, which is likely to be more of a disincentive to the commuter cyclist than those cycling for recreation. Cyclists will always make decisions about which route to take (or whether to make a certain trip at all) according to a number of criteria, including their experience and level of confidence, their journey purpose, and the time they have available. These also include the convenience and safety of access to and from a cycle facility and the relative comfort of the surfaces on a cycle path and the alternative road. Too often there are inadequate maintenance arrangements for cycle paths, which suffer from potholes, obstruction by overgrown vegetation, inadequate sweeping-up of broken glass and other debris, as well as vandalised signing and lighting.

To say that the most successful and well-used cycle facilities are those which offer some distinct net advantage to cyclists is not to say that such facilities need to be large and complex. For example, at the simple level, a gap in a road closure can help to open up a direct link for cyclists which is not available to motorists, as can a short cycle path link between two culs-de-sac. Sometimes, however, in existing built-up areas, the only such connecting paths are narrow footpaths. It is also of course essential to strike a balance between the needs of cyclists and pedestrians. Although both categories of vulnerable road users have much in common vis-à-vis motor traffic there are bound to be some situations where their needs come into conflict and it can be difficult to find the right balance. This is now discussed.

Cyclists and pedestrians: sharing or segregation?

Conflicts are most likely to occur on shared paths, especially narrow ones and, in particular, on shared paths created from what were previously just footpaths. Special problems may also occur where large numbers of pedestrians are to be expected and, most of all, pedestrians with special needs such as the physically or visually handicapped (Williams, 1990). The 'toucan' type of mixed crossings, first introduced experimentally in some British urban areas in 1991, are a fairly cheap and flexible solution for use at sites without large numbers of cyclists or pedestrians. These have push-button operation and their installation can be justified at locations where the Department of Transport has said that normal 'pelican' crossings for pedestrians only could not be justified. They also involve relatively little 'clutter' (Morgan, 1991).

Conflicts are also likely to occur in pedestrianised shopping streets. It is important to remember that, even where actual numbers of recorded collisions between pedestrians and cyclists are fairly few, there may still be a high level of fear among pedestrians, especially the elderly, about potential conflicts. Even where the majority of cyclists behave responsibly, riding slowly or even pushing their bikes through during peak shopping hours, the inconsiderate behaviour of a minority can exacerbate latent worries of pedestrians (Trevelyan, 1992; Bachman, 1987).

To highlight these possible problems is not to say that cycling should never be allowed in pedestrian areas. As in the planning of all special facilities full account has to be taken of local circumstances. These include the length of the pedestrianised area, its width, the relative numbers of pedestrians and cyclists, fluctuations in these levels at different times, and the availability of reasonable safe alternative routes. In Karlsruhe in Germany conflicts with pedestrians on the main shopping street were eased in the late 1980s by the provision of a 'City Route' cycle bypass, taking cyclists around a loop to the south.

More generally, fears about possible conflict between cyclists and pedestrians on shared paths can be a problem but one that can often be alleviated in a number of ways, depending again on the detailed local circumstances (Department of Transport, 1986b). Not only segregation (by level preferably rather than just a white line) but also adequate width for both categories of vulnerable user is essential, if significant numbers of both are to be expected. It also helps to ensure that the surface of both areas is maintained to a good standard so that, for example, pedestrians will not be encouraged to walk on the cyclist area simply because their path is rougher. The provision of clear signing and marking also helps to ensure correct use, although there are still likely to be some of both categories that use the 'wrong' side and complain of the other side weaving or trespassing in front of them. It is also important to have consistent treatment in the layout of cycle paths and footways and not, for example, to cross them over at frequent intervals.

Another way to reduce the likelihood of conflict is to seek out opportunities to promote the interests of both together. Wider and therefore lighter subways under main roads may be more attractive for pedestrians to use than narrow subways designated for pedestrians alone. Special traffic lights installed to help cyclists across main roads should automatically include facilities capable of being used (with a push button) by pedestrians, or, with low numbers of each, by both categories without special parallel provision (Trevelyan and Ginger, 1989).

A common feature of cycle paths, perhaps especially those developed in Germany, is that they have been built at the expense of pedestrians rather than drivers. In Germany the paths have often been created simply by painting a white line down the middle of a pavement, even narrow pavements in the centres and other older parts of towns and cities. In political terms this of course tends to be an easier option than challenging the right of motor traffic to dominate road space. Drivers feel more comfortable that the cyclist has been 'got out of the way', especially if they can then drive faster unperturbed by these 'wobblers'. The common rule in some Continental countries compelling cyclists to use cycle paths where they exist has to some extent been motivated by this kind of attitude, it seems. Even in the Netherlands there is still a reluctance in places to make cycling provision if it slows down drivers or takes away car parking space! (Godefrooij, 1991).

On-road cycling provision

The need to provide for the cyclist by taking space away from the driver is now more widely appreciated, even if political obstacles mean that this is still fairly rare in practice, especially in car-producing countries like France, Germany and Britain with their particularly strong car lobbies influencing transport policies (Hamer, 1987; Monheim and Monheim-Dandorfer, 1991). It seems all too often that the design of traffic infrastructure, especially on main roads, still has to start with the needs of motor traffic, 'the only real traffic', and that only afterwards is any thought given to cyclists.

It is perhaps no coincidence that it has been non-car-producing countries like Switzerland, as well as the Netherlands and Denmark, that have been willing to adopt more radical solutions in favour of the bike. In Switzerland, in cities like Basle and Berne, much has been done in recent years to provide cycle lanes on the carriageway rather than cycle paths, or shared paths, away from the carriageway. These have the advantage of making the cyclist far more visible to the driver, especially important near or at junctions (Klewe and Schallaböck, 1991). It is particularly valuable if these cycle lanes are linked to phases at traffic lights giving priority to cycle movements as well as being kept free of parked cars.

In some Swiss cities such as Basle roads with two or three lanes for motor traffic have been converted to include one or two cycle lanes (one of which is for turning traffic) by removing one lane for motor traffic (Balsiger, 1991; Tschopp, 1991). The political will to do this clearly exists in these cities, but they are the exception.

Here again, the most important aim is to give cyclists an advantage in traffic, in terms of distance and time. Opening up one-way streets for cyclists to ride in the wrong direction, for example on 'contra-flow' cycle lanes, has been quite common in the Netherlands for years (as in Fig. 2.2, an example from Delft) and is also now becoming common in Switzerland and parts of Western Germany. This has helped to provide much more direct links for cyclists on the rather narrower streets often found close to city centres.

At traffic lights, measures like advanced stop lines, or priority arrangements in terms of a cycle aspect giving green to cyclists ahead of drivers, can give cyclists' movements' priority and greatly assist their safety (Wheeler, 1991; Welleman, 1991). UK experience of these is still

Figure 2.2   Contra-flow cycle lane, Delft, Netherlands.

very limited, but mostly good (Morgan, 1991). In some cases it may be possible to include a cycle lane (or cycle path) at a three-arm traffic-signalled junction where the cyclist can bypass the signals altogether.

It again encourages cyclists greatly if their momentum can be interrupted as little as possible. Partly for this reason the Swiss have recently had a policy of reviewing the necessity for Stop signs rather than Give Way signs at junctions (Tschopp, 1991). Any facilities, off-road or on road, that require cyclists to stop and give way frequently will tend to be poorly used since they neglect the fact that a certain speed is essential for stability and keeping upright.

On the highway, cyclists can also benefit from being allowed to use bus lanes, still rare in many cities in Germany but, unusually, rather more common in Britain, as for example in Derby since 1981 where 11 bus lanes (with-flow and contra-flow) were then opened up to cyclists, greatly facilitating cycle movements across the city centre.

For cyclists as well as pedestrians it is important that they are not effectively 'dumped' at dangerous locations, such as on the approach to a roundabout, complex one-way system or other major junction. A cycle path or lane is of limited value if it cannot be safely entered and left. In any case, substantial lengths of cycle path, or other types of cycle route, are more attractive than short isolated stretches. The aim should be to develop continuous routes, with cycle lanes, cycle paths, shared paths and other special facilities linked together with quieter (traffic-calmed) roads to form a comprehensive network. Cyclists on back-street routes need to be given priority as far as possible. To be attractive to cyclists these routes also need to avoid sharp turns as much as possible, to be kept smoothly surfaced, well lit, and free from obstruction by parked motor vehicles. All parts of the network should be well signed and have special measures to help cyclists across busy roads and junctions (Department of Transport, 1986a). These should not be complex or difficult to follow.

Personal security and the use of cycle facilities

The willingness of cyclists (and pedestrians) to use special paths away from the highway, or subways, is influenced not just by their perception of the relative safety these afford in terms of freedom from fears about motor traffic but also in terms of their fears about personal security. As Krause has commented (1991) it is women in particular who are most likely to have these fears. It is not just a matter of affecting their travel at night but also during the day. In particular, narrow and dimly-lit subways with dark corners, and paths leading across fairly isolated parks and other open spaces can be very intimidating, as can largely deserted pedestrianised areas at night.

Solutions to these problems include more sensitive design such as wider subways, with good visibility at the entrances and exits (as emphasised especially in Leiden in the Netherlands), less dense vegetation, improved lighting, and offering people a choice of routes, during the day and at night. The importance attached to directness of a route during the day, offering a useful short cut and avoiding a longer and much more busily trafficked route around the edge of an area may be rated a much lower priority at night or at other times when less people are likely to be around.

Conclusion

In conclusion, it has been noted that cycle paths and other special facilities can offer important contributions to improving cyclists' safety but only if they offer some distinct overall advantages to cyclists, in terms of safety, convenience, comfort, directness and general attractiveness. Cycle paths are particularly important in outer areas with more space and faster traffic, and anywhere where they can result in saving distance and time on cycle journeys. On narrower streets closer to the centres of towns and cities cycle paths are of more dubious benefit, although other measures, including special crossings and traffic-calming techniques, may have an important role. Poor facilities may be worse than no facilities at all, increasing dangers and inconvenience. These may then discredit the cause of cycling provision, making future investment less likely. Regular and thorough maintenance is also essential, both to encourage use and more generally to give cyclists the feeling that they are being respected and not regarded as a second-rate form of transport. Cycling provision must not be made at the expense of pedestrians' safety and a careful balance has to be struck between these, taking full account of local circumstances.

Furthermore, it should never be forgotten that, in most towns and cities, especially older urban areas, cyclists will do most of their cycling on ordinary roads and streets. There they will be intimidated by large and still increasing volumes of motor traffic facilitated by the kinds of 'traditional' motor-traffic capacity maximising policies still often pursued. A serious commitment to encouraging cycling must therefore tackle these wider problems directly and consider how other planning and transport policies should be modified to promote greater equity between cyclists and motor traffic. This challenge is the focus of the next chapter.

Key references

Adams, John, 1981, *Transport Policy: Vision and Practice*, Routledge and Kegan Paul, London.

Alrutz, Dankmar, Fechtel, Hans W., Krause, Juliane, 1989, *Dokumentation zur Sicherung des Fahrradverkehrs*, Unfall- und Sicherheitsforschung Strassenverkehrs, Heft 74, Bundesanstalt für Strassenwesen, Bereich Unfallforschung.

Bracher, Tilman, 1989, *Policy and Provision for Cyclists in Europe*, Commission of the European Communities, Directorate-General for Transport, VII/B-3, Brussels.

Bracher, Tilman, Luda, Helmut, Thiemann, H., 1991, *Zussamenfassende Auswertung von Forchungsergebnissen zum Radverkehr in der Stadt*, Forschung Stadtverkehr, Band A7, Bundesminister für Verkehr, Bergisch Glad-bach/Berlin, Bonn.

Monheim, Heiner and Monheim-Dandorfer, Rita, 1991, *Strassen für alle*, Rasch und Röhring Verlag, Hamburg.

Ploeger, Jan, 1991, *Introductory Speech: Workshop on Bicycle Facilities*, report of proceedings, Velo City '91, Milan.

Thomson, Michael, 1978, *Great Cities and Their Traffic*, Penguin Books, London.

Transport Studies Unit, 1991, *Transport: The New Realism*, TSU, Oxford University.

Other references

Atkins, Stephen, 1989, *Critical Paths: Designing for Secure Travel*, Design Council, London.

Atkins, Stephen, 1991, *Unspoken Decrees – Road Appraisal, Democracy and the Environment*, London Wildlife Trust, London.

Bach, Ole, et al., 1985, *Cykelstier i byer – den sikkerhedmaessige effekt*, Vejdirektoratet, Naestved, Denmark.

Bachman, Peter, 1987, Radfahrer in Fussgangerzonen, *Schweizer Ingenieur und Architekt*, 27–28/87.

Balsiger, Oskar, 1991, *Veloverkehrspolitik am Wendepunkt*, paper presented to the Velo Secur '90 Conference, Salzburg, Austria, 2–5 May, ARGUS, Arbeitsgemeinschaft umweltfreundlicher Stadtverkehr, Vienna.

Bracher, Tilman, 1988, *Subjektive und objektive Sicherheit von Radwegen*, Beitrag zur Internationalen Strassen- und Verkehrskonferenz 'Strassen und Verkehr 2000', Berlin, 1988.

Department of Transport, 1981, *Cycling: A Consultation Paper*, D.Tp., London.

Department of Transport, 1982, *Statement of Cycling Policy*, D.Tp., London.

Department of Transport, 1986a, *Local Transport Note 1/86: Cyclists at Road Crossings and Junctions*, HMSO, London.

Department of Transport, 1986b, *Local Transport Note 2/86: Shared Use by Pedestrians and Cyclists*, HMSO, London.

Department of Transport, 1989, *Making Way for Cyclists: Planning, Design and Legal Issues*, Local Transport Note 1/89, HMSO, London.

Dupree, Harry, 1987, *Urban Transport: The New Towns Solution*, Gower, Aldershot.

Godefrooij, Tom, 1991, *Promoting the Use of the Bicycle: Improving Safety is Not Enough*, paper presented to the Velo City '91 Conference, Milan.

Hall, R.D., Harrison, J.H., McDonald, M. and Harland, D.G., 1989, *Accident Analysis Methodologies and Remedial Measures with Particular Regard to Cyclists*, Contractor Report 164, Transport and Road Research Laboratory, Crowthorne, Berkshire.

Hamer, Mick, 1987, *Wheels Within Wheels: A Study of the Road Lobby*, Friends of the Earth, London.

Harland, D.G., et al., 1986, Footways shared by cyclists and pedestrians, *Traffic Engineering and Control*, May.

Harland, D.G. and Gercans, Raymond, 1991, *Cycle Routes*, paper presented to the Velo City '91 Conference, Milan.

Hartman, Jan B., 1990, The Delft Bicycle Network, in Tolley, Rodney (ed.), *The Greening of Urban Transport: Planning for Walking and Cycling in Western Cities*, Belhaven Press, London, pp. 193–200.

Hass-Klau, Carmen, 1990, *The Pedestrian and City Traffic*, Belhaven Press, London.

Hillman, Mayer and Whalley, Ann, 1983, *Energy and Personal Travel: Obstacles to Conservation*, Policy Studies Institute, London.

Hülsmann, Wulf, 1990, The 'Bicycle-Friendly Towns' Project in the Federal Republic of Germany, in Tolley, Rodney (ed.), *The Greening of Urban Transport: Planning for Walking and Cycling in Western Cities*, Belhaven Press, London, pp. 218–230.

Jansen, Dick, 1988, *Comfort and Speed versus Safety: A Dilemma in the Design of Cycle Facilities*, paper presented to the Velo City '87 Conference, Groningen, September 1987: report of proceedings published by CROW (ed. T. de Wit), Ede, Netherlands, 183–186.

Klewe, Heinz and Schallabök, Karl-Otto, 1991, *Radwege an Strassen*, Monatsbericht des Institut für Landes- und Stadtentwicklungsforschung des Landes Nordrheinwestfalen.

Knoche, Günter, et al., 1981, *Einfluss von Radwegen auf die Verkehrssicherheit, Band 2, Radfahrerunfälle auf Stadtstrassen*. Bundesanstalt für Strassenwesen, Bereich Unfallforshung, Nr. 62, Köln.

Krause, Juliane, 1991, *Die soziale Sicherheit von Verkehrsanlagen – ins besondere Radverkehrsanlagen*, paper presented to the Bonner Fahrrad-kongress, organised by the ADFC (Allgemeiner Deutscher Fahrradclub), Bonn City Council and the Ministry of Traffic and Town Planning, North-Rhine Westphalia, Bonn-Bad Godesberg, 10–11 June.

Kroon, Martin, 1990, Traffic and Environmental Policy in the Netherlands, in Tolley, Rodney (ed.), *The Greening of Urban Transport: Planning for Walking and Cycling in Western Cities*, Belhaven Press, London, pp. 113–133.

Kropman, Jan A., 1991, *Mobiliteit, fietsgebruik en veiligheid*. Instituut voor Toegepaste Social Wetenschappen (ITS), report of Conference, 'Perspectieven voor 15 miljoen fietsers,' 21.11.90, Woerden, Netherlands.

Lind, Magnus G. and Wollin, Staffan, 1986, Bicycle Accidents, *Chirurgica Scandinavica*, Supplement 531.

Ljungberg, Christer, 1990, *Design of Bicycle Facilities from a Cyclist's Point of View*, report of proceedings, Velo City '89 International Bicycle Conference, Copenhagen, 21–23 August, 1989, ed. Niels Jensen and published by the National Agency for Physical Planning, January.

Mathew, Don, 1992, The 10 Best and the 10 Worst Cycling Cities, *New Cyclist* No. 19, March.

May, A., 1991, Integrated transport strategies: a new approach to urban transport policy formulation in the UK, *Transport Review*, 11 (3), pp. 223–247.

Milton Keynes Cycle Users' Group, 1984, *Cycling in Milton Keynes: a User's View*, MKCUG, Milton Keynes, Buckinghamshire.

Ministry of Transport and Public Works (Netherlands), 1979, *The Hague Pilot Cycleway Project 1975–79*, The Hague, Netherlands.

Ministry of Transport and Public Works (Netherlands), 1986, *Evaluation of the Delft Bicycle Network: Summary Report of the Before Study*, The Hague, Netherlands.

Ministry of Transport and Public Works (Netherlands), 1987, *Evaluation of the Delft Bicycle Network plan: Final Summary Report*, The Hague, Netherlands.

Mogridge, Michael, 1990, *Travel in Towns: Jam Yesterday, Jam Today, and Jam Tomorrow?*, Macmillan, London.

Morgan, J. M. 1991, *Cycling in safety?* proceedings and programme Safety '91, Transport and Road Research Labatory, Crowthorne.

Owen, Susan, 1990, *Energy and Urban Form*, Pion, London.

Perraton, Jean, 1968, Planning for the Cyclist in Urban Areas, *Town Planning Review*, Vol. 39 (2), July.

Quenault, S., 1979, *Cycle Routes in Portsmouth – Attitude Surveys*, Transport and Road Research Laboratory Report LR 875, TRRL, Crowthorne, Berkshire.

Quenault, S. and Head, T., 1977, *Cycle Routes in Portsmouth I - Planning and Implementation*, Transport and Road Research Laboratory Report SR 317, TRRL, Crowthorne, Berkshire.

Renner, Michael, 1988, *Rethinking the Role of the Automobile*, Worldwatch Institute, Washington DC, USA.

Social Trends, 1992, *Social Trends 22*, HMSO.

Stores, A., 1980, *Cycle Ownership and Use in Great Britain*, Transport and Road Research Laboratory, Report 843, TRRL, Crowthorne, Berkshire.

Tight, M.R. and Carsten, O.M.J. 1989, *Problems for Vulnerable Road Users in Great Britain, the Netherlands and Sweden*, Institute of Transport Studies, University of Leeds.

Trevelyan, Peter, 1992, *Cycling in Pedestrianised Areas*, Transport and Road Research Laboratory, Crowthorne, Berkshire.

Trevelyan, Peter and Ginger, Mike, 1989, *Cyclists' Use of Pedestrian and Cycle/Pedestrian Crossings*, Transport and Road Research Laboratory Contractor Report 173, TRRL, Crowthorne, Berkshire.

Tschopp, Juerg, 1991, *Massnahmen für den Veloverkehr*, Verkehrs-Club der Schweiz, Ressort Velo, Herzogenbuchsee, Switzerland.

Untermann, Rich, 1990, Why you can't walk there: strategies for improving the pedestrian environment in the United States, in Tolley, Rodney (ed.), *The Greening of Urban Transport: Planning for Walking and Cycling in Western Cities*, Belhaven Press, London, pp. 185–189.

Wheeler, A. H. 1991, *Advanced Stop Lines in Oxford, Newark and Bristol*, Research Report 336, Transport and Road Research Laboratory, Crowthorne.

Welleman, 1991, *The Netherlands National Cycling Policy and Facilities for Cyclists at Signalled Junctions*, Local Authorities Cycle Planning Group Meeting, York, 17 May.

Welleman, A.G. and Dijkstra, A., 1988, *Cyclists and Road Safety in the Netherlands*, in proceedings, International Congress, 'Planning for the Urban Cyclist', Velo City '87, Groningen, published by CROW, Ede, Netherlands, pp. 137–140.

Westerdijk, P.K., 1990, *Pedestrian and Pedal Cyclist Route Choice Criteria*, Drive Project 1031 Report, Traffic Research Centre, University of Groningen, Haren, Netherlands.

Williams, Marian, 1990, Monitoring tactile markings on shared pedestrian–cycle routes, *Traffic Engineering and Control*, 31 (12), December.

Wolf, Jürgen, 1988b, Zur Sicherheit innerortlicher Radwege, *Städte und Gemeindebund 2*, 1988, pp. 54–69.

3 Planning for the bicycle in newer and older towns and cities

Hugh McClintock

Moves towards new directions in transport policy

By the beginning of the 1990s steadily increasing concern about the dangers of global warming and transport's major contribution to it through carbon dioxide emissions had come to encourage a much more critical awareness among transport professionals of the implications of current transport policies. An Organisation of Economic Cooperation and Development Report (OECD, 1990), for example, called for more integration of traffic planning and land use planning, and for a transport shift to public transport as well as a strengthened role for walking, cycling and telecommunications.

In Britain the case for a change of direction was thoroughly argued in 'Transport: the new realism', a report based on the contributions of a wide range of experts in the Transport and Society Project carried out by Oxford University's Transport Studies Unit (TSU, 1991). Its most important message was that it is not just undesirable but impossible to cater for all predicted new transport and travel demand.

The report claimed that there was now far wider recognition of the need to embrace a wide range of new transport policies including traffic restraint, traffic-calming, advanced traffic management systems including driver guidance and integrated signal control, as well as a very substantial increase in the quality and scale of public transport provision. Traffic-calming was seen as important not just to reduce traffic speeds but also as a general strategy to help tilt the advantage in favour of pedestrians and cyclists. This combination of policies should help to improve the quality of life in cities, rather than mobility as such, especially for car users.

The need for new road construction was now seen by the TSU report as following from a consideration of how much traffic to provide for, a decision itself influenced by the combined effect of the policies described. It was quite clear that construction to meet demand should no longer be the core of a transport strategy. The 'new realism' recognised that it was not possible to provide for unlimited car use, thus helping to open up the possibility of other and more realistic directions.

A more radical change in policy had been published in the Netherlands in 1989 in the National Environment Policy Plan (Kroon, 1990), an attempt to develop an environmental strategy fully compatible with the principles of sustainable development. Stabilising carbon dioxide emissions was proposed as a priority national target and, in the transport sector, this meant an increased emphasis on public transport and bicycles.

The proposals drew on the evidence of several studies to show that a considerable proportion of car use in the Netherlands was not 'essential' and suggested that 30–40 per cent of all car rides may be judged as having a reasonable substitute in public transport, the bicycle or telecommunications. The Netherlands is a highly urbanised country, with a high average population density and the Plan felt that nearly half of all car movements are carried out within a reasonable cycling distance (5km) or even reasonable walking distance (2km). Indeed, the Report felt that the use of the bicycle could be encouraged for longer distances as well, up to 10km, as part of its strategy to achieve a considerable increase in the number of kilometres covered by non-motorised transport (Welleman, 1991). This implied the need, among other things, for a great improvement in facilities for cycling (as well as public transport), in order to reduce the attractions of car use.

These incentives were proposed to be reinforced by pricing (increasing variable car costs) and other incentive instruments to influence the choice of transport mode and information and other stimuli to all those involved. The proposals also envisaged reducing parking facilities for commuter traffic through action on volume and regulation, and, increasingly, use of physical planning via concentration on the public transport orientation of land uses, and reducing and managing mobility to achieve shorter distances between where people live, work, shop and spend their free time. Major traffic casualty reduction targets have also been included in the proposals. The radical nature of the policies soon encountered substantial political opposition, showing that it is not easy to change car-friendly attitudes and habits, even in a country like the Netherlands with such a strong cycling tradition!

Implications for cyclists on the general highway network

In practical terms this comprehensive approach also means taking far more account of cyclists' safety and other needs in the design of ordinary roads and streets. However well designed and well maintained special facilities for cyclists are it has now become quite clear that their contribution to the promotion of safe and attractive cycling is limited if cyclists' needs are promptly forgotten as soon as they leave these cycle paths or other special facilities. Apart from the handful of new towns with specially designed and integrated cycleway systems, such as Houten (Netherlands), Västerås (Sweden), or Stevenage (England), it is on ordinary roads and streets that most cyclists will be riding most of the time.

One important way to help cyclists on a wider basis in urban areas is to take full advantage of traffic-calming type schemes. In these schemes, pioneered especially in the Netherlands, Denmark and Western Germany (Cleary, 1991; Hass-Klau, 1990; Keller, 1991, Pharoah, 1990), the focus has been on modifying the layout of a whole street, or even the streets in a whole neighbourhood with the aims of slowing traffic speeds, creating more lively and attractive areas, and helping to reclaim space from motor traffic for other uses including trees and other greenery, playspace and better rights of way for pedestrians and cyclists. Sometimes, as in the 'Tempo 30' areas now very common in Western German towns and cities, measures are limited to the provision of signs and perhaps speed plateaux at the entrance to affected areas. Elsewhere, a wider range of changes are made, involving chicanes, speed tables, ramps, and general carriageway narrowing.

Experience so far in countries with the longest history of such schemes shows that they can make a major contribution to improving the safety of pedestrians and cyclists by reducing the speed differential between their average speeds and those of motor vehicles. By reducing speeds to a maximum of 30km/h, instead of 50km/h, the chances of a fatal or severe accident arising from a collision between a pedestrian or cyclist and a motor vehicle are greatly reduced (see Fig. 3.1). Cyclists and pedestrians can also benefit from the more attractive surroundings which good traffic-calming schemes entail, with a variety of new planting and well designed surface treatment, as shown in the photograph from Heidelberg (Fig. 3.2).

There are also, however, dangers for cyclists in traffic-calming schemes if the details are not sensitively handled (Cleary, 1991). For example, central refuges may succeed in slowing down motor traffic but cycling past them can be very hazardous if insufficient space is left for a motor vehicle overtaking a bicycle. Steeply angled humps can unnecessarily reduce the speed of ordinary cyclists going about their business as well as the speed of car drivers. This may be a particular problem for cyclists carrying children on the back, or parcels, or for any cyclist encountering a feature unexpectedly, for example, just around the corner from a turn. In Germany, in the more radical form of traffic-calming, introduced in areas with the 'house on the ski' sign, walking pace is the speed limit prevailing,

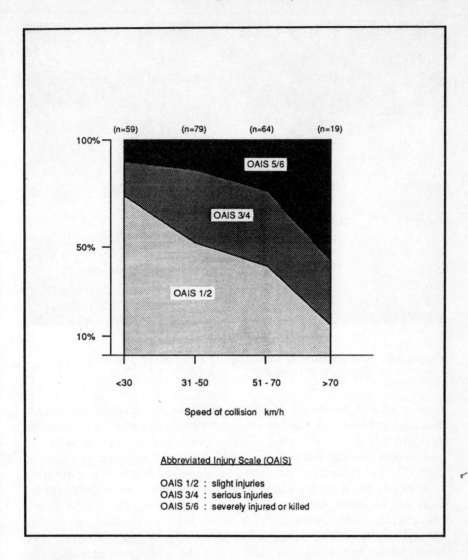

Figure 3.1 The relationship between speed and cycle accident severity.

Source: Alrutz 1989

which has been ruled to mean a limit of 7km/h, i.e. less than a pace that cyclists really need to maintain their momentum without wobbling and falling off!

In general a good principle is as far as possible to exempt cyclists from particular measures. This can be done by leaving a gap between the kerb and any speed hump or plateau, or by including a straight cycle lane to bypass chicanes or central refuges.

Sensitivity to cyclists' needs in design details can be extended to

Figure 3.2   An exceptionally well-designed traffic-calming scheme in the Weststadt of Heidelberg, Germany.

develop into an awareness of how to maximise the potential advantages that such schemes can offer cyclists. For example, central refuges can be provided not just to slow motor traffic speeds and to assist the safety of pedestrians crossing but also to afford some shelter to cyclists making right (UK and Ireland) or left (rest of Europe and North America) turns.

At points where cycle paths or other cycle routes cross ordinary roads, features like speed plateaux can be used to force drivers to slow down. On a wider basis, maintaining as direct links as possible for cyclists through traffic-calmed areas, while effectively forcing drivers to take longer routes can be used as part of a wider strategy to encourage the use of bicycles by giving cyclists priority in terms of distance and journey times (Draeger, 1991).

Given the common problems of finding enough space in the more central parts of older towns and cities to accommodate good standard cycle paths, or even cycle lanes, some use will have to be made of quieter roads and streets as part of the network of designated cycle routes. Traffic-calming can be used as part of a deliberate policy to improve conditions for cyclists on these, and then to connect them as part of a wider cycle network with cycle paths, cycle lanes and other measures. Recent experience in Germany has suggested (Environment and Transport Planning and Planungsgemeinschaft Verkehr, 1991) that, in

Figure 3.3 Cycle paths incorporated with traffic-calming, Mainz, Germany.

narrower streets in urban areas, traffic-calming can in fact make a bigger contribution to cyclists' safety than cycle paths. Cycle facilities and traffic-calming need not be mutually exclusive but can complement each other, as in the use of chicanes and cycle lanes in one of the German model traffic-calming schemes in Mainz-Bretzenheim (Fig. 3.3). A similar scheme in England was introduced more recently in Milton Keynes (Cleary, 1991).

An evaluation of the six German area-wide traffic-calming demonstration projects (Bundesanstalt für Strassenwesen, 1990) also showed broadly positive effects for cyclists from these projects, including a marked reduction in the proportion of cyclists regarded by drivers as 'careless'. By 1991 several German towns such as Freiburg had now introduced 'Tempo 30' zones in all their residential areas, with speed limits of 50km/h retained only on the main residential roads. Such policies help greatly to extend the safety benefits for cyclists.

Traffic-calming schemes in Germany have been mostly limited to residential areas and quieter roads. There have so far been very few schemes to calm traffic on major roads, especially in large towns or cities. This partly reflects the concerns of public transport operators since these roads are more likely to be bus routes but it also reflects continuing pressure to give the momentum of private motor traffic priority over safety for more vulnerable users. However, elsewhere, for example

Denmark, there have been more attempts to introduce traffic-calming on main roads, in some cases as an alternative to the provision of bypasses, and these, as in Vinderup, have helped to increase cycle usage (Pease, 1991).

It is on main roads and, in particular, at main junctions that cyclists are most at risk of accidents and it is at these locations that the main challenge to improving their safety needs to be grasped. Even in the Netherlands junctions often remain dangerous bottlenecks for cyclists and facilities there tend often to be complex and hard to follow (Godefrooij, 1991). It is very important to obtain detailed information on cyclists' perceptions of these problem areas.

Cyclists' safety at roundabouts

As more and more complex arrangements have been introduced in the design of major junctions so cyclists have tended to suffer. Often their safety has been given very little consideration when compared with the need to increase capacity and maintain the momentum of other road users. This has been particularly well illustrated in Britain in studies of cycling at roundabouts (Allott and Lomax, 1991). In terms of general traffic engineering these have offered many benefits, especially for heavy vehicles which can turn much more easily than at most traffic-signal-controlled junctions. However, for cyclists (and motor-cyclists) they can be extremely hazardous, especially large roundabouts (as shown in Fig. 3.4), with recorded accident rates, according to Allott and Lomax, up to 15 times those for cars and two or three times those for pedal cyclists at traffic signals. It is also clear from this study that roundabouts feature high on the list of locations that British cyclists tend to avoid, mainly because they fear they will be at risk from drivers entering the roundabouts at speed and simply not seeing the cyclist in front of them, or not seeing them in enough time to take avoiding action.

Even in Britain roundabouts differ greatly in their design, and the extent of the danger for cyclists will depend on many detailed features, such as entry path curvature, entry width, entry angle and visibility. All of these affect vehicle speed which is critical in determining accident rates and severity.

Considering cyclists' safety at roundabouts on a wider basis it is important to remember that the use of smaller roundabouts, with a maximum diameter of 28m, has elsewhere been commended as a way of increasing cyclists' safety by reducing the speed of drivers entering the junction (Bracher, 1989; Balsiger, 1991). In the Netherlands and Switzerland smaller roundabouts are seen as an important traffic-calming measure, improving cyclists' safety. Clearly much depends on the local conditions and also on the detailed entry geometry. Excessive entry

Figure 3.4 The dangers for cyclists at major roundabouts: Crown Island, Nottingham.

capacity, width of circulatory carriageway and roundabout size can encourage excessive entry and circulatory speeds, especially in off-peak traffic.

The solutions to these problems again need to take full account of local conditions but may involve controlling entry priorities and speeds, and improving drivers' visibility on entry to the roundabout so that cyclists already on the roundabout are less likely to be overlooked. Traffic-calming measures may also have a role here. In some cases there may be scope for peripheral cycle tracks, as in Bremen (Fig. 3.5). These can be linked to special cycle signals to help cyclists across the different arms of the junction. In other cases there may be subways available nearby, suitable for conversion to shared pedestrian or cycle use and linking with the peripheral paths or other 'cyclist bypass' routes in the vicinity. The provision of traffic signals at junctions may also help to facilitate safe cycle movements.

Mini-roundabouts may pose rather less dangers for cyclists (Allott and Lomax, 1991) and have the advantage over traffic lights that, in lighter traffic conditions at least, they are more likely to help cyclists maintain their momentum at the junction.

Figure 3.5 A roundabout redesigned for safer cycle use: Am Stern, Bremen, Germany.

Cyclists and other major junction layouts

It would be wrong to think that conditions for cyclists at major round-abouts are always necessarily worse than at major junctions controlled by traffic signals. In the case of the latter, at major intersections with several arms and many traffic lanes in each direction, there may be particular problems for cyclists wishing to turn across the flow of oncoming traffic (i.e. right in the UK and Ireland, and left in the rest of Europe and North America). And cyclists wishing to go straight on may find themselves in conflict with motor traffic in special turning lanes, especially if these are exempt from signal control.

As mentioned in the last chapter, cyclists' safety at such junctions may be greatly improved by the inclusion of clearly marked cycle lanes, for both straight ahead and turning cyclists, as in Fig. 3.6, which shows a good example in the centre of Basle. Even better is for these cycle lanes to be linked to measures giving cyclists priority over motor traffic when turning. These can take the form of cyclists' 'reservoirs' or advanced stop lines in front of all motor traffic (Wheeler, 1991; Welleman, 1991) or, alternatively, traffic signal aspects which give green to cyclists before drivers (Monheim and Monheim-Dandorfer, 1991).

As well as helping cyclists on the road through the provision of special

Figure 3.6   Cycle lanes at a major junction in the centre of Basle, Switzerland.

facilities it is necessary to modify many other features of road layouts to make them suitable for safe use by cyclists. Particularly dangerous are any features which effectively encourage high speeds by drivers. These include free-flow turning lanes at junctions and slip roads on near-motorway-standard urban main roads. The speeds of turning traffic at other junctions can be reduced by including cycle gaps or 'Velo-weichen' as they are known in Switzerland (Tschopp, 1991). These involve reorganising the layout to force drivers to make a sharper right turn, reducing their speed, while allowing cyclists to slip through with less loss of momentum and far more protection from motor traffic. This can also help cyclists going straight on. Moreover, both road design and markings should make it easier for drivers to expect to see cyclists.

Even with the improvements brought about by better gears, cyclists are still sensitive to gradients, as well as to loss of momentum, and sensitivity is also required in dealing with this. That is one reason why it may often be more suitable, space permitting, when providing a cycle crossing of a main road, for that to take the form of a subway, with a height of no more than 2.5m, rather than a bridge over a road where headroom of at least 4.5m and more probably 6m needs to be maintained. This makes it more difficult to provide approaches for cyclists with a reasonably rideable gradient, that is, of not more than 5 per cent.

Figure 3.7   Cycle-sensitive highway design near Winterhur station, Switzerland.

Where cycle paths are provided alongside a road going under a railway, canal, or other road, there is similarly no need to drop the level of the cycle path as much as that of the road, as recognised in many locations in the Netherlands and on the main road by the railway station in the Swiss town of Winterthur (see Fig. 3.7). This, with adjoining measures including cycle lanes, is an excellent example of a cycle-friendly road layout.

Cyclists and general traffic management

There are a number of other ways in which cycling can effectively be encouraged, by ensuring that cyclists are not automatically subjected to the same restrictions as motor traffic. These include road closures where often cyclists can be helped with a simple cycle gap (kept free from parked cars or other obstructions) to maintain a direct and fairly quiet route, again giving them a relative distance (and perhaps also time) advantage over drivers. Similarly, there may often be good reasons for introducing turning bans for drivers which, if applied automatically to cyclists, can result in their having to take unnecessary detours, eroding the attractions of the bike for short journeys.

Several Swiss cities such as Basle and Berne have recently developed a strong awareness of how cyclists' needs can be promoted in a wide variety of schemes. For example, the right for cyclists to use one-way streets in the 'wrong' direction is now particularly common in some German and Swiss cities (Alrutz et al., 1991). In Basle cyclists on one two-lane one-way street have been helped by exempting them (and buses and taxis) from the ban on straight ahead movements by general motor traffic on the right-hand lane.

Cyclists can also benefit greatly from wider traffic management policies to exclude motor traffic from certain areas, for example city centres. In some cases, as in Gothenburg (Sweden), Groningen (see Chapter 9) and Bremen, these have taken the form of dividing the central area or historic core into a cell system, with movements by most motor traffic between the cells forbidden and access being permitted only from the peripheral roads. Cyclists, however, are still allowed through between the cells, again helping them to maintain direct routes, and thus making cycling relatively more attractive.

Car-free cities and car-free axes

Even more radical are schemes which aim at the creation of so-called 'car-free' cities. This usually means attempts to exclude as much motor traffic as possible (that is, excluding delivery and emergency vehicles, and possibly hotel traffic) from the central cores, usually in places of strong historic character such as Lübeck and Münster in Germany. Lübeck (Schunemann, 1991) has one of the most far-reaching such policies, introduced at weekends only from 1991 and intended to apply to the whole week, as from 1993. Cyclists are exempt from such restrictions and are also helped by policies to improve cycle access to the central core from the rest of the urban area, as well as to increase the provision of cycle parking facilities at a number of points, including many on part of the 'freed' road surface.

One of the important aims of such 'car-free' city policies is to restore the character of the historic core of cities which over the years has been more and more swamped by motor traffic, whether moving or parked. This character has been eroded not only by the motor vehicles themselves but also by the clutter to serve them, such as wider tarmac areas for road space and parking, and forests of traffic signs and markings. If, as in pedestrianised areas, such policies are accompanied by the reintroduction of traditional materials in the road surface (although not rounded cobbles!), the reclamation of green areas lost for car parking, and more tree and shrub planting, cyclists can also be greatly helped by the much quieter and more attractive conditions that ensue.

Car-free axes are important as well as car-free cities. One example of this was the creation of a car-free east–west route in Tilburg in the Netherlands as part of the Dutch Government's major cycle route experimental scheme in the late 1970s. This entailed a through route making use of sections of street limited for through motor traffic, as well as cycle paths, bridges and subways. Another excellent example is the Promenade in Münster, where a most attractive route for pedestrians and cyclists has been created through the linear park area that straddles the inner core (Innenstadt). This was previously part of Münster's fortifications.

Cyclists and other traffic policies

Other elements of the cycle network can be formed from permitting cyclists to share bus lanes, as in Derby and Berlin (see Chapters 4 and 11), provided that there is adequate width, i.e. a minimum of 4m. Bus lanes, coupled with bus priority measures at traffic lights, are increasingly being combined with traffic restraint-measures linked to the encouragement of drivers to leave their cars at park-and-ride sites on the peripheries of cities. Apart from the specific benefits to cyclists from being allowed to avoid congestion, and speed their journey times, through using such facilities, cyclists can also gain through the overall reduction in traffic in city centres. In Oxford, extensive provision of bus lanes (and park-and-ride sites), as well as cycle lanes and some other special cycling facilities, have helped to generate what appears to be the largest increase in cycling of any British city in recent years (Mathew, 1990). Even more impressive is the example of Freiburg where a large increase in cycling since the mid-1980s has gone hand in hand with a series of major measures to extend and market the public transport system. These, and extensive traffic-calming, have helped to generate some of the biggest recent increases in cycle usage of any German city.

Adults who used to ride bikes many years ago and who would like to take up cycling again can be encouraged by an awareness of the possibilities to promote cycling in other traffic policies. For example, schemes to promote car-pooling through shared use of cars for commuting must involve some register of users' preferred origins, destinations and travelling times which could also be used to organise a 'bike-mate' scheme. In these, such 'born-again' or novice cyclists are matched up with experienced riders who can advise them on the best route and the best way to negotiate traffic on their regular journeys.

Cyclists can benefit from other wider traffic management policies intended to ensure that access to facilities does not depend on personal motorised transport. Even if they do not persuade drivers to sell their cars they may at least persuade some that the ownership of a second car in their household is not necessary and that the bike and public transport

can represent attractive and worthwhile alternatives. Even if car ownership does not decrease, it is important to try to reduce the use of the car
by some people for some types of trips, as well as to reduce the length
of their trips. This is a fundamental lesson from Dutch experience and
could, given the right political commitment, be applied in other countries
with similar high levels of car ownership (Heynen, 1992).

The development of cycle networks

In the ideal situation every single road and street in a city would be made
'cycle-friendly'. A more realistic aim, however, is to deploy all these
kinds of measures to move towards the development of a cycle network.
A cycle network, rather than a cycle path network, should be the aim,
since the latter term can imply the completion of a quantity of cycle
paths, regardless of their quality or real contribution to cyclists' safety.
A cycle network will use good quality cycle lanes, cycle paths or shared
paths, by the highway and off-highway, for example, running by rivers
or canals, across parks and other open spaces, where they can be fitted
in. It will also use traffic-calmed streets and pedestrianised areas with
cycle exemptions to form a comprehensive network for both daily cyclists
and leisure cyclists to use. This should link all parts of the urban area,
both the city centre, residential, shopping and all kinds of employment
and education areas, as well as provide safe links to the surrounding
countryside.

Links in the network should be continuous and as direct as possible,
easy to follow, with plenty of clear and well maintained direction signs,
with smooth and well swept surfaces. Particularly valuable are links
which give cyclists a distinct advantage for their journeys by overcoming
major barriers such as main roads, railways, canals and rivers. This
means considering the scope for special bridges, as on the south
Cambridge route (see Chapter 7), or subways or underpasses if sensitively
designed and well lit for non-motorised users, with safe cycle route
connections via the rest of the network to the most popular destinations
for cyclists. Politicians are still far more likely to support funds for new
road bridges or underpasses than for similar connections for cyclists and
pedestrians but such cycle facilities can be of great benefit. They can be
of particular value in promoting safer routes to schools, where perhaps
some of the greatest potential for increases in cycling lies.

In choosing the links that will eventually form this network it is important to have a full understanding of the routes now used by cyclists,
whether officially or unofficially, and also to be aware of the locations
that they avoid as being too dangerous, or are generally reluctant to use
unless there is no alternative for certain journeys. It is misleading just to
rely on recorded accidents since these may give a very false picture of the

distribution of serious problem spots, as measured by cyclists' own views on where it is and is not fairly safe to cycle. This underlines the importance of consultation with local cycling groups and all likely users of sections of the network, including local schools and colleges and major employers.

Account also needs to be taken of the origins and destinations of cyclists' trips, for example the places that cyclists are most likely to want to reach, including entertainment and leisure centres and swimming baths. The desire lines of potential users must be considered. Such analysis should take account of future land use changes and potential new major developments and redevelopments. Some parts of a cycle network may be created fairly readily, for example, with minor upgrading of an existing path, while others may be achievable only in the longer run. This category includes cycle schemes designed to be an integral part of major new road or junction changes or new cycle paths to be included in the plans for redevelopment of particular plots of land. It is vital to ensure that these links are safeguarded, through being included in development plans for an area and in development briefs for particular sites so that the opportunity to build them is not lost when the development or redevelopment actually occurs. Cycle schemes can be promoted as part of a number of wider schemes, for environmental improvement, for derelict land reclamation, for canalside or riverside enhancement, or for the opening up of new employment, residential or recreational areas.

It is also essential that all schemes for new roads, for road widening and for general traffic management are appraised for their likely impact on cyclists, as well as pedestrians, as these too can open up useful opportunities to promote safe and attractive cycling. Without this kind of auditing there is a serious risk of creating new blackspots for cyclists and disrupting the continuity of network routes, for example, big new roundabouts or new roads that truncate back streets or paths used by cyclists. This underlines the need for the cultivation of a wider 'cycle awareness' in central and local government so that all officials automatically, in the context of other initiatives, 'think bike'. This wider cycle awareness will be helped by having an appropriate administrative framework, allowing for coordination between different departments. It is also important to get early commitment to safeguarding routes, for example in local development plans and development briefs, even if the routes may not be built for some time. In this way it may be possible to erode some of the considerable time and effort that can be needed for the implementation of even minor cycle schemes. Consistency in cycling policy is also helped by having a regular specific financial allocation for cycling schemes, to be drawn on in addition to funding for cycle measures as an integral part of other types of traffic and development schemes.

Cycling provision in new towns and cities and lessons for older urban areas

In the development of new suburbs or other new settlements there may be particularly good opportunities for the inclusion of good standard cycle routes, including segregated crossings of main roads, safe paths built to adequate standards and with segregation where substantial numbers of both cyclists and pedestrians are anticipated. Such considerations were very much exploited in the development of the Delft suburb of Tantoft (Hartman, 1990) and, most impressively of all, were one of the main principles in the planning of the new town of Houten in the Netherlands near Utrecht (Meilof, 1988).

In Britain several new towns have made some attempt to include cycling provision in their original plans (Dupree, 1987). These included Harlow and Stevenage in the first new towns developed after 1945, and, since 1970, the major expansion of Peterborough. That it is more difficult to include plans for good cycling provision if cycling is not considered from the start is illustrated by the experience of Milton Keynes. There, the redway system of shared paths for cyclists and pedestrians was grafted on to the Master Plan in the mid-1970s, a few years after the basic 1km grid layout had been fixed and development had started. This has meant that gradients on the redways have often actually been greater than those on the roads, one of the features that have made the redway system, although one of the most extensive examples of cycling provision in Britain, also one of the most criticised (Milton Keynes Cycle Users' Group, 1984).

In developing a cycle network much can be learnt, in older and newer towns and cities, from the experience of Delft (Hartman, 1990). In addition to focusing on the need to help cyclists overcome the major barriers between different parts of the city, and thus making their journey distance and time shorter, policy aimed to develop a hierarchy of routes, serving neighbourhood, district and city-wide levels, as illustrated in Fig. 3.8. This can help to ensure that cyclists will always find a safe route nearby for any of their journeys. It also shows recognition of the importance cyclists attach to not having to go too far out of their way, and is a concept which can be a very useful guide in planning cycle networks in other cities, depending on their structure and topography. In hillier cities, for example, it may be more appropriate to think in terms of a spine or spines of main cycle routes, connecting to a series of feeder routes, avoiding the steepest terrain.

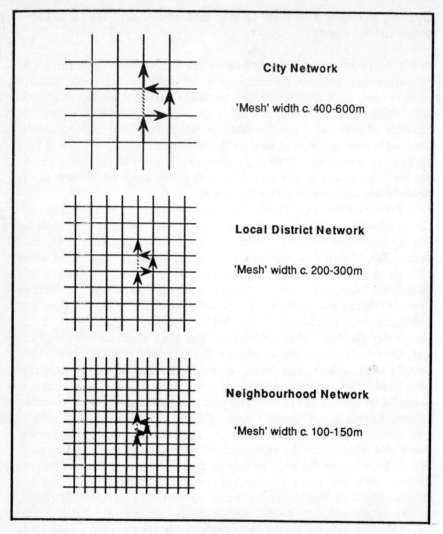

Figure 3.8 Delft cycle network hierarchy. Principles of its development at city, district and neighbourhood levels and the influence of missing links.

Source: Dutch Ministry of Transport (VENW) 1987

Planning policies to encourage shorter trips in cities

Although the achievement of good standards of cycling provision is certainly much easier in new towns, if considered from the outset, than in older urban areas, planning policies generally can do much in the longer run, as well as the short term, to reduce the length of trips and favour the use of the bicycle. For example, policies which favour the development of large out-of-town shopping facilities effectively tend to encourage car use by undermining the viability of smaller shopping centres closer to the centre, and therefore within easier walking and cycling distance. Higher densities in general can encourage more walking and cycling trips, although with blocks of flats the incentive to use bikes may be eroded without secure storage space for bikes. Indeed, this is important in any housing.

The trend towards the development of larger facilities of various kinds has, along with the increase in car ownership, tended to erode the attractions of bicycle use. This is especially the case when such facilities are not only further away, but hard to reach safely and lacking in secure cycle parking, while providing ample space for free car parking. By contrast, policies which promote higher density and the provision of facilities within easy walking or cycling distance can help reduce the attractions of car use (European Community, 1990). This is especially true if linked to a reversal of the recent trend towards the centralisation of facilities, especially education and health institutions, at greater average distances from people's homes (Elkin, McLaren and Hillman, 1991). Encouragement of shorter trips and use of non-motorised travel can also be helped by a reversal of the common trend in the centres of British towns and cities, in particular, to drive out residential uses and the relatively greater absence there of other than commercial, administrative and cultural land uses.

Land use policies of this kind need to be coordinated with measures to constrain car usage. These include traffic policies such as the reduction of the provision of car parking places, both on-street and off-street, and especially those catering primarily for car commuters. Car parking charges also have an important role here (Apel and Lehmbrock, 1990). At the same time, bike access and bike parking can be provided at major public transport interchanges while car parking there is restricted. The costs of fuel as well as of parking are significant. Enforcement measures against speeding drivers by the police, as well as through physical measures in traffic-calming schemes are also important, and perhaps need also to be complemented in future by 'vehicle-calming' measures to prevent motor vehicles from travelling at excessive speeds.

Publicity and promotion of cycling schemes

Publicity measures to make known the existence of any cycle facilities need to be extensive, including wide distribution of attractive leaflets, and special features in the local media, with some based around special events such as opening ceremonies and mass rides along the routes. Publicity should be directed at likely users, including local schools and colleges and major local employers. Publicity needs to be undertaken at two levels, both to erode the image of the bicycle as a second-rate means of transport, and also to make people aware of the new opportunities to use it safely. Opinion formers are often behind public opinion in their wish to see cycling promoted (Brög and Erl, 1991). Not only does the bike often have a generally poor public image but in addition its economic potential is usually underestimated. A German survey found that one-third of all cycle trips were to shops and that cycling customers were those with the greatest shopping frequency (Monheim, 1989).

Improving the positive image of the bike can be encouraged by mass cycle rides, guided tours of new facilities, and other cycling events. Also important are the opening up of bicycle shops, cafes or bicycle stations (see Chapter 4). It is also important to promote the regular use of bikes for official duties by local authority staff, and to encourage well-known local figures to be seen riding bikes regularly!

Even better is when local employers can be persuaded to complement new cycle schemes by steps such as the provision of secure cycle parking on their premises, showers and storage facilities for their cycling employees, and mileage allowances for employees using their bikes on official business. They may also offer loans for employees for purchasing bikes. More helpful still are decisions by employers to provide secure cycle parking for their employees at the same time as reducing the number of car parking spaces. Cycling needs to be fully integrated in 'staff alternative travel schemes'.

Decisions on choice of means of transport can of course be influenced in a number of ways, including the provision of financial incentives, at both national and local level. These include the levels of taxation on both the purchase costs and running costs of cars. Also important are the prices charged for use of public transport. With the strong bias in transport policies favouring car use these, whether positive or negative influences, have also tended in most cases to inhibit use of bicycles. Employees using bikes on official business have not found it as profitable as using their cars, particularly if they are in possession of a company car where their social and leisure use of the car is subsidised as well as their official use (Greenpeace, 1991).

What is important is to get all the fiscal incentives to work consistently with transport policy rather than, as is so often the case, to work in a fragmented way and often in conflict with each other. This includes decisions by governments on taxation both on the fixed and variable costs of running cars, and subsidising fares, and, at local level, on the scale of fees to be paid for car parking for commuters, shoppers and other users, short-stay and long-stay.

In recent years there has been much talk about road pricing as a possible method of traffic restraint in the most congested cities. Practice with such schemes is still limited but it would appear as though a package of

measures in connection with road pricing could ensure that some of the
revenues raised are used to increase support for cycling as well as public
transport.

Conclusions

In this chapter we have seen that an effective policy to promote the use
of bicycles in towns and cities needs to go beyond the provision of good
cycle facilities. It must also mean ensuring that all roads and streets are
as safe and comfortable as possible for cyclists to use, and that the
opportunities to promote safe and attractive cycling are exploited in a
wide variety of highway planning, traffic management and other town
planning schemes. Traffic-calming in particular offers major potential to
improve cycling conditions but only if it is handled sensitively in its
detailed design. The same is also true in the design of major junctions.
Efforts on all these kinds of measures are important in the development
of a cycle network, tailored to local conditions, and involving close
consultation with cyclists, taking advantage of their detailed knowledge
of local opportunities and possibilities. It is also important to have
knowledgeable and dedicated staff, backed by strong political commitment and a large and specific cycling budget. Lastly, it has been argued
that the opportunity to encourage cycling will be greater if cycling policy
is integrated with other measures affecting transport policy and the
choice of mode, including fiscal incentives and publicity measures. These
must be directed at overcoming the second-rate image of the bicycle as
well as highlighting the new opportunities for safe and attractive cycling
opened up by the development of comprehensive cycle networks. In the
long run, cycle use will also be greatly facilitated by planning policies to
secure the location of local facilities within easy walking and cycling
distance.

Key references

Allott and Lomax, 1991, *Cyclists and Roundabouts*, report commissioned for the
Cyclists' Touring Club by Allott and Lomax, Birmingham, CTC, Godalming,
Surrey.
Bracher, Tilman, 1989, *Policy and Provision for Cyclists in Europe*, Commission
of the European Communities, Directorate-General for Transport, Brussels.
Bracher, Tilman, Luda, Helmut, Thiemann, H., 1991, *Zussamenfassende Aus-
wertung von Forschungsergebnissen zum Radverkehr in der Stadt*, Forschung
Stadtverkehr, Band A7, Bundesminister für Verkehr, Bergisch Glad-
bach/Berlin, Bonn.
Bundesanstalt für Strassenwesen, 1990, *Forschungsvorhaben Flächenhafte Ver-
kehrsberuhigung*, 5. Kolloquium, Ergebnisse aus den Modellgebieten und

Erfahrungen andere Städte vom 16–17.5.90 in Ingolstadt, BASt, Bergisch Gladbach.

Cleary, Johanna, 1991, *Cyclists and Traffic-Calming: A Technical Note*, Cyclists' Touring Club, Godalming, Surrey.

Draeger, Werner, 1991, *Tempo 30 – Vorteile für den Radverkehr*, report of proceedings, Velo Secur Conference, Salzburg, May 1990, ARGUS (Arbeitsgemeinschaft Umweltfreundlicher Stadtverkehr), Vienna.

Elkin, Tim, McLaren, Duncan and Hillman, Mayer, 1991, *Reviving the City: Towards Sustainable Urban Development*, Policy Studies Institute and Friends of the Earth, London.

Godefrooij, Tom, 1991, *Promoting the Use of the Bicycle: Improving Safety is Not Enough*, paper to the Velo City '91 Conference, Milan.

Monheim, Heiner and Monheim-Dandorfer, Rita, 1991, *Strassen für alle*, Rasch und Röhring Verlag, Hamburg.

Organisation of Economic Cooperation and Development, 1990, *Environmental Policies for Cities in the 1990s*, OECD, Paris.

Transport Studies Unit, 1991, *Transport: The New Realism*, TSU, Oxford University.

Welleman, A.G., 1991, *The Netherlands National Cycling Policy and Facilities for Cyclists at Signalled Crossings*, Local Authorities Cycle Planning Group Meeting, York, May.

Other references

Alrutz, D. et al., 1989, *Dokumentation zur Sicherung des Fahradverkehrs*, Bundesanstalt für Strassenwesen, Bergisch Gladbach.

Alrutz, D. et al., 1991, *Radverkehr in Einbahnstrassen*, Planungsgemeinschaft Verkehr, Hannover.

Apel, Dieter & Lehmbrock, Michael, 1990, *Stadtverträgliche Verkehrsplanung: Chancen zur Steuerung des Autoverkehrs durch Parkraumkonzepte und Bewirtschaftung*, Deutsches Institut für Urbanistik, Berlin.

Balsiger, Oskar, 1991, *Velo am Wendepunkt*, report of proceedings, Velo Secur Conference, Salzburg, May 1990, ARGUS (Arbeitsgemeinschaft Umweltfreundlicher Stadtverkehr), Vienna.

Brög, Werner and Erl, Erhard, 1991, *Verhaltensbeeinflussung nach dem Public Awareness-Konzept-dargestellt am Beispiel der Fahrrad-Förderung*, Socialdata, Institut für Verkehrs- und Infrastrukturforschung GmbH, Munich.

Dupree, Harry, 1987, *Urban Transport: The New Towns Solution*, Gower, Aldershot.

Environment and Transport Planning & Planungsgemeinschaft Verkehr, 1991, *Cycle Safety: A Comparison Between German and British Towns*, ETP, Brighton.

European Community, *Green Paper on the Urban Environment*, COM (90) 218 EC, Brussels.

Greenpeace, 1991, *Company Car Costs*, Greenpeace, London.

Hartman, 1990, The Delft Bicycle Network, Chapter 13 in R. Tolley (ed.), *The Greening of Urban Transport: Planning for Walking and Cycling in Western Cities*, Belhaven Press, London.

Hass-Klau, Carmen, 1990, *The Pedestrian and City Traffic*, Belhaven Press, London.

Heynen, Pascal, *Travelling Cleaner*, Transport 2000, London.

Keller, H., 1991, Progress of Traffic-calming in German towns and cities, *Transportion Planning Systems*, Vol. 1 (2), 61–69.

Kroon, Martin, 1990, Traffic and environmental policy in the Netherlands, in Rodney Tolley (ed.), *The Greening of Urban Transport: Planning for Walking and Cycling in Western Cities*, Belhaven, London.

Mathew, Don, 1990, Oxford's Traffic Restraint, *The Surveyor*, Vol. 175 (5126), 3 October.

Meilof, R.W., 1988, *Town Planning: How to Stimulate Bicycle Traffic*, report of proceedings, Velo City '87 Conference, Groningen, CROW, Ede, Netherlands.

Milton Keynes Cycle Users' Group, 1984, *Cycling in Milton Keynes: a Users' View*, MKCUG, Milton Keynes.

Monheim, Heiner, 1989, *Die Rolle des Fahrrads in der Stadtentwicklung und Verkehrssanierung. Stadtbauliche Bedeutung, Investionsbedarf, Arbeitsmarkteffekte*, Kongress zur wirtschaftlichen und ökologischen Bedeutung des Fahrradverkehrs, Münster, 23 August.

Owen, Susan, 1991, *Energy-Conscious Planning*, Council for the Preservation of Rural England, London.

Pease, Jack, 1991, Studies into bypass benefits sharpen growing debate, *Local Transport Today*, No. 60, 24 July, pp. 10–11.

Pharoah, Tim, 1990, *Traffic-Calming and Strategies in Europe*, 'Traffic Calming in Theory and Practice' Conference, East Midlands Conference Centre, Nottingham University, May.

Roberts, John, 1989, *User-friendly Cities*, TEST (Transport and Environmental Studies), London.

Royal Town Planning Institute, 1991, *Transport Growth and Planning Policy*, RTPI, London.

Schunemann, Helmut, 1991, *Autofreie Altstadt und Prioritäten für den Umweltverbund am Beispiel Lübecks*, Bonner Fahrradkongress, 10–11 June, Bad Godesberg.

Tschopp, Jürg, 1991, *Massnahmen für den Veloverkehr*, Verkehrs Club der Schweiz, Basel, Switzerland.

Wheeler, Albert, 1991, *Advanced Cycle Stop Lines in Oxford, Newark and Bristol*, Transport and Road Research Laboratory Research Report 336, TRRL, Crowthorne, Berkshire.

4 Cycling and public transport

Hugh McClintock

Cycling and public transport: partners not rivals

Promoting use of the bicycle in cities does not mean a concentration on maximising the number of cyclists. Policies for the promotion of cycling need to be balanced with those to promote the other environmentally-friendly modes of transport: walking and public transport. All of these types of transport have suffered from the domination of the private car in our cities and all need to be promoted in the context of wider policies to make cities quieter, safer, cleaner and more attractive places in which to live, to work and to relax.

Cycling, walking and public transport each have their specific requirements if they are to maximise their potential, and the way in which this potential is maximised, to the detriment of private car traffic, must be worked out in relation to the differing circumstances in different towns and cities. This means taking account of the size of urban areas, the length of journeys, and local climatic factors. Social and demographic characteristics of the local population may also be important, for example, the proportion of older people, as they may especially be more inclined to use public transport than to cycle if the terrain is hilly.

The achievement of higher levels of cycle use in towns and cities will generally be easier in smaller ones than in large ones, because of the greater average trip distances in the latter. However, what is also very important, particularly in larger cities and conurbations, is the development of policies which encourage the combined use of these environmentally-friendly modes as a serious alternative to the 'convenience' of private car use. To achieve this requires a common recognition, by cyclists, public transport operators, planners and politicians that the bicycle and public transport are partners and not rivals. Without this recognition the motor car will be the winner.

As mentioned in Chapter 2, the domination of most Western cities by the motor car has often meant that very large areas have become devoted to motor traffic movement and car parking and other facilities required by private car use. This has been true even in higher density European cities, but particularly true of most cities in North America and Australia (Newman and Kenworthy, 1989). Public transport has a particularly important role in improving urban structures through freeing space which would otherwise be used for roads and parking. Although the bicycle requires much less space than the car for its movement and parking, on grounds of space requirements alone, public transport and, in particular, light rapid transit systems are the most efficient users of space for movement. Well subsidised and well promoted comfortable, reliable and frequent modern public transport can attract car occupants, reducing congestion. Such policies can be even more effective in reducing congestion when linked to appropriate pricing and management policies for short- and long-term car parking (Apel and Lehmbrock, 1990). The space freed from reducing car traffic can be used both to improve provision for the bicycle and also to extend pedestrian precincts, giving those on foot more opportunity to enjoy the urban scene without constant fear of intrusion from motor traffic.

Recognition of the concept of cycling and public transport as partners and not rivals requires an awareness of the common advantages of both, as more efficient users of space and energy, and also of the relative advantages and disadvantages of each.

The bike, free from the constraints of fixed lines, stops and schedules, is particularly suited for short trips in fairly flat areas, that means for distances of up to 2–3km, although also with a large number of trips up to 5km and, with good infrastructure and topographical conditions, increasingly up to 10km. For distances up to 3km, in particular, the bike is almost always able to achieve shorter journey times than bus travel, allowing for a typical walk of 400–500m to the bus stop and usually a short wait for the bus (Grabe/VOV, 1985). For longer distances, and, in particular for distances over 5km, the bus, tram and especially the train will in most cases give faster journey times, unless services are infrequent and journey times slow and unreliable.

Cycle access to and from railway stations

Dutch transport policy is now looking to increase the role of the bicycle at the expense of some bus trips for distances of up to 5km (Welleman, 1991). In that densely populated country, 60 per cent of all trips by bus, tram and metro are of this distance or less. Official thinking now regards these short trips as determining the capacity required during the rush hour and also that they cause a major part of public transport operators' losses. Moreover, as part of the Bicycle Master Plan 1991–95 there is a specific aim to improve cycling to and from stations. About one-third of rail passengers typically arrive by bike, and sometimes 50 per cent, but the aim is now to achieve an increase in the number of cycle-borne passengers by 15 per cent by 1995.

Many Dutch people also use a bike when they complete their rail journey, to go on to their destination, according to a survey (Bracher et al., 1991, p. 88). This kind of travel habit, bike–ride–bike, or 'sandwich' travel, is also very common in Denmark, with people often reducing the risk of theft of the bicycle left at the destination station by leaving an old bike there and keeping their best bike at home, for home-based trips. — For the cyclist such combinations offer the advantage of being able to complete their journeys with a faster door-to-door journey time than if they relied on public transport alone, or public transport and walking. As the same Dutch survey showed, average distances of all kinds of trips to stations are likely to be significantly longer (3.7km) than those at the end of the rail trip (2.9km). This suggests that it is the former in particular that offer potential for cycling. The latter may have more potential for leisure than daily cyclists, especially if marketed as part of a package tour.

To maximise the potential for combining cycling and public transport it is essential that attention is paid to improving each part of the total transport chain involved in such trips. As with any chain this transport chain is only as strong as its weakest link. For example, the weakest link may often tend to be the last one, the link between arrival station and workplace, and especially if the cyclist's employer is not actively trying to encourage cycling through the provision of secure cycle parking, showers and changing facilities.

Analysing each link in this chain means starting by ensuring that the cyclists can store their bikes safely and conveniently where they live. This tends to be more of a problem in cities where a large proportion of the population live in flats (Luers, 1985) with no separate garage space.

The next step in the chain is the journey to the station (or bus or tram halt). It is important that account is taken of these movements in any plans for the development of cycle networks. There is a need to analyse any particular bottlenecks or other hazardous locations which discourage cycle access to stations and other transport interchanges and to include cycle facilities or traffic-calming measures to assist these locally focused movements, taking account of the main area of origin of these cyclists. The aim should be to provide safe, direct, convenient and comfortable cycle access right up to the next link in the chain, the cycle parking area. This may mean enabling cyclists to share subways or ramps, or to provide lifts, a measure like ramps which may also improve access for the handicapped. Appropriate solutions will vary according to local circumstances but may, space permitting, also include the provision on flights of steps of a trough at the side to make it easier for cyclists to push their bikes up and down. Any facilities provided need to be clearly signed and well publicised.

Providing short- and long-term cycle parking at stations

Both the fear of theft or tampering and the convenience of use will be important factors in determining the level of usage of cycle parking facilities. Too often any cycle parking which has been provided has been of the wrong type, with stands supporting only one wheel and not the whole frame. Too often stands have been provided which are far too close together (i.e. less than 700mm) which makes it very hard to get bikes in and out without getting entangled with the next one. Although weather protection is also important this has sometimes been given too much weight at the expense of convenience of use, making it very hard to get in to hold the front of the bike, without bumping the user's head. Good lighting, in the vicinity of the stands and by approaches, is also vital to help reduce the risk of theft. Parking within station buildings may mean that separate weather protection is not required and the cycle stands can more easily be supervised by station staff.

The convenience for cyclists, and therefore the incentive to combine cycling and public transport, is maximised by the provision of small groups of stands close to each station entrance, and this can also help to reduce the menace to pedestrians of cycles left in a disorderly manner. Moreover, as Brunsing comments (1990), cycle parking facilities need to be designed in such a way that they blend into surroundings but also remain in full view of the public.

In the Netherlands, the standard of cycle parking at stations has for many years been fairly high and in Western Germany major improvements have been made in some areas in recent years, as for example in the cities in North Rhine-Westphalia covered by the Rhein-Ruhr Transit Authority, VRR (Gyukits et al., 1986). At many stations, including both main and suburban ones, and including new park-and-ride sites on the edge of the urban area, extensive, attractive and fairly secure covered cycle parking has been provided. The provision of good bike-and-ride facilities at some stations in Munich has helped to generate large increases in the number of cycle-borne passengers in a place with a weaker cycling tradition than many cities elsewhere in Germany.

Reducing cycle theft at cycle parking areas

While it is impossible to eliminate the problem of cycle theft from concentrations of parked bikes it is possible in various ways to reduce it. One way is to erect stands at convenient locations likely to be overlooked by many passers-by. Using translucent materials to cover the cycle stands helps to make them weather-proof while being much more likely to deter thefts than cycle sheds with dark corners in out of the way locations. Providing stands that can support all of the bicycle and to which the

Figure 4.1 Well-designed covered cycle parking outside Cologne main
station.

main frame and, preferably, both wheels can be locked also reduces the
likely incidence of cycle theft. A good example, at Cologne Station, is
shown in Fig. 4.1. Use of bicycles rather than cars for access to public
transport trips is also encouraged by erecting the stands as close as possible to the platforms and with direct access from the cycle parking area.
Clear signing and lighting are also important, as well as protection from
bird droppings in some stations!

With the steady increase, on the one hand, of cycle theft and, on the
other, in the value of many bikes now purchased, it seems that more
cyclists are willing to pay a charge for secure parking of their bikes,
when left for longer term periods. This has encouraged some public
transport authorities to respond by providing cycle lockers or boxes.
Experience suggests (Froitzheim, 1990; Schäfer-Breede, 1987) that these
can be popular, if the charges are considered reasonable by potential
users and if management problems can be overcome. In particular, there
seem to be problems with coin-operation, which can attract vandals, and
also in catering for casual customers. It seems to be easy to work out
arrangements for cyclists willing to rent lockers on a regular basis, of at
least a week, and preferably a month or quarter. Lockers also have the
advantage for those wishing to complete their journeys entirely by public

transport of enabling them to safely leave not just their bicycle but also their pump, lights, rainproof clothing, helmet and other accessories.

There are other potential problems with cycle lockers which need to be addressed in the light of particular local circumstances. These include the extra space requirements, compared with orthodox cycle parking provision, and the rather intrusive nature of the design of some types of locker in certain settings, especially on streets and other outdoor locations. These need to be handled sensitively.

'Bicycle stations' and other cycle hire facilities

The most ambitious types of cycling provision at stations are to be found in the Netherlands where cycle parking at even quite small urban stations has for years been combined with cycle hire and repair facilities. By 1989 there were 92 of these 'bicycle stations' in the Netherlands. In large urban areas their services often include advice to cyclists about choice of routes for daily and touring purposes, and also the sale of maps, guides and accessories. This concept of bicycle stations is now spreading elsewhere, especially in Denmark and Germany. In Germany, the first such bicycle station was developed in the early 1980s on the square in front of Bremen main Station, and several other cities have now made similar provision, usually the result of initiatives from cycling groups rather than from the Deutsche Bundesbahn or other public transport operators.

One advantage of bicycle stations, especially if linked to extensive and guarded cycle parking areas, is greater security for cyclists, without the need for expensive and more space-consuming cycle lockers. Another advantage, of appeal both to public transport operators and pedestrians, is that it enables the large number of bikes frequently left in the vicinity of central stations to be much more economically and tidily parked, with less intrusion in the urban environment and less in the way of pedestrians than if they are left locked to every post and railing in the vicinity, regardless of how inconvenient or unsafe that is for pedestrians. With the continued increase in popularity of cycling it is quite common, even without improved provision, to see around 1,000 bikes left around main stations in Germany and Switzerland, with far more in some cases. An extreme example in Germany of this 'bicycle pollution' is Münster where the problem of the proliferation of parked bikes became so great, with well over 3,000 bikes (Froitzheim, 1991) being left in and around the station area, that the City Council has built a special multi-storey cycle parking facility. This is the first in Germany, although such facilities have been provided for some years in Japan, where both the lack of space and the increase in cycle usage in the 1980s became even more serious (Replogle, 1983; Schafer-Breede, 1987).

Cycle hire facilities are very common at stations in several Continental countries, and not only at main railway stations. Widespread cycle hire helps casual users, as well as commuters, especially in tourist areas. In addition to being normal practice in Dutch towns this has been a long-standing tradition at Swiss stations (Tschopp, 1988) where Swiss Railways, SBB/CFF, introduced cycle hire in the 1950s as a service for travelling salesmen. In recent years demand at Swiss stations has grown steadily, with the growth of leisure. By 1991 cycle hire facilities were offered by no less than 600 stations, that is, most stations in the country (Froitzheim, 1990).

Cycle parking at suburban stations and bus/tram stops

The number of bikes left parked around any public transport stop can be a rough guide to likely demand but, in general terms, away from central stations the next priority for cycle parking are suburban stations towards the edge of the urban area. In these locations average distances from homes to train or other public transport stops are likely to be greater than in residential areas closer to city centres, and, with often lower average densities and a greater preponderance of relatively spacious one-family houses, with garages and often garden sheds, space for storage of bikes is likely to be fairly easy. By contrast, in residential areas closer to the centre, public transport frequencies, especially of buses, are likely to be higher, and with greater average density of building, spaces for keeping bikes securely in homes may also be more limited. Train, and tram and bus stops in particular are more likely to be within easy walking distance of homes.

It is therefore particularly in outlying and lower density residential areas that bike-and-ride provision can be of benefit, not just to cyclists but also to public transport operators. For the latter the main benefit is that it can extend the range of customers within convenient travelling distance of the public transport stop. For those walking, a normally maximum acceptable distance of 700m has been suggested in Germany (Bracher et al., 1991) whereas a distance of 2km is quite acceptable for a cyclist wishing to continue by public transport. On this basis, encouragement of bike-and-ride can increase tenfold catchment areas of local stations (Bracher et al., 1991).

Minimal transfer distances and times between cycle parking and the waiting area can encourage greater public transport use. Cyclists know they can rely on finding a secure and convenient place to leave their bikes, without having to resort to railings and poles. Better cycle parking at stations can also encourage greater train use by cyclists (Gyukits, 1986).

Demand for cycle parking at particular stations can also be influenced by the fare zones structure operating in certain city-wide or conurbation transport systems. In Zurich, for example, it has been observed that there is a heavier demand for cycle parking at the last station within a particular fare zone, as people use their bikes to make a rather longer trip to catch their train, rather than go to a nearer station and pay a higher fare!

Bike-and-ride with bus-based park-and-ride

Bike-and-ride provision may also be made in connection with bus-based park-and-ride, as well as at railway stations and tram stops. A good example of this in England is York, with a well sited cycle parking area both near the main entrance to its major park-and-ride site to the southwest of the city, and close to the bus stops. It also has cycle path access. Experience in Oxford has shown two kinds of cycle passengers, those that come on their bikes and then continue by bus and also those who come by car with bikes in the boot, who then park their cars and complete their journey by bike!

Not least of the many potential advantages from the promotion of bike-and-ride is a reduction in space requirements compared with the major park-and-ride developments now being pursued in many European cities. Park-and-ride developments may help to reduce pressure for commuters to drive into city centres, but still may be of limited value in reducing inessential car use by people who have no need to use their car in the course of their work. German experience shows that 60 per cent of park-and-ride customers live less than 4km away, little more than the longest distance, 3.5km, that most cyclists are prepared to ride to a bike-and-ride site (Froitzheim, 1991). Although park-and-ride is promoted as a very important way of luring drivers from their cars experience shows that it may even attract people who previously made the whole of their journey by public transport.

In so far as park-and-ride developments do succeed in enticing drivers away from their cars for part of their total journeys this may be at the expense of traffic and living conditions generally in the area around the park-and-ride site. Large park-and-ride sites entail the allocation of large tarmac areas for drivers, often on valuable land that might be better used in other ways. In Germany some sites now include special multi-storey car parks, and even smaller sites may themselves generate substantial extra traffic in the vicinity in peak hours, often in areas that have hitherto been relatively unaffected by the intrusion of motor traffic. Any time benefits that drivers gain from using public transport for the main part of their trip may be eroded by congestion when they return and want to drive away from the park-and-ride site. This spreading of congestion, unless linked to bus priority signals and other special measures, may also add to a risk that park-and-ride promotion detracts from the promotion of other public transport services, and their improvement. Froitzheim has commented that 'Park and Ride is a luxury solution for relatively few drivers.' (Froitzheim, 1991).

Furthermore, improvements in terms of car access to park-and-ride sites may be at the expense of creating safer access for cyclists to the same bus or train stops. At many public transport stops of course there will simply not be room for official encouragement of park-and-ride, while bike-and-ride provision, needing only about one-tenth as much space per parked vehicle, may be much easier to accommodate. Indeed, encouragement of bike-and-ride may help to reduce the problems of unofficial park-and-ride that, with serious increases in traffic congestion, have often increasingly plagued suburban railway stations, often to the intense annoyance of local residents. Where bike-and-ride is promoted alongside official park-and-ride it is important to give preferential siting to the cycle parking provision rather than to locate cycle stands in peripheral parts of the car park where they will be inconvenient, insecure and thus poorly used by cyclists. Preferential siting of cycle parking also gives a message to drivers of what is officially regarded as most important, especially if reinforced by good publicity and marketing. By contrast, badly sited cycle parking and indeed poorly designed cycle parking facilities in general, with unsafe, inconvenient and ill maintained cycle access, give a message to cyclists that their needs are not being taken seriously and that they are just second-class transport users. Bike-and-ride must be well publicised and signed, and its use will also be encouraged by a perception among drivers that they stand a poor chance of getting a parking place.

Carriage of bikes on trains

The provision of cycle parking at stations may be a relatively problem-free form of bike-and-ride promotion compared with the improvement of arrangements for carrying bikes on public transport. In many countries, and perhaps especially in Britain, these arrangements have got much worse in recent years, with the relatively low investment in railways (and other public transport) and with the fact that the new rolling stock which has been introduced has often made the carriage of bikes impossible or extremely difficult, even outside peak hours. Different services, local and Intercity, have their own regulations and restrictions, and the growing complexity of these have made the carriage of bikes on trains very difficult. These have driven away potential passengers and helped to fuel a large increase in sales of cycle carriers for cars! In most Continental countries the picture is not so bleak and indeed major improvements have been introduced. In the Netherlands, for example, the Nederlandse

Spoorwege, until the mid-1980s, charged disproportionately high fares in order to discourage passengers from taking their bikes with them but has in recent years reversed this policy, especially on long distance trains. Denmark also has done much to lift restrictions, especially outside peak hours (Koop, 1990).

In terms of urban cycling, the main theme of this book, this deterioration is very regrettable, especially when the use of bicycles overall for rail-based journeys is also discouraged by lack of secure and convenient cycle parking at the station of origin. In Continental countries, at least, there are some signs of improvement for carrying bikes on local trains, with experience tending to undermine the fears of some railway personnel about the delays for train timetabling from loading and unloading bikes. In several cities, the carriage of bikes on urban trains and even trams is now permitted, at least outside peak hours and at weekends, and in quite a few cases, such as the new Zurich S-Bahn line opened in 1990, good provision, with special hooks, has been made for carrying bikes in special compartments, along with other luggage. In Germany, Berlin has in recent years been at the forefront of measures to integrate cycling and public transport (Bracher, 1991) with free bicycle travel for regular ticket holders, an important incentive for cyclists to buy season tickets, even if they are less regular public transport users. In Berlin there has also been a general easing of restrictions on both its S-Bahn and U-Bahn (overground and underground urban railways) systems, with several positive initiatives to accommodate more bikes, especially on the S-Bahn, which is particularly important for leisure traffic (see also Chapter 11).

Carriage of bikes on trams

One of the most impressive examples of arrangements for carrying bikes on public transport services is in Basle. For some years tram drivers have been quite willing even in peak hours to carry broken-down bikes, and the carriage of bikes outside peak hours is now well established. In the case of two tram lines, 10 and 12, bikes can be carried at any time, along with prams and wheelchairs, in a special low-floored compartment in the centre of the tram. Appropriate logos painted on the platform indicate where cyclists and wheelchair and pram users should wait to use these. Most impressive in Basle is the special 'bike-and-ride' tram trailer, for carrying up to 25 bikes, that can be rented by groups at weekends on tram line 10 which runs out into the nearby attractive countryside of Alsace. In Germany the carriage of bikes on trams has faced more prohibitions but is now becoming more common, and not just outside peak hours (Bracher, 1991).

Figure 4.2   Carriage of bikes on the rack and pinion railway serving the hilly suburb of Degerloch, Stuttgart, Germany.

Carriage of bikes on buses and taxis

Comprehensive consideration of the potential for combining cycling and public transport also needs to include other means of public transport such as buses, ferries and taxis. This is especially important in cities with less dense rail networks. There have been several experiments, not always whole-hearted and successful, in the carriage of bikes on buses, either in the boot, on prongs or in trailers, for both leisure and commuting purposes (Brunsing, 1990; Karl, 1986). Cities like Bremen and Brunswick in Germany have introduced successful experiments in converting buses to carry bikes for weekend leisure trips, and a similar experiment was started in the English cities of Liverpool and Manchester in 1990 for recreational bike and bus access to the Peak District National Park. In Denmark it is compulsory for taxis to be able to carry a bicycle, and in Germany it is common in some very hilly places for cyclists to ride their bikes downhill and, when going uphill, to take their bikes by taxi! In Stuttgart, a particularly hilly city, this is very much encouraged on the track railway to the southern suburb of Degerloch, where a special plat-form designed to carry bikes, loaded by cyclists themselves, is carried in front of the driver on the line from Marienplatz in the city centre (see

Fig. 4.2). A similar facility exists on the Postlingerbahn in Linz in Austria (Rauh, 1990).

Even though the more successful arrangements for enabling cyclists to carry their bikes on trains and buses have tended to be for leisure rather than daily urban cycling there is an important relationship between the two. People who take up leisure cycling may feel safer than launching out on their own in a busy urban area, especially if they are part of a group. This experience can then give them the confidence and skill to try riding a bike for some of their daily trips as well.

Sharing road space with buses and trams

Experience in Basle shows the importance in other ways of the joint promotion of cycling and public transport, including the potential for promoting both together in terms of traffic management. For example, such provision in Basle has included the conversion of a two-lane road into a one-lane road for general traffic while the second lane is reserved for buses and bikes, as well as turning motor traffic.

Shared use of bus lanes by bikes and buses is common in several places in England including Derby, Nottingham and London, and some German cities like Berlin, as well as Denmark and Sweden. This can take various forms: it may involve simple shared use of with-flow or contra-flow bus lanes or the provision of cycle lanes next to a simple bus plug (bus-only lane) or 'bus sluice' as they are known in the Netherlands. In these, abuse by private motor drivers is deterred by the installation of a shallow pit wide enough to exclude cars but narrow enough for buses to negotiate.

On-street running of trams has traditionally been feared by some cyclists who worry about getting their wheels caught in the tracks (Davies, 1989). Although posing less of a problem to the now more popular mountain bikes this can still be minimised with sensitive design. A white line or kerb, or other change in surface or texture, can be used to warn cyclists when they are riding too close to the tram line. At crossing points, cyclists, whether on roads, cycle lanes or cycle paths, can be encouraged to cross the tracks at right angles, rather than at a sharp angle, with approaches realigned if necessary to provide for this.

It is important when considering any traffic management measures to give advantage to buses or trams to consider the potential for applying the same priority to cyclists, as for example with traffic lights that let buses or trams start ahead of motor traffic at junctions. Links between 'cell' systems in city centres, designed to restrict through movements by private motor traffic, as in Bremen or Gothenburg, can be maintained for cyclists as well as buses to make their journeys more direct and convenient.

Where there is vigorous promotion of public transport as well as cycling, it seems that there is likely to be a greater growth in cycling than in places that rely largely on the provision of cycling infrastructure alone. For example, Oxford has, in the last twenty years, done more than most British cities to restrain the growth of traffic in its city centre. Transport policies have included the provision of bus lanes and the development of peripheral park-and-ride sites to reduce traffic on narrow central streets. While motor traffic overall in the city has increased steadily, the levels in the city centre have remained constant, but the amount of cycling has doubled (Mathew, 1990).

An even more impressive example is Freiburg, just west of the Black Forest. Concern about the dangers of 'Waldsterben' (death of trees) from motor traffic emissions produced particularly strong local pressure in the mid-1980s to reduce motor traffic growth. Transport policies were then changed, with greatly increased investment in both cycleways and new and better tram lines. Within a few years the shares of the total modal split accounted for by both cycling and public transport grew significantly, with cycling increasing to 27 per cent of all trips (Gobel, 1988). The share of daily trips undertaken by private car has also been reduced by the introduction in recent years of increasing varieties of 'environment tickets' giving large discounts for regular public transport use in the city, and now, the whole region. These have been based on similar concepts pioneered in Basle and other Swiss cities and, like those, have been heavily marketed. As in other areas of cycling policy, this underlines the need for policy-makers not to take a too blinkered approach but to cultivate a wide awareness of the opportunities for promoting cycling in the course of implementing measures with other primary purposes.

Conclusion

Given the increasing evidence of the very adverse social and environmental effects of the domination of Western cities by the motor car it is essential that cycling and public transport are seen as complementary rather than rival modes of transport. The aim of this policy should be to build on the complementary strengths of both 'environmentally-friendly' modes of transport to offer an attractive combined package that will offer a serious alternative, in terms of convenience and door-to-door travel times, to car travel. This means, above all, good quality and well-designed cycle parking, with easy connections to train, tram and bus services. It also means paying attention to the scope for other possible improvements in each link in the 'chain' of a trip. Furthermore, it means encouraging the provision of cycle hire at transport interchanges and 'bicycle stations'. It also means increasing rather than decreasing the opportunities for passengers to take their bikes with them on both short and long distance trains and buses, and introducing imaginative and well-publicised initiatives to encourage this. Finally, in terms of shared use of road space, cyclists, buses and trams can benefit, especially in a context of general restraint of private motor traffic.

Key references

Bracher, Tilman, 1991, *The Bicycle and Public Transport Mode*, paper presented to the Velo City '91 Conference, Milan, November.

Bracher, Tilman, Luda, Helmut, Thiemann, Hans-Jorg, 1991, *Zussamenfassende Auswertung von Forschungsergebnissen zum Radverkehr in der Stadt*, Forschung Stadtverkehr, Band A7, Bundesministerium für Verkehr, Bergisch Gladbach/Berlin, Bonn.

Brunsing, Jurgen, 1990, Public transport and cycling: experience of modal integration in West Germany, in R.S. Tolley (ed.), *The Greening of Urban Transport: Planning for Walking and Cycling in Western Cities*, Belhaven Press, London.

Froitzheim, Thomas, 1990, *Fahrradstationen an Bahnhöfen. Modelle, Chancen, Risiken*, Schriftenreihe des AFC-Nordrhein-Westfalen, Düsseldorf.

Froitzheim, Thomas, 1991, Kuckkucksei und hässliches Entlein: Park-and-Ride contra Bike-and-Ride, *Verkehrszeichen* 4/1991, pp. 15–20.

Koop, Eigil, 1990, *On the Recent Engagement of Bicycles and Trains in Denmark*, in Niels Jensen (ed.), Velo City '89 proceedings, National Agency for Physical Planning, Copenhagen.

Replogle, Michael, 1983, *Bicycles and Transportation: New Links to Suburban Transit Markets*, Bicycle Federation of America, Washington, DC.

Schäfer-Breede, Klaus, 1987, *Kombinierter Personenverkehr – Bike and Ride*, Contributions to a Conference in Essen, 1986, organised by the ADFC (Allgemeiner Deutscher Fahrradclub), Bremen.

Other references

Alrutz, Dankmar, Fechtel, Hans. W., and Krause, Juliane, 1989, *Dokumentation zur Sicherung des Fahrradverkehrs*, produced for the Bundesministerium für Verkehr by the Bundesanstalt für Strassenwesen, Bereich Unfallforschung, Bonn.

Apel, Dieter and Lehmbrock, Michael, 1990, *Stadtverträgliche Verkehrsplanung. Chancen zur Steuerung des Autoverkehrs durch Parkraumkonzepte und - Bewirtschaftung*, Deutsches Institut für Urbanistik, Berlin.

Davies, David, 1989, Light Rapid Transit: implications for cyclists, *Cycle Touring and Campaigning*, June/July.

DSB (Danish State Railways), *Cykelparkering og cykelcentre – et idekatalog*, DSB Styregruppen for cyckelparkering, Copenhagen.

Gobel, Norbert, 1988, *Freiburg – Kommunalpolitische und verwaltungstechnische Durchsetzung der Verkehrsumteilung*, in Fahrrad – Stadt – Verkehr, I, Conference Report, Darmstadt.

Grabe, W. and Verband Öffentlicher Verkehrsmittel (VÖV), 1985, *Das Fahrrad als Ergänzungsverkehrsmittel des ÖPNV*, VÖV-Schriften 1.68.2, Reihe Technik, Düsseldorf.

Gyukits, H. et al., 1986, *Planung und Betrieb von Fahrradboxen im VRR (Verkehrsverbund Rhein-Ruhr)*, Gelsenkirchen, Germany.

Hanel, K., 1986, *Sachexpertise Infrastruktur – Servicestationen – Fahrradverleih – Fahrradhandel*, Modellvorhaben Fahrradfreundliche Stadt, Werkstattbericht 16, Umweltbundesamt, Berlin.

Hanton, Alistair and McCombie, Steve, 1989, *Provision for Cycle Parking at Railway Stations in the London Area*, London Cycling Campaign.

Heynen, Pascal, 1992, *Travelling Cleaner*, Transport 2000, London.

Karl, Jürgen, 1986, Mit dem Fahrrad in Bus und Bahn, *Verkehrszeichen* 3/1986, pp. 46–50.

Luers, A., 1985, *Reiseantrittwiderstände, speziell der Einfluss wohnungsnaher Abstellmöglichkeiten auf den Verkehrsanteil des Fahrrades*, in Perspektiven des Fahrradverkehrs – International Planungsseminar auf Schloss Laxenburg bei Wien.

Mathew, Don, 1990, New Way Ahead for Oxford – A Balanced Transport Policy, *The Surveyor*, Vol. 175 (5126), 3 October.

Newman, Peter W.G. and Kenworthy, Jeffrey R., 1989, *Cities and Automobile Dependence: A Source book*, Gower, Aldershot.

Patschke, Wolfgang, 1987, Entwicklungspotential der Systemverknüpfung Fahrrad und Schiene, in Schäfer-Breede, Klaus (ed.), *Kombinierten personenverkehr: bike and ride*, Berträge und Materialen zu einer Tagung in Essen 1986, Allgemeiner Deutscher, Fahrrad-Club Bremen.

Ploeger, Jan, 1988, *Access to the City*, report of proceedings of the Velo City '87 Conference held in the Martinhal Conference Centre,

Groningen, (ed. T. de Wit), CROW, Ede, Netherlands.

Rauh, Wolfgang, 1990, *Das Fahrrad im Verkerhr: Wegweiser zu einer fahrradgerechten Organisation des Strassenverkehrs*, Arbeitsgemeinschaft umweltfreundlicher Stadtverkehr (ARGUS) and Verkehrsclub Österreich (VCÖ), Vienna, Austria.

Tschopp, Jürg, 1988, *Bike and Ride and the Introduction of the Green Reduction Card. Basle, a Success Story in Stimulating Use of Public Transport and the Bike*, report of proceedings of the Velo City '87 Conference, Groningen, CROW, Ede, Netherlands.

Tschopp, Jürg, 1991, *Massnahmen für den Veloverkehr*, Verkehrs-Club der Schweiz (VCS), Herzogenbuchsee, Switzerland.

Umweltbundesamt, 1983, *Fahrrad und Öffentlicher Verkehr*, Modellvorhaben fahrradfreundliche Stadt, Werkstattberichte Nr. 4, Umweltbundesamt (Federal Office of the Environment), Berlin.

Welleman, A.G., 1991, *The Netherlands National Cycling Policy and Facilities for Cyclists at Signalled Junctions*, paper given to the meeting of the Local Authorities Cycle Planning Group, York, 17 May.

5 Getting the right balance in cycling policy

Hugh McClintock

Introduction

The emphasis in the last three chapters has been on physical measures which can help to encourage cycling and make it safer. However, whether or not these infrastructure measures do indeed have any success depends to some extent not just on how well they are designed, built and maintained, but also on the way in which they are, or are not understood and accepted by cyclists. A particular kind of special facility may be technically correct, and indeed very sophisticated, but will fail if it is not based on a realistic understanding of cycling techniques and of the wide range of people who ride bicycles, and their needs. Although some needs differ for different kinds of cyclist, some are important for all, such as smoothness of ride, the ability to maintain balance, the ability to maintain momentum as much as possible, and the need to avoid complex manoeuvres (Franklin, 1988). The cyclist has been described as 'a chauffeur, tightrope artist and engine all in one' (Ploeger, 1991).

With cycling, as with broader traffic management measures, human factors are of great importance in the extent to which road safety is improved, whether objectively in terms of accident statistics, or subjectively in terms of the perception of the users, that is, in terms of their sense of greater freedom from danger. In measures to assist cyclists, as with other road safety measures, what appear to be appropriate measures to promote safety or reduce the likelihood of accidents can simply not work or adversely influence other manoeuvres in an unintentional way, depending on various human factors including attitude, behaviour and reaction (Singleton, 1991).

To start with, in planning any measures to assist cyclists it is important to have a clear understanding of how cyclists may differ in their choice of route and in the relative importance they attach to directness, time saving, convenience and safety. Some of these factors have been discussed in earlier chapters. If these differences in likely users are not taken into account, as well as having a full understanding of the bicycle's advantages and limitations, there is a greater likelihood of any special measures to assist cyclists worsening rather than lessening dangers for cyclists, and also of creating or exacerbating rather than reducing the likelihood of conflict with other users. For example, unrealistic assumptions about the length of delays cyclists are willing to tolerate at red cycle signals may encourage them to cross on red at times when they are not expected by drivers, resulting in more bad feeling and more accidents.

Influences on cyclists' riding behaviour

Traffic planners are often ignorant of the fact that different cyclists travel at different speeds, depending on their age, constitution, fitness and experience (Krause, 1986; Bracher, 1989). The journey purpose is also significant for speed with cyclists on leisure and shopping trips mostly riding slower than those going to work or education, more likely to be under pressure of time. Also important are the amount of baggage carried, and whether a child is carried behind, or indeed whether a trailer is towed. Lightweight bikes with a wide range of gears are also of course likely to be ridden faster than sturdier and heavier roadsters, especially popular in the Netherlands, without gears or with few gears. The growing popularity of mountain bikes, for urban commuting as well as leisure use, is also increasingly important. With their wider handlebars, adequate width for manoeuvre is especially important.

With faster cyclists typically riding around at twice the speed of the slowest, narrower paths that do not have space to permit overtaking will be most likely to be avoided by the former. Cyclists who are more confident riders and keener on speed will tend to give a higher priority to maintaining their momentum, at the cost of safety, in traffic. Depending on the volume, speed and composition of motor traffic on alternative routes, they will be more likely to shun cycle paths if these offer a less smooth surface and if the momentum of riders in using them is more likely to be interrupted by frequent requirements to give way or stop. They will tend to be more frustrated by the frequent longer delays at cycle signals than ordinary traffic lights, and, at a dual carriageway crossing, having to wait separately for green at cycle lights to cross these.

Also not well understood by traffic planners are the differing physical and mental burdens of cyclists (Ploeger et al., 1990). A cyclist's speed depends on the rider's own capability, on topography and on weather. He points out that cyclists with the same performance, doing 30km/h on the flat with no wind, will manage only 15km/h on a 3 per cent slope and with a head wind of 3m/second. Cyclists riding uphill or against a head wind are more likely to wobble. Traffic planners with a driving background tend to forget this. Providing extra width or planting or other measures to screen out some of the side wind should be considered.

Implications of variations in behaviour by different groups of cyclists

Cyclists have a reputation of being instinctive anarchists in relation to traffic rules. A survey of public attitudes to traffic regulation in Britain (Jones, 1990) found that a large number of cyclists admitted to infringements of traffic law that they would be unlikely to commit as drivers.

A German survey of riding behaviour by Pauen-Hoppner (1991) showed the large number of traffic law infringements by cyclists but stressed that it would be wrong to seek the origins of deviant behaviour only among cyclists and not also among aggressive drivers and drowsy pedestrians. Moreover, cyclists' attitudes to traffic regulations are certainly influenced by the fact that the common motor traffic orientation of traffic planning has often meant that cyclists' needs have been overlooked, effectively encouraging poor observance by cyclists of traffic rules. For example, one-way systems are created involving cyclists having to use much longer and often more dangerous routes. This encourages riders to use these streets in the wrong direction. New roads are built, or old roads widened, cutting off quiet back streets that cyclists have been using, with no remaining possibility for safe crossing. This can encourage illegal use of pedestrian subways or overbridges. Other roads are closed, and turning bans introduced in order to control general motor traffic, but often at the expense of both convenience and safety for pedal cyclists.

This motor vehicle bias commonly applies both to the layout of roads and also to traffic rules. For example, there are situations when cyclists find it very difficult safely to obey rules requiring them to give hand signals when turning. Indeed, obeying such rules can actually result in cyclists being more at risk in some situations, for example, when they need to slow down on a slope before making a sharp turn.

It is true that there may often be a minority of cyclists that show no sense of responsibility towards other road users, and even, apparently, little concern for their own safety when ignoring red lights or other priority arrangements. However, it is important not to be so blinded by anger at this behaviour as to overlook what, for many cyclists, will be the good reasons for not always following the rules. At large junctions cyclists, for example, may be inclined to edge forward before lights have turned green, in order to be able to negotiate their next manoeuvre in more safety. This may well reflect a lack of sufficient time in the phasing of the signals for them, rather than drivers, to complete their manoeuvres.

It should be remembered that the differential in speed between cyclists and cars has steadily increased in recent years with the major improvements in acceleration and braking performance of cars. This has probably encouraged many drivers to drive with a fiercer style than previously, and in most cases apparently oblivious of the intimidating effect this can have on cyclists, for example, when they shoot away from traffic lights. This kind of behaviour is probably all the more likely in countries where most drivers have no recent experience of being cyclists, or none at all, as in much of Southern Europe. Drivers, especially young male drivers, often drive with deliberate recklessness (Manstead, 1991), showing complete ignorance of the potentially very dangerous effects of the car's physical combination of mass and speed.

The 'speed culture', with car advertisements often emphasising the speed potential of their machines, regardless of prevailing speed limits, has tended to reinforce this highly irresponsible mentality, along with spacious design standards of urban roads. It has also been suggested that faster and more aggressive driving may have been fostered in part by the concentration of road safety measures, like seat belts, stronger car bodies, anti-lock brakes and crumple zones, on ones aimed mainly at drivers and car occupants (Briese, 1991). Through the phenomenon of 'risk compensation', drivers, feeling more protected and confident, then adjust their behaviour to new levels of risk perception, putting more vulnerable road users more at risk (Adams, 1985). Eighty-five per cent of recorded accidents to pedal cyclists in the UK involve a car (Morgan, 1991), a similar level to that found in Germany (Environmental and Transport Planning and Planungsgemeinschaft Verkehr, 1991). Most take place in daylight, not at night-time with inconspicuous cyclists, as drivers often tend to imagine, and occur at or near junctions. In the majority of cases involving an adult cyclist, the driver is primarily at fault (Mills, 1989).

Drivers often have little understanding of the real basis of cyclists' apparently deviant behaviour. For example, cyclists using a one-way cycle path in the wrong direction may do so because it in fact offers them a safer route than having to cross twice over a main road, or because in some other way it offers them a safer route than what is officially available. The illegal use of one-way streets in the wrong direction, or pedestrianised areas, may be the result of a lack of safe and reasonable alternatives for cyclists. Conflict between pedestrians and cyclists may arise because of poor separation or maintenance arrangements or because insufficient space has been allocated for both groups, while space for motor traffic remains undiminished. Rather than simply condemn all signs of non-compliance with the traffic rules it is essential that traffic planners study these clues for the very useful evidence they can yield of cyclists' desire lines, on the one hand, and, on the other, of areas they avoid as being too dangerous. Such behaviour may also reveal evidence of poor design, encouraging conflicts rather than making them less likely.

Inadequacies of accident statistics as a measure of road safety

A careful analysis of the problem areas for cyclists should not be based just on an analysis of recorded accidents and their locations. In the first place, as emphasised by several studies in different countries, for example in Britain (Mills, 1989), Denmark (Odense Kommune, Magistratens 2, Afdeling, 1979), Sweden (Västerås Kommun, Gatukontoret Trafikavdelingen, 1983), the official accident records in respect of cyclists tend both to underestimate greatly, and to misclassify, cyclist accidents. This underestimation, or 'Dunkelziffer' (dark figures), as they are referred to in Germany, is particularly pronounced for accidents involving no injury, no motor vehicle, and for those on minor roads. Hospital records of cycle accidents tend to be more comprehensive than those of the police which, in the case of cycle accidents can result in up to 74 per cent of slight and 61 per cent of serious accidents being missed (Mills, 1989). These findings suggest that official police statistics commonly tend to underestimate greatly the actual number of cycle accidents.

Even when using official accident statistics it is very difficult to arrive at firm conclusions about trends in accidents, especially when absolute figures are related to the amount of cycling in different countries, by different groups, on cycle paths, major roads and minor roads. Morgan (1991, p. B2) provides a clear illustration of this when he notes that 'the estimated amount of cycling in a particular year can be changed drastically by the next year's reestimates'. This happened, he notes, in the official UK Department of Transport's Transport Statistics figures for 1987 and 1988 which gave a retrospective reduction in that year's casualty reporting rates of 32 per cent! He added that

Coupled with the vagaries of accident reporting, this adds up to great uncertainty about accident rates, the relative risk in cycling, and even about whether the accident rate is increasing or decreasing.

There is certainly a serious cycle accident problem. Even in the UK where cycling accounts for only 2.5 per cent of all journeys, pedal cyclists account for 5.5 per cent of all road user fatalities (British Medical Association, 1992, p. 45), meaning that cycling carries a comparatively higher risk of death than other modes of transport. Moreover, the general trend for some years in Britain has been for accidents to cyclists not to decline when there has been a fall in recorded traffic accidents generally. However, there is a danger in official accidents being used to exaggerate the dangers of cycling in relation to other road users. The 'lower' rate of accidents to drivers is for a start boosted by a lack of allowance for the fact that there is no cycling on motorways, roads with a relatively low accident record, and also that there are no child drivers. For child cyclists the rate is particularly high, but, with this group total deducted, the differential then narrows considerably. In the UK the risk of injury for pedal cyclists has changed little since the early 1980s, while it has fallen for all other road users (Morgan, 1991, p. B1). However, though their risk per mile is great, people who cycle have only a slightly higher than average risk of injury per year compared with all travellers and a slightly lower than average risk of death. Casualty rates also have to be linked with distance travelled, in so far as reasonable data on this are reliable. A study of pedal cyclist casualty rates per distance travelled found a rate 10 times as high in Great Britain as in the Netherlands (Tight and Carsten, 1989). Using numbers of trips or time exposure as the comparative basis, however, gives rather less unfavourable results than the 'traditional' approach of accident rates per passenger kilometre (British Medical Association, 1992).

A more radical view, emphasised by Hillman (1991) is that the risk to all road users should be taken account of in any analysis of the safety of different modes, i.e. by 'externalising' as well as 'internalising' the danger, i.e. taking account of the dangers inflicted by different modes as well as ones inflicted *on* them. This would reveal very different correlations between the rates for large, sturdy vehicles and for unprotected road users. The logic of this conclusion is, Hillman says, that cycling should be promoted as a form of transport that keeps the risk of death among other road users to a minimum, as well as reducing the volume and speed of motorised vehicles.

Even if the accuracy of official accident statistics was more trustworthy, there would still be a need to remember that they can be misleading because accidents are an unreliable if not misleading measure of safety or danger, as Adams, in particular, has argued (1985, 1988). As Adams says: 'Danger cannot be measured directly but its presence can be detected by its influence on behaviour.' This means that people tend to avoid altogether the locations they regard as most dangerous. This is then reflected in low accident figures for those locations.

It is therefore important to gather evidence of cyclists' subjective perceptions of the safety of different locations, to complement official police and hospital accident records. This can be done from questionnaire surveys of cyclists, from observation and from consultation with local cycling groups. Understanding subjective safety is important not just to get a fuller picture of where major improvements are needed to get cyclists to ride at all but also, on the other hand, of where their subjective sense of safety may not be justified by objective conditions and where they need reminding of the risks they face. For example, there is a danger with some off-highway cycle paths, and shared pedestrian–cycle paths, that they encourage a false sense of security and therefore poor riding behaviour, which increases the risks both to the riders themselves and to other riders and pedestrians. Improving cyclists' safety should not be seen in isolation. There is little merit in providing a facility which improves cyclists' safety by making pedestrians significantly more at risk, while motor traffic remains largely unrestrained.

Cyclists' safety and drivers' speeds

Many studies have confirmed that high speeds are the greatest safety threat to cyclists (Monheim and Monheim-Dandorfer, 1991, p. 284), and that higher speeds are much more likely to result in serious injury to cyclists, as discussed in Chapter 3. Cycle accidents outside built-up areas are much less common but are much more likely to be fatal than in urban areas because of higher average speeds. Lower speeds by drivers give far more time for reaction to unexpected happenings, and for avoiding action, if necessary. In her Anglo-German study of Cycle Safety (Environmental and Transport Planning/Planungsgemeinschaft Verkehr, 1991), Hass-Klau concluded that German experience showed that a quarter of all accidents could have been avoided if motor vehicles had obeyed the speed limit. She also found that a combination of strict police enforcement of speed limits and widespread traffic-calming was the main explanation for the good safety record for cyclists in Heidelberg.

Problems in assessing the impact of road safety measures

In addition to the problems in relying on accident statistics in arriving at useful conclusions about cyclists' safety or 'unsafety', and even more, in trying to make valid international comparisons, with the varying definitions of categories of accidents, there are also major problems in defining the effects of various road safety strategies. Hillman, Adams and Whitelegg state (1991, p. 98) that 'there is much dispute and confusion in the road accident literature about the impact of various road safety measures'.

Morgan commented (1991, p. B3) that during the 1980s 'there have been various cycle safety campaigns, new British Standards and legal requirements for cycles and equipment and the introduction of road schemes intended to help cyclists'. Yet, he says, 'the number of cyclists killed and injured has fluctuated with no discernable long term trend', suggesting that 'these safety measures have at best mitigated worsening conditions for cyclists on the roads'.

One reason for the uncertainty over the impact of particular engineering 'accident remedial' measures is the phenomenon of 'accident migration' or 'redistribution of risk'. There is reason to believe that any success in reducing accident rates for motor car occupants has been at the expense of the safety of vulnerable road users (Adams, 1990; Briese, 1991). There may therefore be a redistribution of risk rather than a reduction. As Adams also strongly argues (1985) there is very good reason to believe that, due to the operation of 'risk compensation' potential safety benefits are consumed as performance benefits. This means that the driver of a car with improved braking will rely on this improved performance to leave braking until later. Similarly, wearing seat belts may make drivers feel safer, encouraging them to drive faster. In both cases the safety of vulnerable road users is likely to be made worse. This will tend to reduce the accident rate for the latter, but may result in other evidence of increased danger such as a rise in the amount of accident damage to motor vehicles and insurance claims. Reducing the number of crashes might therefore be a more sensible aim than reducing the number of accidents.

Adams' theory is based on the premise that at any given time there will be a level of risk that an individual is prepared to tolerate, or even seek. This means that safety improvements which do not alter people's tolerated level of risk will tend to be nullified by behavioural reactions which tend to nullify the level of risk. This means that the value of safety improvements will tend to be ended when people feel safer and engage in more risky behaviour. For example, it has been alleged by Adams that devices such as seat belts may encourage drivers to drive faster and that requiring cyclists to wear reflective clothing or helmets may encourage them to ride in places where they would not otherwise ride. Accident rates may therefore be mainly determined, he argues, by individuals' propensity to take risks, where they have the chance to do that. In the case of cyclists (and pedestrians), the difficulties of improving their safety are compounded by the fact that it is difficult to curb their flexibility in movement, manoeuvrability and direction (Hillman, Adams and Whitelegg, 1991, p. 102).

A further dimension of uncertainty is the large number of wider influences on road safety. These include the density of traffic and building development, the amount, speed and composition of traffic, the amount of motor traffic in relation to total traffic, and the width and straightness of roads. Apel et al. (1988), after a detailed study of urban traffic factors in the accident statistics for 80 European towns and cities, concluded that the type, size and state of development of major roads and the percentage of motor traffic in relation to overall traffic volumes are the principal factors determining accidents in urban areas. In addition, they stated, the relative accident frequency of a district depends on the width of the carriageways, the extent of the road network and the percentage of main roads, especially in residential and mixed use areas.

They also concluded that the individual cyclist runs a smaller risk in towns and cities with a high proportion of cycle traffic. This is contrary to a common attitude among many 'traditional' traffic planners that any encouragement to people to cycle will inevitably mean more accidents.

Several studies have confirmed that there is often a clear problem of perception of cyclists by drivers, with some drivers apparently finding cyclists invisible (Environmental and Transport Planning/Planungs-gemeinschaft Verkehr, 1991). That this happens, even when the cyclist has bright clothing and other conspicuity aids, raises the matter of what Singleton (1991) says is often the missing factor in accident histories, that is the feelings experienced or actions taken by the driver (or other road user) immediately prior to the accident, including whether they are suffering from stress, illness, aggression or fatigue. The impact of these is also affected by personality factors or stresses resulting from life experiences such as work or personal relationships. In any case, Singleton has suggested that drivers tend to focus their attention on the sources of perceived danger and miss other less obvious conflicts. In the case of drivers this means that they do not see smaller, less threatening ones, such as pedestrians and cyclists, and is one reason for the frequent occurrence on major roundabouts of incidents where drivers entering fail to see a circulating cyclist (Allott and Lomax, 1991). A lesson from this, Singleton suggests, is the need to redesign road layouts to draw the attention of drivers more towards the source of conflicts, especially with vulnerable road users. For example, roundabouts may be made safer for cyclists by enlarging the central island or by squaring the approaches. Drivers tend to arrive at roundabouts too fast, expecting to go, not stop, leaving too little 'observation time' to take in details. Traffic-calming measures on roundabout approaches may therefore also help, by reducing entry speeds. This is especially important for inexperienced drivers who seem to find roundabouts the most difficult type of junction to deal with.

In assessing the relevance of road safety strategies used in one country for anywhere else, account has to be taken not only of differing legislation but also of the differences in community values which underpin such legislation and its enforcement. For example, in Britain there has been a marked increase in recent years in social attitudes to driving under the influence of alcohol. However, attitudes to this matter are still quite different from those common in Scandinavia where it is quite accepted for people to report to the police about neighbours who they fear are in danger of driving under the influence of alcohol.

Because laws are a reflection of a community's values they will not be effective without a tacit acceptance of those laws by the majority and available infrastructure to permit the enforcement of them (McKay, 1989). Awareness of this will have a very important bearing on what road safety strategies, for cyclists or other road users, will have an impact in any particular society. At the same time, as Bracher has argued (1989, p. 95) a greater acceptance of traffic rules can be achieved only if both the cycling infrastructure and traffic rules inspire cyclists' confidence and contribute to the comfort, ease and safety of cyclists. Where cyclists and motor traffic meet, the road design must allow both sets of users to see each other clearly, and must reduce the speed differential between them.

The main aim of cycling policy, including road safety strategies directed at cyclists, should therefore be to create a travel environment which protects the vulnerable road user. This will be assisted by analysing the safety position of each road user separately, looking both at rates and numbers. If each user is not considered separately there is a danger of targets being set only for the reduction of absolute numbers of accidents, as in the UK for a one-third accident reduction from 1987–2000 (Department of Transport, 1987) and for these being met at the cost of pedestrians and cyclists (West-Oram, 1991). Despite the claims that it is surprising that traffic accidents have in general declined as motor traffic has increased, he argues that this decrease is precisely because of the increase in car traffic. Far more trips are made by car, and far fewer on foot or by bicycle, disguising the fact that cyclists and pedestrians have been that much more at risk for each of the trips they do still make. To go just by absolute figures of accidents gives a very distorted picture of the whole road safety situation, he also emphasises.

In the light of these qualifications about the effectiveness of strategies for improving cyclists' safety, the merits and demerits of certain strategies are now discussed, and their value in reducing the 'unsafety' of cycle use. These are as follows:

1. *Protection* Since most serious pedal cycle accidents happen in traffic and involve motor traffic it seems logical to suggest that these can be reduced by protecting cyclists from the dangers of traffic, especially on faster roads. Brighter clothing and conspicuity aids can certainly help, as also can side barriers on lorries to reduce the dangers of cyclists being sucked in under them, especially when lorries turn. However, a critical question arises here about the balance between protecting the likely victims and other measures to reduce the source of the dangers. In addition to being a point of contention in the debate over the merits of segregating cyclists in traffic (see Chapters 2 and 3) this has been well illustrated in the debate on the use of helmets by cyclists (British Medical Association, 1992; Bracher et al., 1991).

Advocates of helmets maintain that the head is the most injured part of the body (86 per cent of cycle injuries in Britain) and that wearing a helmet will reduce the likelihood of serious injuries, at least when cyclists fall off their bikes, or when they are in collision with motor vehicles travelling at slow speeds. The common objection of many cyclists to helmet use is first of all that their effectiveness is very limited when motor vehicles are travelling at more than about 20km/h. Furthermore, it is felt totally wrong in principle to put the onus of protection on to the cyclist without any attempt to enforce lower speeds by the driver. There is also a fear among some cyclists that wearing a helmet (or even wearing reflective aids) may encourage drivers to drive with less consideration, under the misconception that the cyclist is now much better protected (McCarthy, 1990). Furthermore, there is the fear that the safety of cyclists not wearing a helmet will now be more at risk because they will be less obvious to drivers. As the BMA report acknowledged, the case for wearing cycle helmets is that much stronger as regards child cyclists, many of whom tend to have accidents from falling off their bikes, rather than from collisions with motor vehicles. In such cases helmets can offer very worthwhile protection.

Much of this debate reflects uncertainty as to how risk compensation will operate with measures like helmets. Will they encourage drivers to be more or less considerate? Will they encourage cyclists to be more careless? It is still too early to produce firm evidence about this but it is certainly clear that in other ways the growing dangers of motor traffic have tended to put disproportionate burdens on to more vulnerable road users. This is particularly well illustrated in the case of children and the increasing limitations on the geographical extent of their activities, as documented by Hillman, Adams and Whitelegg (1991). They showed risk compensation in operation on a large scale, with a far lower proportion of children being allowed by their parents to go out on their own, on bicycles or on foot. Even allowing for the fact that this confinement, and restriction on the growth of children's independence, reflected parents' worries about the dangers of assault on their children, as well as from increased traffic, its conclusions were an alarming indictment on the extent to which we have allowed the effects of motor traffic to dominate our urban areas. Protection has been achieved, but at a high price in terms of loss of independence, freedom and adventure.

The danger with protection strategies is that, as the same authors say, they impose heavy performance penalties upon vulnerable road users, since their main aim is to improve the safety of vehicle occupants. Barriers restrict the direct routes of cyclists and pedestrians, and they are often routed via distinctly inhospitable subways and bridges. These inspire fear of, and deference to, other traffic. If people do, the authors argue, routinely adjust their behaviour in response to increases or decreases in safety or danger, then to seek to reduce accidents by reducing danger is to chase a chimera. It is vital not to lose sight of the distribution of the road accident risk burden or changes in its distribution over time.

2. *Education* Given the apparent lack of knowledge of good cycling

and driving techniques it is easy to emphasise education as of key importance in improving cyclists' safety. Certainly, getting across the notion
that individuals should take responsibility for their own and other
people's road safety is important. This can help instil more responsible
attitudes and influence behaviour positively, for example in correct posi-
tioning and signalling on the road and at junctions. Training is
particularly important for children who lack control skills and the
maturity to judge speeds adequately, yet in the UK about half of them
do not get any training (Department of Transport, 1990). Road safety
training needs to be available for adults returning to cycling after many
years as non-cyclists, as well as to younger age groups. It is also helpful
if this can include some basic instruction in cycle maintenance since a
poor state of repair can also contribute to cycle accidents. A fear of cycle
theft may have aggravated this by encouraging more people to ride
unroadworthy machines (Bracher et al., 1991).

Despite the apparent benefits of much road safety education, there are,
as with other road safety measures, doubts about these claims, especially
in the longer run. For example, road safety education can breed responsible attitudes but also overconfidence on the one hand, or insecurity on
the other. Studies of the effectiveness of the British National Cycling
Proficiency Test, generally taken by children aged 9–11 (Darlington,
1976), have differed on whether it is of any benefit even in the short
term, but agree that long-term benefits are particularly questionable,
especially given that it may well lead young cyclists to think they are
safe, encouraging them to cycle more and increasing their exposure to
risk. Moreover, the fact that children have passed the cycle test may give
them and their parents the impression that the children will now be safe
to cycle on main roads. This perception is particularly dangerous if the
parents themselves are not confident cyclists, able and willing to ride
with their children to help entrench responsible behaviour. There seems
to be a particular problem with 12–15-year-olds, especially males (Downing, 1985) who like to do stunts and ride recklessly and who in general
show riskier riding behaviour, testing themselves against their environment.

Mills (1989) has suggested that education should take account of
gradual change, with age, in the cycling environment, with information
on the correct procedures to undertake certain specific manoeuvres, for
example making right turns and negotiating roundabouts, as well as
defensive riding techniques. For drivers, education should focus on junctions and overtaking behaviour with cyclists, as well as generally
encouraging them to be aware of cyclists.

Other research (for example, Carsten et al., 1989) has confirmed that
drivers tend to drive too fast for the road conditions, and display a lack
of recognition that they are driving a potentially lethal weapon (West-
Oram, 1991). Speed (1990) found in her research on drivers' and cyclists'

attitudes that many drivers were poor judges of cyclists' speed movements and that motor vehicle drivers less than 30 years old displayed poor road skills, perception and tolerance towards cyclists. She called for much greater emphasis in training on the needs of the vulnerable road user.

These findings underline the danger of road safety education putting too much emphasis on the victims protecting themselves, without also tackling the more difficult problems of bad driving and, in particular, excessive speeds. Some educational programmes have tended to encourage cyclists to defer to unlawful behaviour by drivers rather than take steps to tackle the real problem of drivers causing accidents, often the result of their impatience, recklessness, or, even worse, drunken driving.

There may be a particular problem with drivers' attitudes in countries like the UK where many drivers have not ridden a bike for many years. Making drivers do some bicycle riding as part of their driver training certainly therefore has its attractions as a way of inculcating greater understanding. Since, as McKay (1989) says, the reality is that everyone learns about traffic from experience and then that experience sets their behaviour patterns, some drivers, at least, might get some understanding from cycling themselves! A reasonable co-existence of drivers and cyclists is also probably helped by a public recognition of the importance of cycling, still so lacking in many countries.

3. *Legislation* Legislation has an important role in setting the framework for good traffic behaviour, including cycling, provided that it is based on the aspirations and values of the community, and that it is enforced. The laws and traffic rules must take account of all user groups and should complement physical measures (as far as possible self-enforcing), such as traffic-calming techniques to encourage lower speeds. Enforcement of drink-driving legislation is also of particular importance for the most vulnerable road users. Enforcement of traffic laws (sensitive to cyclists' needs) should also apply to cyclists, for example punishing those riding without lights after dark or other irresponsible behaviour.

New technology may have an increasingly important role in enforcement, especially of speed limits, as speed control cameras have already begun to show.

Also important is a certain minimum level of understanding for cyclists' plight from the legal system rather than the incidents that have occurred, for example, in magistrates' courts in England, of some magistrates' apparently being more intent on questioning cyclists' rights to be on the streets at all than to punish grossly irresponsible driving.

4. *Environmental Change* The physical provision of infrastructure for cycling must be based firmly on the need to encourage mutual respect of cyclists and other road users. Large-scale traffic-calming schemes, as

experience in Germany and several other countries now shows (Cleary, 1991), are most likely to result in a decline in both the number and the severity of accidents. A study of English urban safety management schemes suggested that they could reduce cycle accidents by one-third (Mackie, Ward and Walker, 1990). It is also important (Briese, 1990) that these measures, and any cycle infrastructure, should not slow down cyclists unduly or this will undermine the potential for cycling to represent a real alternative to driving. Safety and speed should not, he insists, be seen as opposing criteria.

This underlines the importance of Hass-Klau's conclusion that good quality infrastructure has a positive effect on cycle usage and correlates with a lower accident risk for the individual cyclist. Similarly, Bracher emphasises that safe traffic infrastructure for cyclists must enable vehicle drivers to see each other properly, and must not encourage a lack of attention by either, as in technically perfect arrangements, which because of their complexity or long delays are not observed by road users as planned (Bracher 1989, p. 99). Streets must be designed to support good, slower and calmer driving, and not to undermine it.

In the longer term, the role of environmental change can assist road safety as a whole, particularly for vulnerable road users, by forming part of a wider land use planning approach to reduce mobility, encourage shorter trips and the use of less harmful means of transport than the private car (Briese, 1991; Godefrooij, 1991).

Conclusion

The provision of infrastructure for cyclists must take account of their likely understanding and acceptance of such measures. Both physical infrastructure and traffic rules must be based on a clear understanding of the characteristics of cycling as a means of transport and the varying needs of different cyclists. While continuing to develop effective educational and training programmes to encourage good cycling and driving behaviour, policy-makers must be aware of the limitations of these and of the many ways in which current traffic policy and traffic rules do not accord with cyclists' needs. Individual responsibility is important in improving road safety and preventing accidents, as well as public policy, but there is a real danger of simply trying to promote safer cycling by putting disproportionate burdens on cyclists rather than drivers. The reduction of traffic speeds by drivers, both through physical measures and greater police enforcement, can result in a very great increase to cyclists' safety. In the longer term, changes in land use planning and other measures to reduce the need to travel should particularly help the most vulnerable road users, that is, pedestrians and cyclists.

Key references

Alrutz, Dankmar, Fechtel, Hans W., & Krause, Juliane, 1991, *Dokumentation zur Sicherung des Fahrradverkehrs*, Unfall- und Sicherheitsforschung Strassenverkehr, Heft A74, Bundesanstalt für Strassenwesen, Bereich Unfallforschung, Bergisch-Gladbach.

Bracher, Tilman, 1989, *Policy and Provision for Cyclists in Europe*, Commission of the European Communities Directorate-General for Transport, Brussels.

Bracher, Tilman, Luda, H., Thiemann, H., 1991, *Zussamenfassende Auswertung von Forschungsergebnissen zum Radverkehr in der Stadt*, Forschung Stadtverkehr, Band A7, Bundesministerium für Verkehr, Bergisch Gladbach/Berlin, Bonn.

Briese, Volker, 1991, *Verkehrssicherheit: Anspruch und Wirklichkeit*, Bonner Fahrradkongress, Mensch – Umwelt – Fahrrad: Die Zukunft des Stadtverkehrs, 10–11 June, Bonn.

British Medical Association, 1992, *Cycling: Towards Health and Safety*, Oxford University Press.

Environmental and Transport Planning & Planungsgemeinschaft Verkehr, 1991, *Cycle Safety – A Comparison between German and British Towns*, ETP, Brighton.

Godefrooij, Tom, 1991, *Promoting the Use of the Bicycle – Improving Safety is Not Enough*, paper presented to the Velo City '91 Conference, Milan.

Hillman, Mayer, 1991, Cycling – false premises for policy formation, *Town and Country Planning* 60 (12), December.

Mills, Paula J., 1989, *Pedal Cycle Accidents – A Hospital Based Study*, Research Report 220, Transport and Road Research Laboratory, Crowthorne, Berkshire.

Other references

Adams, John, 1985, *Risk and Freedom: The Record of Road Safety Regulation*, Transport Publishing Projects, Cardiff.

Adams, John, 1988, Evaluating the effectiveness of road safety measures, *Traffic Engineering and Control*, July–August.

Adams, John, 1990, *Risk Compensation, Risk Homeostasis and Traffic Safety Measures*, report of proceedings, Velo City '89 Conference, Copenhagen, (ed. Niels Jensen), National Agency for Physical Planning, Copenhagen.

Apel, Dieter et al., 1988, *Stadtverkehrsplanung Teil 4: Verkehrsicherheit im Städtevergleich*, Institut für Urbanistik, Berlin.

Briese, Volker, 1990, *The Fast Bicycle – An Important Political Demand or a Safety Risk?*, report of proceedings, Velo City '89 Conference, Copenhagen, (ed. Niels Jensen), National Agency for Physical Planning, Copenhagen.

Carsten, O.M.J., Tight, M.R., Southwell, M.T., with Plows, B., 1989, *Urban Accidents: Why Do They Happen?: Report of a Study on Contributory Factors in Road Traffic Accidents*, Automobile Foundation for Road Safety Research, Basingstoke, Hampshire.

Cleary, Johanna, 1991, *Cyclists and Traffic-Calming: A Technical Note*, Cyclists' Touring Club, Godalming.

Darlington, O.J., 1976, *Children Cycling*, County Council of Hereford and Worcestershire Highways and Transportation Planning Department, Worcester.

Davis, Bob, 1992, *Death on the Streets: Cars and the Mythology of Road Safety*, Brefi Press, Tregaron, Wales.

Department of Transport, 1987, *Road Safety: The Next Steps: An Interdepartmental View of Road Safety*, D.Tp., London.

Department of Transport, 1990, *Children and Roads: A Safer Way*, HMSO, London.

Directorate-General for Transport, 1991, *The Report of the High Level Expert Group for a European Policy for Road Safety*, Directorate-General for Transport (DG VII), Commission of the European Communities, Brussels.

Downing, Charles, 1985, *Pedal Cycle Accidents in Great Britain*, report of proceedings, 'Ways to Safer Cycling' Conference, April 1985, D.Tp., London.

Draeger, Werner and Hahn-Klockner, H., Leichtigkeit, Sicherheit und Akzeptanz von Radverkehrsanlagen, Vorurteile – Thesen – Tatsachen, *Städte und Gemeindebund* 11/1987, pp. 608–616.

Franklin, John, 1988, *Cyclecraft: Skilled Cycling Techniques for Adults*, Unwin Hyman, London.

Godefrooij, Tom, 1988, *Increasing the Visibility of Cyclists: How, Why, How Not, Why Not?*, report of proceedings, Velo City '87 Conference, 'Planning for the Urban Cyclist', Groningen, (ed. T. de Wit), CROW, Ede, Netherlands.

Hall, R.D., Harrison, J.H., McDonald, M., 1989, *Accident Analysis Methodologies and Remedial Measures with Particular Regard to Cyclists*, Contractor Report 164, Transport and Road Research Laboratory, Crowthorne, Berkshire.

Harland, D.G. and Gercans, R., *Cycle Routes*, paper presented to the Velo City '91 Conference, Milan.

Hillman, Mayer, Adams, John, Whitelegg, John, 1991, *One False Move: A Study of Children's Independent Mobility*, Policy Studies Institute, London.

Jones, Peter, 1990, *Traffic Quotes – Public Perceptions of Traffic Regulation in Urban Areas*, Transport Studies Unit, Oxford University, published by HMSO, London.

Krause, Juliane, 1986, *Kritische Partner im Verkehr*, Institut für Städtebau Wohnungswesen und Landschaftsplanung der Technischen Universität Braunschweig.

Local Authorities Association, 1990, *Road Safety Code of Good Practice*, Local Authorities Association.

Mackie, A.R., Ward, H., and Walker, R.T., 1990, *Overall Evaluation of Area-Wide Schemes*, Urban Safety Report, Research Report 263, Transport and Road Research Laboratory, Crowthorne, Berkshire.

Manstead, A.S.R., 1991, *Social Psychological Aspects of Driving Behaviour*, paper to the Annual Conference of the British Psychological Society, University of Manchester.

McCarthy, Mark, 1990, *Cycling and Risk*, report of proceedings, 'Cycling and the Healthy City' Conference, organised by Friends of the Earth, Hammersmith Town Hall, London, 27 June.

McKay, Murray, 1989, Strategies for safety, *Local Transport Today*, 7 March.

Monheim, Heiner and Monheim-Dandorfer, Rita, 1991, *Strassen für alle*, Rasch und Röhring Verlag, Hamburg.

Morgan, J.M., 1991, *Cycling in Safety?*, proceedings and programme, Safety '91, Transport and Road Research Laboratory, Crowthorne, Berkshire.

Odense Kommune, Magistratens 2. Afdeling, 1979, *Born pa Skolevejen: Born i trafikken*, Odense.

Pauen-Hoppner, Ursula, 1991, *Cyclists' Behaviour and Experiences – Insider Stories on the Question of Safety*, paper presented to the Velo City '91 Conference, Milan, November.

Ploeger, Jan, 1991, *Bicycle Facilities*, paper presented to the Velo City '91 Conference, Milan.

Ploeger, Jan et al., 1990, *Wegwijzer Fietsvorzieningen: Uitgangspunten en plan-vorming*, Stichting Centrum voor Regelgeving en Onderzoek in de Grond-, Water- en Wegenbouw en de Verkeerstechniek (CROW), November.

Plowden, Stephen and Hillman, Mayer, 1984, *Danger on the Road: The Needless Scourge*, Policy Studies Institute, London.

Preston, Barbara, 1990, The safety of walking and cycling in different countries, in Tolley, Rodney (ed.), *The Greening of Urban Transport: Planning for Walking and Cycling in Western Cities*, Belhaven Press, London.

Preston, Barbara, 1991, *The Impact of the Motor Car*, Brefi Press, Tregaron, Wales.

Quimby, A., Downing, C. and Callahan, C., 1991, *Road Users' Attitudes to Some Road Safety and Transportation Issues*, Contractor Report 227, Transport and Road Research Laboratory, Crowthorne, Berkshire.

Rothengatter, J.A. and de Bruin, R.A., 1987, *Road Users and Traffic Safety*, Van Gorcum, Assen/Maastricht, Netherlands.

Ruwenstroh, G., Kuller, E.C., Gersemann, D., 1986, *Regelabweichendes Verhalten von Fahrradfahrern*, Bundesanstalt für Strassenwesen (Bereich Unfallforschung) Nr. 142, Bergisch-Gladbach.

Singleton, David, 1989, The influence of human factors in road safety engineering, *Journal of Traffic Medicine* 89 (17), pp. 3–4.

Singleton, David, 1991, *Adjusting Drivers' Focus of Attention to Reduce Vulnerable Road User Casualties*, report of proceedings of the International Conference on Traffic Safety and the Vulnerable Road Users, New Delhi, India, January.

Speed, Liz, 1990, It's all a question of attitudes, *Cycle Touring and Campaigning*, October/November.

Tight, M.R., Carsten, O.M.J., 1989, *Protection for Vulnerable Road Users in Great Britain, Netherlands and Sweden*, Working Paper 291, Institute of Transport Studies, University of Leeds.

Västerås Kommun Gatukontoret, Trafikavdelingen, 1983, *Trafikäkningar 1982*, Västeras, Sweden.

West-Oram, Frank, 1989, Measuring danger on the road, *Traffic Engineering and Control*, November.

West-Oram, Frank, 1990, Casualty reductions: whose problem?, *Traffic Engineering and Control*, September.

West-Oram, Frank, 1991, The one-third reduction target, *Traffic Engineering and Control*, July–August.

Wolf, J., 1988, *Modal Split und Verkehrsunfallstatistik im Städtevergleich*, Sammelband zum internationalen Kongress, Fahrrad – Stadt – Verkehr, 2–3 April 1987, Frankfurt am Main, ADFC Hesse, Darmstadt.

PART II

PRACTICE

6 Nottingham

Hugh McClintock with Ian Chatfield and Johanna Cleary

Introduction: cycling and transport policy in Nottingham

The name of Nottingham, situated in the East Midlands about 200km
north of London, has long been linked to the bicycle, because it is the
home of Raleigh, still the largest cycle manufacturer in Great Britain.
The Nottingham conurbation, including surrounding suburbs such as
Arnold, Beeston and West Bridgford, has a population of about 450,000,
nearly half that of the county of Nottinghamshire as a whole.

In terms of car ownership and cycle use the county is fairly average
for the UK. The 1981 census recorded a level of 3.92 per cent of trips
to work by bike. This was less than one-third of the county with the
highest level, Cambridgeshire (13.27 per cent). The rate for Nottingham
City, 2.9 per cent, was even lower. It is also fair to note, however, that
several other counties had much lower levels and also that there are parts
of the conurbation where nearly 10 per cent of trips to work were
recorded as being made by bicycle (Chatfield, 1991). Nevertheless, it is
true to say that Nottingham's reputation as 'the home of the bicycle' has
not been reflected in any strong tradition of regular cycle use.

More significant is the reputation of Nottinghamshire since the early
1970s as a place with a stronger than average public transport commitment. Nottingham was one of the first places in Britain to abandon
1960s plans for major road building. In 1974 it achieved much national
publicity for its radical 'zone and collar' project. This was a system of
bus lanes and traffic light restraint of other motor traffic. It was abandoned in 1975, after substantial local opposition, but it is still regarded
by some people as an idea that was basically sound but which public
opinion in general was not yet ready to accept.

Another pioneering 'environment-friendly' early-1970s transport
initiative was the extensive pedestrianisation of shopping streets in the
city centre. At the time it was one of the most extensive of any British
city and it has recently been expanded.

Although most of the bus lanes introduced as part of the zone and collar scheme were abandoned with it, public transport has remained relatively cheap and good in Nottingham. Forty per cent of journeys to work were made by bus in 1991. Current plans aim to increase this further, with more radical measures including the reintroduction of bus lanes, but making these more effective through sophisticated traffic-signal controls including bus priority signalling. Some of these will be on routes into the city from park-and-ride sites.

Other current major transport initiatives include plans for what is claimed to be Europe's first High Occupancy Vehicle lane, for 3km on Mansfield Road, a main radial route north of the city centre, and, particularly important, the Light Rapid Transit network (LRT). The first LRT line, extending 12km from the Midland station to Hucknall in the north-west, is due to open in 1995. There are several proposals for further lines to form a larger system. The LRT system will also be connected to the reopening of passenger services on a disused railway line via Hucknall to Mansfield in the north of the county, to be known as the Robin Hood Line. The first stretch of this is due to open in 1993.

Car commuting is to be discouraged in other ways too, such as the raising of charges for all-day car parking in the centre, the extension of park-and-ride, and pioneering schemes for car sharing and car pooling.

Cycling initiatives in Nottingham

Like most Western cities Nottingham experienced a decline in cycle use throughout the 1950s, 1960s and early 1970s. However, unlike most other urban areas, especially older towns and cities, it did see one local initiative to encourage cycling. Raleigh Industries and the City Council commissioned a report from Eric Claxton, who had been the designer of the cycle network in Stevenage New Town some years previously, to make recommendations on providing for the cyclist. His report 'Nottingham: Home of the Bicycle' (Claxton, 1974) proposed a system of cycle priority streets, somewhat similar in concept to the abortive experimental cycle scheme in Portsmouth of the early 1970s (Quenault and Head, 1977: Quenault 1979). Unfortunately, his ideas were regarded as impractical and the report was not well received. The incipient interest in cycling was stillborn and several years followed with no action, giving other urban areas such as Bedford, Middlesborough and Cambridge a head start. The County Council's then Director of Planning and Transportation was reluctant to promote cycling at all, believing simply that cycling was a dangerous activity which should not be encouraged.

There was, however, some renewed interest by the end of the 1970s. At national level the Government, in its 1977 Transport White Paper, had given a lead in announcing its Innovatory Cycling Schemes budget. This was maintained after the 1979 change from Labour to Conservative

Government and resulted in the publication of the Department of Transport's Cycling Consultation Paper in 1981.

In Nottingham there were concurrent moves to form a cycling campaign group, encouraged by Friends of the Earth, Transport 2000 and the Cyclists' Touring Club, similar to those recently launched in London, Edinburgh and Bristol. 'Pedals' was launched in May 1979. Its early small successes included the erection of groups of cycle stands in the city centre, and other minor improvements were followed in late 1981 by the County Council's decision to promote a 6km cycle route linking the city centre with Clifton to the south-west. This initiative was to be half-funded by the Department of Transport Cycling Innovatory Scheme budget. It was a reflection of the strong commitment to cycling of the Labour group which took control of the County Council in May 1981 and, in particular, of the personal enthusiasm of Malcolm Lee, the then County Environment Committee Chairman. This change of policy also reflected careful lobbying of the local Labour Party in the period beforehand. Indeed, this lobbying was of critical importance in that change. Since then, it is probably fair to say that Nottinghamshire's cycling initiatives have enjoyed a fairly broad measure of support among councillors of all parties, especially as its pro-cycling reputation increased, thus helping the development of a much stronger and more consistent cycling commitment than among most other local authorities. From this period onwards it was clear that cycling was creating considerable kudos for Nottingham, and this has continued to grow steadily.

Initially only about one-third of the Clifton cycle route actually comprised any kind of cycle path or even shared paths with pedestrians. The rest consisted of roads closed to through motor traffic, or other quieter roads. The route had two signalled cycle crossings and made good use of an old toll bridge across the River Trent between The Meadows and Wilford. After the imposition of a series of increasing weight restrictions this had been closed to motor traffic when Clifton Bridge was widened. This bridge, and the connecting former road, Queen's Drive (now Queen's Walk), carried an important gas main. It was therefore decided to rebuild the bridge. Cyclists as well as pedestrians were to be permitted to use the new bridge, which was reopened in 1982 (Department of Transport, 1987; Chatfield, 1983; McClintock, 1983; Thompson and Layfield, 1985). The Clifton route had been introduced as a one-year experiment but was soon made permanent after clear evidence that it was helping to divert cyclists from more dangerous alternative routes. It was in general well-liked by users, pedestrians as well as cyclists, despite several detailed criticisms (McClintock, 1983, 1985). The total cost of the route, as opened in September 1982, was £60,000.

One major focus of criticism was the confusing arrangements for cyclists and pedestrians at the crossing of Waterway Street, near the city

Figure 6.1   Queen's Walk, Clifton cycle route, Nottingham, footway and cycle path.

centre. Here the paths for cyclists and pedestrians crossed over twice in quick succession and both groups then faced a dangerous unsignalled crossing on Meadow Way. These criticisms resulted in a series of changes, including the upgrading of this crossing to a signalled cycle crossing, parallel to a pelican crossing, in 1987. Another improvement was the resurfacing of Queen's Walk, a very pleasant tree-lined former radial road through The Meadows from which motor traffic had been diverted in 1978, by a very attractive separate cycle path and footway, with segregation by level. In addition, the grass verges were widened. This scheme (Fig. 6.1) was completed in late 1983 and was the largest of several cycle schemes in Nottingham assisted by Central Government Urban Programme funding.

Most of these were implemented by the City Council who had also adopted a commitment to cycling in the early 1980s. They have helped to implement several minor 'feeder' routes, as well as upgrading some important paths in their parks for shared use by cyclists and pedestrians. These have helped to open up quieter and more direct routes for cyclists away from main roads. 'Pedals' lobbied hard for commitment to cycle routes in the city and other local plans. This acceptance in principle has helped to safeguard sections of routes for later implementation, helping to ward off threats to break up route continuity by other development proposals. This has helped to build up the total network of routes locally. Indeed, the city local plan contains proposals for several routes that are still to be developed, helping to make the extension of the network more likely.

The main changes on the Clifton route, mentioned above, reflected an awareness of the need to take account of pedestrian movements in the detailed planning of cycle schemes and the likelihood of pedestrians being attracted to use cycle crossing facilities, especially where there was no provision for them to cross. It was clear from the studies of cyclists' and pedestrians' attitudes to the route that segregation by level was distinctly preferred to unsegregated shared paths or segregation by white line alone with the consequent inclination of both groups to get in the way of each other (McClintock, 1983, 1985).

The success of the Clifton route encouraged the County Council to make a bid for the Nottingham conurbation to be selected for one of the Department of Transport's proposed cycle route network experiments, announced by Kenneth Clarke, the then Secretary of State for Transport, and a local MP, in January 1982 (Department of Transport, 1982). Preparation of Nottingham's submission was made easier by the publication of two reports by Pedals with proposals for major cycle routes (Pedals, 1980, 1981). The former focused on the flatter area in the south and south-west of the conurbation, from West Bridgford round to Beeston and including The Meadows, Wilford, Clifton and Lenton. The later report extended these proposals to cover the whole conurbation.

Refined versions of several of these route proposals, along with a few others, featured in the County Council's submission, which also took account of more detailed information on existing cycle flows and the most frequent locations of cycle accidents. This was another reason for focusing on the flatter area of the conurbation, closer to the River Trent valley, as this also has most of the busiest roads. The locations of major generators and attractors of cycle journeys were also more specifically taken into account, as well as the aim of providing safe, attractive and convenient links between them. It was, furthermore, considered essential that continuous high quality facilities be provided and that investment be concentrated in areas which already had a relatively high level of cycling (Chatfield, 1991).

There was in fact a total of about 10km of old cycle tracks already existing in Nottingham, mostly concentrated along the outer ring road (Clifton Boulevard) and University Boulevard, south of the campus. There were also two isolated lengths of old cycle path on Arnold Road on the north side of the city. The Pedals reports had proposed that these be upgraded and extended to form part of longer routes, being combined with shared paths, signed sections on quieter streets and special crossing measures at junctions. The adopted Nottingham network scheme followed these principles and generally aimed to make good use of tried

Figure 6.2   Queen's Road, Beeston 'toucan' crossing, Nottingham.

and tested measures rather than further innovatory measures which have been a separate part of the Department of Transport's programme. It has not always been clear, however, what is 'innovatory' and what is merely a refinement of existing measures. There have in any case been some later changes to the Nottingham network in the form of experimental schemes such as the 'toucan' combined pedestrian and cycle signalled crossings. Introduced in Nottingham as part of a national pilot programme of such measures in 1991, these involved the conversion of two signalled cycle crossings on Queen's Road in Beeston (Fig. 6.2) and Sherwin Road in Lenton.

Following discussions with the Department of Transport, the details of the original network routes were changed and it was not until the spring of 1986 that the first new special facilities, linked to two new cycle signals, were opened. The Department of Transport Greater Nottingham

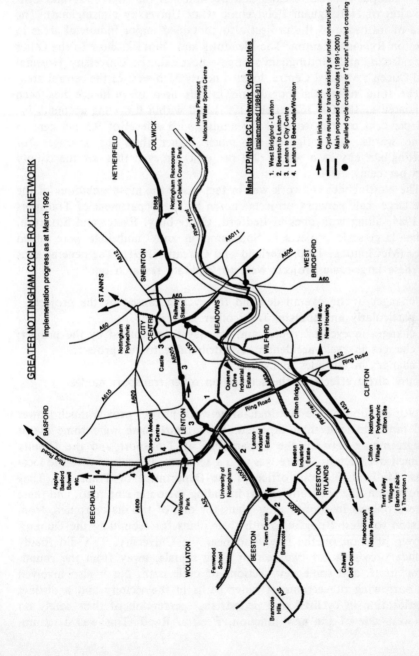

Figure 6.3 Greater Nottingham: cycle route network developments as at early 1992.

cycle route network project has comprised four strategic routes situated in the generally flat area within 2–3km. of the River Trent (see Fig. 6.3). This area contains the city centre with the Lace Market, its historic core, the residential areas of Clifton, Wilford, West Bridgford, The Meadows, Lenton, Beeston, Wollaton and Beechdale as well as Nottingham University's campus between Lenton and Beeston and the city centre and Clifton sites of Nottingham Polytechnic (City University Nottingham). The area of influence of the project also contained major industrial areas in Beeston Rylands, Lenton, The Meadows and Dunkirk, close to the Outer Ring Road, and Nottingham's largest hospital, the University Hospital and Queen's Medical Centre, located nearly 3km west of the central area.

The total residential population in this area of influence has been estimated at 105,000 (Chatfield, 1991) and within it cycling accounts for 5.5 per cent of trips to work by adults, with a level of 9.5 per cent in some wards. Both figures are much higher than the averages for Nottingham city as a whole (2.9 per cent) or even that for the county (3.9 per cent).

The Nottingham Network was in fact easily the most ambitious of the five large-scale network projects chosen by the Department of Transport in 1984, along with ones in Bedford, Canterbury, Exeter and Stockton. Other large-scale projects in Southampton and Cambridge were added later (McClintock, 1990; Harland and Gercans, 1991). The general aims of these large-scale projects were to facilitate research on:

1   changes in the overall demand for cycling caused by the project, particularly any transfer from other modes;
2   changes in cyclists' routes and journey times caused by the project;
3   changes in cycle accident rates attributable to the project;
4   changes in attitudes to cycling;
5   any direct effects of the scheme on other transport modes.

Implementation of the Nottingham network project proved much slower and more difficult than expected. For a start there were some major disagreements between the Department of Transport and the County Council over details. There was also a series of difficulties with the local (East Midlands Region) office of the Department of Transport. They were responsible for trunk roads, including the outer ring road, and there were problems in coordinating plans for one of the major routes, from Beeston to West Bridgford, with their plans for rebuilding the Dunkirk flyover junction on the ring road near the University. This did finally include provision for two sets of cycle signals, away from the roundabout itself, and some new sections of cycle path, but it also involved the narrowing of sections of older paths in the vicinity and a distinct deterioration in cyclists' and pedestrians' perception of their safety on the west side of the new junction, Beeston Road. This was a natural crossing point for cyclists on the ring road cycle track, as well as for local pedestrians and, in particular, parents walking their children to the nearby primary school. All suffered.

In contrast to the commitment of the Department of Transport, nationally, in promoting the UK's largest cycling project, this incident made it clear that, so far as the Department of Transport's Regional Office was concerned, providing increased capacity for motor traffic was still the dominant consideration. The needs of more vulnerable users merited very little serious attention. This was in complete contrast with the thrust of the 1981 Consultation Paper and its aims in designating Regional Cycling Officers to ensure that cyclists' needs were fully taken into account in future trunk road schemes.

At the time of the announcement, in 1984, of the large-scale network schemes, it had been expected that work would be completed by 1987. In the event the last scheme forming part of the Nottingham network, the most complex project, was not finished until the spring of 1991. In addition to the particular problems with the Department of Transport's Regional Office there was a more general problem of coordinating cycle schemes with other new road and road widening works, as on Abbey Street in Lenton. The final cost of the project, comprising about 37km of cycle route (including many stretches of signed, quiet back-streets as well as cycle paths and shared paths) was £700,000. This included the installation of nine signalled cycle crossings, or segregated parallel cycle and pelican signals (two of which were later converted to toucan crossings), and also one completely new bridge for cyclists over the River Leen at Lenton. One of the routes also made use of an existing foot-bridge, converted to shared use, the suspension bridge over the River Trent between The Meadows and West Bridgford (see Fig. 6.4).

In assessing the experience of the Nottingham network project it is important to remember that the official Department of Transport/ Nottinghamshire County Council project, with its four major routes, is only part, albeit the most extensive part, of the total cycle planning developments in the Nottingham area. The Clifton route, for example, had been the first major step forward. The County Council, at its opening in 1982, claimed that it was 'the longest cycle route in the UK to be completed as a whole'. As mentioned above, the value of that route was soon to be augmented by a series of other changes, on Meadows Way and Queen's Walk.

Despite the difficulties with the Department of Transport's Regional Office it is only fair to point out that it was responsible for some improvements to the older cycle paths on Clifton Boulevard, albeit in response to local pressure. While Kenneth Clarke MP was still a Minister at the Department of Transport in 1981, it also committed itself to what proved to be one of the most successful cycle schemes in Nottingham, the Clifton Lane cycle track between Wilford and Clifton alongside the

Figure 6.4   The suspension bridge over the River Trent between West Bridgford and The Meadows area in Nottingham, converted from sole pedestrian use, and one of several existing features incorporated in the Nottingham network.

A453 trunk road, the main road to and from the M1 and A42/M42 motorways. This included the replacement of a section of old cycle path which had been buried when that road was dualled in the early 1970s. The replacement scheme included extensions to connect both with Wilford village and with the ring road cycle tracks at Clifton Bridge, as well as a signalled cycle crossing.

The Clifton Lane cycle path took cyclists right away from the busy road and the major roundabout at Silverdale and also included a new bridge over Fairham Brook. Together, these have greatly improved the perception of safety of Clifton-bound cyclists, especially the large number of students going to and from the Clifton site of the Polytechnic (City University Nottingham). It was built to a high standard, with very few minor road or access crossings. The fact that it runs alongside land excluded from building because of the danger of flooding from the Trent helped the maintenance of priority and thus momentum for cyclists. It represents an excellent example of where a good standard cycle path can give a very substantial improvement for cyclists.

The path has also proved popular with leisure cyclists, including families. This value was reinforced by the links to the riverside shared paths built by the City Council from Wilford under Clifton Bridge. These now run through very attractive scenery near the river towards the older part of Clifton and beyond.

Several complementary cycling initiatives have been taken by Nottingham City and other local District Councils such as Rushcliffe, covering the West Bridgford area, and Broxtowe which includes Beeston, west of the city. The City and Rushcliffe have helped to implement sections of the Trent south bank riverside, on the west and east sides of the built-up area, and a largely traffic-free route which by 1993 should extend to the large and still expanding National Water Sports Complex at Holme Pierrepont to the east of West Bridgford.

Much of the land within Nottingham's city boundary is owned by the City Council, and its attitude as landowner to using land for cycle paths has not always been as constructive as might be expected from its official planning policy. Nevertheless, the City Council has helped to provide a series of feeder links, both cycle paths and shared paths, within different parts of the built-up area, especially The Meadows and Lenton. Indeed several of these initiatives have been on the north side of the city, such as the signed back route to the inner-city neighbourhood of Radford. With the County Council they have provided numerous small-scale but very worthwhile measures such as cycle gaps in road closures and groups of cycle stands in the city centre and at other locations such as swimming baths, libraries and leisure centres. The City has also opened up to cyclists some wider paths in parks, especially Colwick Park in the east, Wollaton Park in the west, and Woodthorpe Grange to the north of the city centre. Other such links, for example across The Forest, are planned with the similar aim of opening up safer, more direct and more attractive routes for cyclists. In addition, cycle paths have been provided as part of general environmental improvement and landscaping schemes. Examples are the River Leen path between Basford and Bulwell in the north-west and the path by the Beeston and Nottingham Canal at Lenton. Further progress in establishing official canalside routes has, however, been frustrated by the attitude of the British Waterways Board. Another important City scheme has been the Sneinton Greenway. This was started in the early 1990s on former railway land east of the city centre. This links to other routes in Colwick Park and Daleside Road out towards Netherfield. Together these routes have extended several earlier stretches of continuous route, forming part of the wider cycle route network in the Nottingham area. The Nottingham network has come to encompass a far larger number of routes than the official Nottingham network project.

Monitoring of the official Department of Transport/ Nottinghamshire County Council cycle network

The plethora of cycling initiatives in Nottingham has been far more extensive than any other older British town or city, with the probable exception of London under the GLC, discussed in Chapter 8. In fact it could be said that Nottingham is way ahead, in terms of provision on a per capita or per kilometre of road basis. It has also, as Harland and Gercans have noted (1991), made the evaluation of the Nottingham official Department of Transport network project particularly complex, compounded by its much longer than expected implementation period. The main monitoring study by the Transport Research Laboratory (TRL) on behalf of the Department of Transport was started in October 1985 by JMP Consultants (1991). Because of the likelihood of a long period between 'before' and 'after' surveys it was agreed to undertake some interim annual monitoring. Accordingly, monitoring surveys were undertaken in two-week periods each October from 1986 to 1989, following the 'before' surveys in exceptionally dry weather in October 1985.

The 'before' study was designed to ascertain existing flows, attitudes and characteristics of cycling in Nottingham before the development of the official network and included:

1   counts of cyclists at 14 screen line stations together with a further control site situated outside the area of influence of the network;
2   interviews with cyclists crossing a screen line;
3   direct interviews with approximately 1,000 students at Nottingham University and the city centre site of Nottingham Polytechnic (City University Nottingham);
4   direct interviews with approximately 1,500 residents in the West Bridgford, Beeston and Wollaton areas;
5   surveys of journey time by cycle, public transport and private car;
6   counts of traffic flow at four counting stations;
7   weather records;
8   accidents.

There were several main conclusions arising from the Consultants' evaluations:

a)   during the implementation period cycle accidents increased in the north and east of Nottingham but remained stable or decreased in areas served by the network, despite increases in general traffic;
b)   between 1985–90 cycle flows in general decreased in the Nottingham area, although these figures may have been slightly distorted by the exceptionally dry weather in the 'before' survey period;
c)   if the effects of adverse weather conditions are discounted, cycle

flows in Nottingham compare favourably with the national trend
between 1985–89 and flows on the cycle route network itself showed
that no fall occurred there;
d) decreases in cycle flows showed a strong correlation with the amount
of heavy rain experienced;
e) female cyclists and those on shopping or education trips seemed
more willing to use the new facilities;
f) many cycle routes do not use the most direct path and journeys and
can take longer on those parts of the network where adjacent main
road alternatives exist;
g) students and householders from areas well served by cycle routes
tended to perceive cycling as being safe and cycle more themselves
when compared to those in other areas;
h) the surveys showed no direct correlation between growth in cycle
ownership and cycle flows, in contrast to the growth in car ownership and motor vehicle flows.

The final counts and surveys for the TRL were carried out in the autumn
of 1990, which was in fact some months before the completion of the
last official network facility. In any case, experience elsewhere shows that
it takes time for cyclists to learn about and adjust their route choice to
new facilities (Westerdijk, 1990). It might therefore have been helpful if
the TRL surveys had been concluded a year later, to reduce the risk of
inaccurate conclusions being drawn through premature analysis. Nevertheless, these findings in general made clear that the implementation of
the official Department of Transport/Nottinghamshire County Council
network has provided important benefits for local cyclists. Even if the
project did not result in encouraging very substantial numbers of new
cyclists it did have important benefits in encouraging people to switch
from more dangerous routes. The annual fluctuation in flow on the
network routes in Nottingham, as in Bedford (Harland and Gercans,
1991), was much smaller than the fluctuations in cycle flow on the
parallel roads. The various facilities have clearly, by and large, helped to
make cyclists, especially female cyclists, feel safer and this is also an
important achievement.

Discussion of monitoring results and lessons for wider application

The relative success of Nottingham's cycle schemes has almost certainly
been helped by the fact that almost all have been based to some extent
on proposals from local cyclists and that there has been close consultation with them as well as with other groups at all stages, from initial
design to final implementation. This has also helped to provide valuable

feedback on detailed problems. Teething problems can so easily occur even on well-designed schemes, and the appropriateness of both basic concepts and detailed design and operational features needs to be very carefully assessed in the light of the way schemes are actually built and used. There has also been regular consultation with other groups such as the disabled, and early consultation on general design features, for example on shared facilities. This has helped to reduce, although not eliminate, conflicts.

There are, however, a number of reservations about the achievement of the network. Many are also applicable to the wider cycle network in the Greater Nottingham area. Although the majority were satisfied with the facilities as provided, the TRL surveys showed (Harland and Gercans, 1991) that a number of improvements were suggested, particularly better lighting, better segregation from pedestrians, improved drainage and more maintenance. Lighting was seen as especially important on off-road paths, at remote locations, and, most particularly, on unsegregated shared paths.

Nottingham's record in the maintenance of cycle facilities would not appear to have been markedly better than elsewhere. There have been particular problems with cycle route direction signs and overgrowing vegetation on off-highway cycle paths. Maintenance appears often to have fallen into a void, with different agencies apparently being much more unwilling to accept responsibility than for maintenance of roads on the one hand, or footpaths and footways on the other. It is also true that the standard of road maintenance remains a common source of complaint for cyclists, especially in the many situations when they have no alternative but to ride on roads. Quieter back streets signed as part of designated cycle routes are often even less smooth than main roads, eroding their value as attractive alternatives. Obstruction by parked cars also sometimes reinforces this disincentive, especially for faster cyclists.

Proper maintenance as well as good detailed design and construction are fundamental to successful cycle schemes. Nottingham's experience suggests that a gulf all too often exists between the good intentions of scheme designers and the much lower level of commitment of those responsible actually for building and maintaining the schemes. All too frequently they appear to lack even a basic understanding of cyclists' needs, such as a smooth surface, and crossings where the kerb is flush with the road. Even in Nottinghamshire it has been clear that the level of commitment to cycling and awareness of how to make provision for it vary greatly, between different engineers, planners, agencies and politicians.

Where cycle paths ran close to the carriageway cyclists on the carriageway were asked in the TRL surveys why they were not using the adjoining cycle facility. Most of the carriageway cyclists preferred the road because the surface was better and there were fewer obstacles, particularly fewer pedestrians. This attitude was stronger in the case of one of the Nottingham schemes, Castle Boulevard, where the alignment of the cycle path near the city centre was much constrained by the presence of an attractive group of trees, as well as pressure from local shops for the retention of kerbside car parking.

Whereas the construction of some new cycle facilities can substantially reduce journey times, the experience of many of these, including several in Nottingham, has been that the routes tended to increase journey time. This is perceived as a disadvantage by the more experienced and confident cyclists, who tend to rate speed and directness as their most important criteria in route choice. Less confident cyclists will rate safety more highly than a quicker journey time, provided that the time penalty is not too high. Timing on cycle signals is therefore critical, it would seem, as some cyclists are unwilling to wait long to cross, especially if traffic flow on the road they are crossing is low. This apparently impatient behaviour is reinforced by cyclists' concern at cycle signals as to whether they have been detected. The use of push buttons and 'wait' messages that light up, as at pelican and toucan crossings, has not been generally authorised by the Department of Transport at cycle crossings.

It is important to evaluate the development of cycle facilities, or even a cycle network, in the wider context of traffic trends in the area, as the Nottingham experience clearly shows. Even where a substantial cycle network has been completed cyclists will almost certainly still need to ride on ordinary roads and streets, without any kinds of special facilities, for much of their journeys. The level of traffic growth in Nottingham during the main cycle network implementation period, 1985–90, was particularly high, 19.4 per cent, as compared with 9.2 per cent over the same period in Bedford (Harland and Gercans, 1991). As the same authors commented.

Increasing numbers of motor vehicles suggest more opportunities for cyclists to give up cycling and travel by car, and increased traffic implies increased discomfort and risk for those cyclists who continue cycling on the roads.

The general level of traffic growth becomes even more significant if, as might be suggested, it has been accompanied by an apparent deterioration in driving standards due to frustration with increasing congestion, thus putting vulnerable road users even more at risk. This kind of perception is one reason why, in Nottingham as elsewhere, fewer parents have been willing to allow their children to cycle to school, with often a very significant amount of 'escort' traffic around schools as parents drive children there instead of letting them walk or cycle (Whitelegg, Adams and Hillman, 1991). Fear of cycle theft at schools, as elsewhere, reinforces this disincentive to use bikes regularly.

In considering the contribution of the official Nottingham cycle network project to the safety of local cyclists in general an important fact to bear in mind is that this effort has been concentrated in one part of the conurbation. This area is generally less intensively built-up with more open space and underused space, both within and outside highway boundaries. Although a few smaller cycle schemes have been introduced elsewhere such as the River Leen path between Basford and Bulwell in the north-west, and gaps in road closures and 'cycle slips' in traffic management schemes in areas like Forest Fields, Basford and Hyson Green, the overall progress in these areas is much less marked. This relative neglect reflects a number of factors including the smaller amount of cycling in this part of the city, its much steeper average topography (especially around Mapperley and Arnold), its greater density of building and its generally narrower main roads with less 'spare' space in which good standard cycle paths could be incorporated. Even the area's disused railways, which elsewhere have offered useful alignments for cycleways in built-up areas, were fragmented some years ago and used for other purposes. To some extent this relative neglect also reflects less political commitment to cycling, for example in Gedling Borough which includes Arnold and Mapperley. It also seems clear, however, that the cycle accident rate in this part of the area has been greater and there are now plans to give cycling provision more attention in future.

Another largely neglected area is the city centre. In the early 1970s, as already mentioned, Nottingham had an extensive pedestrianisation scheme, with through traffic diverted onto the surrounding inner ring road. However, relatively little thought was given to maintaining safe and convenient routes for cyclists within the central core, apart from three bus and cycle only links. With the general growth of traffic over recent years the inner ring road has become even more dangerous to ride on and a greater barrier for safe cycling to and from the city centre. A few improvements were introduced in the 1980s such as the Canal Street cycle crossing (part of the Clifton route) and modifications to the Maid Marian Way pelican crossing to permit its use by cyclists (itself very controversial in an environmentally sensitive area), but the problem has still to be fundamentally addressed. The approach to the Canal Street crossing has remained difficult, especially for northbound cyclists, and was in fact made harder with the inclusion in 1985 of a bus lane in the junction. This seems generally confusing and dangerous for all types of road user and finding a solution has been tied up with wider traffic and redevelopment plans in the whole area between the Broad Marsh and the Midland station.

It is true that a number of groups of cycle stands were erected in the city centre by the end of the 1980s but these are hard to ride to safely and legally. Recent proposals for further pedestrianisation in the central core, near the Council House by the Old Market Square, and on the 'tourist trail' route between the Lace Market and the Castle (Castlegate and Low Pavement) have also threatened further difficulties for cyclists. This tourist route is an important and indeed the only route for cyclists between east and west across the city centre. There are also problems still to be resolved in accommodating cycle movements near the alignment of the new tram system whose first line is due to open across the city centre in 1995.

The TRL surveys of the official network routes found that pedestrians said they were not adversely affected by the presence of cyclists and about three-quarters of those interviewed were in favour of more such routes (Harland and Gercans, 1991). Although the County Council have emphasised the importance of consultation with different groups, including those representing the disabled, the mixing of cyclists and pedestrians has on several occasions proved contentious in Nottingham, as elsewhere. Anxieties about the shared use of existing pedestrian facilities nearly killed off the Clifton route proposals, in the autumn of 1981. It was finally agreed that cyclists should dismount at two narrow sites, a river bridge and a subway under the outer ring road. Another particularly controversial problem surfaced in 1987 when Beeston High Road, part of the proposed cycle route across the south of the conurbation from West Bridgford to Beeston, was pedestrianised. Cyclists were allowed to ride through most of this pedestrianised shopping street, but without any clear demarcation, and it was plain that this was resented by many pedestrians, along with complaints about abuse by delivery vehicles (McClintock, 1988; Milton and Howarth, 1989). Following strong local pressure from Broxtowe Borough Council it was decided to ban all traffic, including ridden bikes, through the area between 10.00 a.m. and 4.00 p.m.

It can be argued that Nottingham's experience underlines the importance of considering pedestrians' needs in conjunction with those of cyclists. This was a clear lesson gained from the Waterway Street and Meadows Way crossings on the Clifton route, discussed above. Several of the new signalled crossings introduced in the mid-1980s were, at least initially, for cyclists alone, even when local residents wanted a pedestrian crossing at the same location. By the late 1980s the County Council had realised the importance of providing new crossings for pedestrians at the same time. This should in future prove easier with the new style 'toucan' crossings which permit a more flexible, less cluttered and much cheaper type of joint cycle- and pedestrian-signalled crossing.

Conflict between pedestrians and cyclists can of course often arise simply because of inconsiderate behaviour by one group or the other. Cyclists in Nottingham complain about poor driving standards just as much as elsewhere in Britain and, similarly, the letters columns of local newspapers are no less full of readers' horror stories about cyclists riding through red lights, using no lights after dark and riding on pavements. Indeed it is possible that the conversion of some stretches of footway into shared paths may have helped to encourage some cyclists to regard all pavements as open to them, especially where detailed design features do not discourage such abuse. It seems, moreover, that the ratio of male to female cyclists in Nottingham is particularly high and, since male cyclists tend to be more confident and go faster, these may tend to make pedestrians feel more at risk from cyclists than elsewhere!

It is also important to appreciate, however, that bad riding behaviour and conflict between cyclists and pedestrians has in some instances been effectively encouraged by poor design. An example of this is on the rebuilt stretches of ring road cycle path near the University. The Department of Transport's Dunkirk flyover rebuilding scheme has some points which are below their own recommended standards on shared provision (Department of Transport, 1986). In contrast, the best designed segregated cycle paths and footways, such as Queen's Walk on the Clifton route, have shown no real evidence of conflict, with the vast majority of cyclists and pedestrians being satisfied (McClintock, 1983, 1985). On other shared paths, with white line segregation, cyclists have often complained about pedestrians straying onto their side, particularly if there are few signs and markings to demarcate clearly the respective areas for each. Clearer segregation is clearly preferable above a certain threshold number of cyclists and pedestrians.

There is no doubt that, compared with other British towns and cities, Nottingham's cycle planning experience is very extensive and much has been learnt about detailed design features and maintenance since the beginning of the 1980s. Judged by the best Continental experience, however, the defects are much more apparent. Many are perhaps the result not of the lack of finance but of the Department of Transport's general reluctance to allow the use of features common in cycle planning practice in countries such as the Netherlands and Denmark. Examples of this include detailed cycle track junction crossing layouts and marking arrangements, and also their unwillingness to permit the use of red cycle aspects on signalled cycle crossings and toucan crossings.

Although most other countries in north-western Europe have now realised the importance of area-wide traffic-calming schemes in reducing motor traffic speeds and thereby contributing to the safety of the most vulnerable road users, there have so far been few signs of Nottinghamshire acting on this awareness. The County Council was not among those councils who were quick to take advantage of the Department of Transport regulations authorising 20mph (30km/h) lower speed limit zones. Although Nottinghamshire has been proud of its accident remedial scheme work, which has included road-safety-based traffic-calming measures such as the provision of central refuges, the safety of cyclists has not always featured highly in the detailed design. An instance is on Woodborough Road, north-east of the city centre, where in 1987 cyclists complained that such features allowed insufficient space for drivers to pass them safely. It remains to be seen to what extent these criticisms are taken into account in future traffic-calming work in the area. This has the potential to yield great benefits for cyclists' behaviour, if sensitively handled (Cleary, 1991).

This underlines the importance of taking into account cyclists' needs in all traffic planning and highway management, not only in the provision of special cycling facilities, but also in assessing all new road and traffic management proposals for their likely impact on cyclist (and pedestrian) safety. In Nottingham, no less than elsewhere, roundabouts are still commonly included in road layouts in new developments, such as at Gamston and Compton Acres in West Bridgford, despite the evidence of their dangers for cyclists (Allott and Lomax, 1991). The inclusion of cycle paths in the early stages of these housing developments, at least, has been only rather half-heartedly pursued. This relative inconsistency stresses the importance of a sustained effort to ensure that cycling is not overlooked in everyday traffic management and highway and town planning. It is also important to ensure that cycle routes for longer term development are safeguarded in local development plans. All planners and engineers need to be encouraged to adopt a 'cycle awareness' so that opportunities to promote cycling are fully exploited in all major development and redevelopment schemes, for example, in the provision of 'missing links' in longer routes. Too often cycling is still seen as marginal to main traffic problems, with public transport improvements far more likely to be mentioned than cycling when changes in current transport strategies are discussed. 'Traditional' attitudes of highway engineers are slow to change, but this change is necessary before the infrastructure can be modified to help cyclists.

Another area with much scope for improvement in future cycling provision in Nottingham is the creation of safer links between the urban cycle route network and the surrounding countryside. Links have already been provided on the west and east sides of the built-up area, with the completion of sections of the riverside path on the south bank of the Trent, including safe passages under the very busy road bridges such as Clifton, Trent and Ladybay. However, these need to be extended, with more connections to the urban routes. Even more importantly, though, there is still very little that has been done to facilitate safe rideable access to nearby countryside in the rest of the conurbation. Such links, when developed, could be joined to other longer distance regional and subregional leisure routes as well as to railway stations, thus encouraging non-car-based recreational trips and a more 'environment-friendly' pattern of tourism. The County Leisure Services Department in Nottinghamshire is keen to promote this.

Relatively little has been done so far in Nottingham to encourage combined use of cycling and public transport, apart from the provision of very limited cycle parking facilities at the main railway station. The projected completion of the Robin Hood line to Mansfield and subsequent completion of the Light Rapid Transit to Hucknall offer good opportunities for exploiting this potential, at least in terms of off-peak, access for bikes on trains and trams. The provision of secure and generally attractive cycle parking at major public transport stops, especially those further out from the city centre, is another objective.

Although provision of cycle stands in the city centre and at facilities such as leisure centres, libraries and shopping centres has become common, it is far from universal and many workplaces still lack good secure cycle parking. The City Council has published, in conjunction with Pedals, several editions of an Advice Note on this topic, but cycle parking provision has not been made mandatory and relatively few developers have acted on the advice.

One of the most important features of cycling initiatives in Nottingham since the early 1980s has been the attempt at a wider promotion of cycling than by the provision of special facilities alone. This has shown some awareness, at least, of the importance of trying to develop a 'cycling culture'. Each of the major cycle schemes has been the subject of extensive publicity and promotion, with leafletting of local households, cycling group members, schools and local media.

Pedals, with local council support, produced a local cycling guide, the Pedal Pushers' Guide to Nottingham. First produced in 1983, a second edition went on sale in 1991. This publication was supported by Raleigh who also assisted with another Pedals publication, a 'Cyclists' Code' leaflet published in 1988, to encourage safer use of shared paths. This was also produced in conjunction with the County Road Safety section.

Interest in cycling locally, perhaps always more latent than elsewhere because of the Raleigh connection, has been greatly helped by the County Council Leisure Services Department's involvement since 1983 in coordinating a programme of guided cycle rides. With leaders from local cycling groups, County Council staff and other volunteers, these are of various lengths and destinations and take place in the spring and summer of each year. By the early 1990s, assisted by the Nottingham Health Authority, they were attracting record levels of participation in the north as well as the south of the county. The Leisure Services Department has more recently built on this experience with the publication of 'self-guided' round-the-county ride leaflets, of particular appeal to recreational cyclists.

The highlight of the Leisure Services Department's cycling promotion, however, has been the organisation each summer of the Great Nottinghamshire Bike Ride. This event, started by Pedals in 1982, has now become a regular annual event, a circular mass ride from Nottingham to Newark and back. By 1991 it attracted more than 5,000 riders. There is a choice of routes: a full ride of 80km (50 miles) or a half-ride of 30km (18 miles). The shorter route particularly appeals to families with younger children and less confident adults who are willing to take up cycling, or are trying it again for the first time in many years. This event and the guided rides have almost certainly encouraged more people to buy bikes and to use them, at least for occasional leisure trips. Cycling in groups often gives more confidence and enjoyment. Combined with the popularity of mountain bikes these events may, locally at least, have helped to give cycling a more acceptable and positive image for adults than that described in the TRL report on Attitudes to Cycling a few years ago (Finch and Morgan, 1985). They also help to combat the common negative image of cycling in the local press, prevalent in Nottingham as elsewhere, with cyclists regularly being portrayed as irresponsible road users.

Conclusions

Great progress has been made with cycle provision in Nottingham but there is still much room for further improvement. This will require sustained political pressure from local cyclists and local councils. A general conclusion which can be drawn about all the Department of Transport's major cycle route network projects is that it is very easy to underestimate the time and effort needed to implement an extensive facility for cyclists such as a route or network (Harland and Gercans, 1991). These authors went on to say that:

The highway authority and the planning authority need to liaise closely so that the necessary consents can be obtained in a logical and planned sequence. Ample time should be allowed for explaining the scheme both to local people and the agencies representing the interests of affected groups such as pedestrians, blind and partially sighted people, and other disabled people . . . .

This conclusion certainly reflects the experience of Nottingham. This project was originally intended to be completed by 1987 but in practice was not finished until the spring of 1991. Many of the other smaller schemes in the area have also faced many implementation problems, with long delays even for minor improvements.

Given the general low esteem in which the bicycle is held in the UK, however, and the weaker cycling tradition compared to some other European countries, Nottingham's cycle planning achievements certainly stand out from other British towns and cities, even if there is still room for much further improvement. Within that part of the conurbation which has benefited most from cycling provision, whether funded by the Department of Transport, County Council or other local authority, much of great value has been achieved, even if the results may not appear spectacular in terms of encouraging new people to take up cycling as a regular form of daily transport. Many of the new facilities, perhaps especially the signalled crossings, are well appreciated, even if both the detailed design of some and the maintenance of most of them could be improved. Many lessons have been learned both about the value of special facilities and about detailed design features and many more recent cycle schemes clearly show awareness of the limitations of earlier attempts. This has been helped by a changed political climate in which, both locally and nationally, cycling and environmental factors generally are taken much more seriously, along with a recognition among many politicians and traffic planners of the importance of restraining private car use.

Nottingham's experience underlines the fact that other transport and planning policies are needed to complement special facilities. The contribution of its special facilities, even in the network area of influence, has been clearly constrained by the overall growth of traffic in the area. Promoting cycling as a serious means of daily transport and as a leisure activity must mean tackling this more directly and taking advantage of many opportunities in all transport planning and traffic management to 'think bike'.

References

Allott and Lomax, 1991, *Cyclists and Roundabouts: A Review of literature*, Cyclists' Touring Club, Godalming, Surrey.

Chatfield, Ian, 1983, The Clifton Cycle Route, Nottingham: Planning and Implementation, *Journal of the Institute of Highways and Transportation*, August–September.

Chatfield, Ian, 1991, *The Development of a Cycleway Network in Nottingham, U.K. and the Results of a Before and After Study into its Effects*, paper presented to the Velo City '91 Conference, Milan, November.

Claxton, Eric, 1974, *Nottingham: Home of the Bicycle*, Raleigh Industries Ltd. and Nottingham Corporation.

Cleary, Johanna, 1991, *Traffic Calming: a Technical Note*, Cyclists' Touring Club, Godalming, Surrey.

Department of Transport, 1982, *Cycling Policy: Statement by the Secretary of State for Transport*, D.Tp., London.

Department of Transport, 1986, *Local Transport Note 2/86: Shared Use by Pedestrians and Cyclists*, HMSO, London.

Department of Transport, 1987, *Clifton to City Centre Route, Nottingham. Design, Implementation and Monitoring*, DTP, London.

Finch, Helen and Morgan, John, 1985, *Attitudes to Cycling*, Transport and Road Research Laboratory Report RR14, TRRL, Crowthorne, Berkshire.

Harland, D.G. and Gercans, R.A., *Cycle Routes*, paper to the Velo City '91 Conference, Milan.

JMP Consultants Ltd., 1991, *Nottingham Urban Cycle Route Project: After Study Summary Report*, Transport and Road Research Laboratory (TRRL), Crowthorne, Berkshire.

McClintock, Hugh, 1983, *Clifton Cycle Route, Nottingham: A Survey of Cyclists' Attitudes*, Institute of Planning Studies, University of Nottingham.

McClintock, Hugh, 1985, *Clifton Cycle Route, Nottingham: A Survey of Pedestrians' Attitudes*, Institute of Planning Studies, University of Nottingham.

McClintock, Hugh, 1988, Reconciling rights of way, *The Surveyor*, Vol. 170 (5007), pp. 20–21.

McClintock, Hugh, 1990, Planning for the bicycle in urban Britain: an assessment of experience and issues, Chapter 14 in R. S. Tolley (ed.), *The Greening of Urban Transport: Planning for Walking and Cycling in Western Cities*, Belhaven Press, London.

Milton, Hugh and Howarth, C. Ian, 1989, *Analysis of Cyclists' Behaviour: Beeston High Road*, TRRL Report WP/RS/82, Accident Research Unit, Psychology Department, University of Nottingham.

Pedals (Nottingham Cycling Campaign), 1980, *Nottingham – Cycle City: Proposals for a Major Cycling Experiment in Nottingham*.

Pedals (Nottingham Cycling Campaign), 1981, *Bike City Bikeways: Proposals for a Network of Cycle Routes for the Nottingham Conurbation*.

Quenault, S., 1979, *Cycle Routes in Portsmouth III: Attitude Surveys*, Transport and Road Research Laboratory Report LR875, TRRL, Crowthorne, Berkshire.

Quenault, S. and Head, T., 1977, *Cycle Routes in Portsmouth I – Planning and Implementation*, Transport and Road Research Laboratory Report SR317, TRRL, Crowthorne, Berkshire.

Thompson, Stuart and Layfield, Roger, 1985, *Nottingham: Clifton to City Centre Cycle Route – A Study of Cycling Behaviour*, Report WP (HSF) 20, Transport and Road Research Laboratory, Crowthorne, Berkshire.

Westerdijk, P.K., 1990, *Pedestrian and Pedal Cyclist Route Choice Criteria*, Drive Project V1031, Traffic Research Centre, University of Groningen, Netherlands.

Whitelegg, John, Adams, John and Hillman, Mayer, 1991, *One False Move*, Policy Studies Institute, London.

7 Cambridge

Andrew Wallace

Introduction

The University city of Cambridge has a population of approximately 100,000, including over 10,000 students. The River Cam provides the focus for many of the city's leisure activities such as punting and rowing. There are many walks, cycle routes and picnic spots along the banks of the river and in the nearby meadows.

Cambridge attracts shoppers not only from within the city, but also from the surrounding area and villages. It offers a mixture of historic shopping streets and purpose-built shopping centres. There are both large and small stores, more individual shops such as craft, antique and book shops and also a daily market.

The city is a major employment centre. It has a thriving tourist trade and also major service employers such as the University, a leading teaching hospital, a Central Government office and three Local Government headquarters. Along with its well established aeronautical and electrical engineering companies, Cambridge has seen a very rapid growth in the number of high technology firms in the area. This growth, which has become so pronounced that it has become known as the Cambridge Phenomenon, has also led to a corresponding increase in the use of the highway network, particularly at peak times.

The city therefore consists of both commercial and academic premises which provide origins and destinations for traffic of all types. Being on the edge of the East Anglian Fens, the terrain is flat and the climate relatively dry which make conditions ideal for cycling.

The road network of Cambridge is of a ring and radial pattern with the central area bounded by the River Cam (or Granta) to the north and west and by the railway a little further out to the east. The road bridges over these boundaries tend to be narrow and congested particularly at peak times. As a result, cyclists have for many years shared the footbridges with pedestrians. As these footbridges form part of a network across green areas and common land, cyclists have to a large extent also shared this network. Although these routes are fairly extensive, cyclists

Table 7.1 2-way peak hour cycle flows, Cambridge, 1948 and 1991.

| | 2-way peak hour flows | | | |
| | 1948 | | 1991 | |
Street	Cycles	Motor vehs.	Cycles	Motor vehs.
Magdalene Street	1475	396	454	1217
Victoria Avenue	1369	667	285	926
Lensfield Road	574	390	407	1610
Newmarket Road	877	526	354	3255

cannot travel far before having to cross or ride along a heavily trafficked road. Thus they also have to share the same routes with, and negotiate the same junctions as, motorised vehicles.

Cambridge has a long history of cycling and it is almost as difficult for us to visualise the enormous numbers of cyclists during peak hours in 1948 as it would have been for people then to imagine the numbers of motorised vehicles in the rush hour today. The contrasts are clearly shown in Table 7.1.

The final report of the Cambridge Transportation Plan (Travers Morgan and Partners, 1972) stated:

Cambridge is famous for its bicycles. The swarm of cycles in Trinity Street and King's Parade, the gowns and books and bicycle baskets are an essential part of the flavour of the University Town.

Cambridge's bicycles are associated with its function as a University Town but it would be a mistake, however, to neglect consideration of the use of bicycles in other parts of the City and by other than residents of the University. Household residents account for 71 per cent of daily cycle trips and about 76 per cent of daily cycle miles.

This report also stated that in 1967, on a typical weekday in the study area, 121,220 trips were made by bicycle (22 per cent of all trips). Of these, 90,480 (75 per cent) were made by people living in the city.

The 10 per cent sample census of 1971 showed that more city residents went to work by bicycle than by car and that 30 per cent of Cambridge residents who lived and worked in the city cycled to work. Comparative figures elsewhere were: Peterborough, 25 per cent, Norwich, 13 per cent, Portsmouth, 10 per cent and Stevenage, 9 per cent.

In 1975 Cambridge City Council, at the invitation of Cambridgeshire County Council, produced the Cambridge Cycleways Report (Cambridge City Council, 1975). This report laid down the following objectives against which any proposals should be judged:

1 To extend wherever possible the system of routes for bicycles in order to separate the cyclist from road users.

2   To provide where necessary some means of giving the cyclist protection and/or priority on existing roads and junctions where separate cycleways are not feasible.

In attempting to achieve these objectives, the report stated that they must be compatible with other transportation objectives as detailed in the County Council's Transport Policies and Programme and that cycle facilities must come within the financial resources likely to be allocated for this purpose. The report went on to say that the provision of facilities for cyclists on existing roads and junctions should not result in any severe impediment which would interfere with the free flow or safety of other road users, in particular, public transport. Some restriction of other traffic might be possible provided that alternative routes were available.

The conclusions and recommendations of this report are summarised below:

- the most effective way of improving conditions for cyclists in the city is the construction of relief roads in order to provide alternative routes for restraint measures;
- the proposed cycle network must be a combination of different facilities;
- the limited money available must be used wisely to bring the greatest benefit in areas of greatest need;
- proposed short-term and long-term cycle networks with an early start to implementation on several identified elements in the short-term network;
- approaches to be made to the Department of Transport offering Cambridge as a suitable city for research and experimental schemes aimed at improving conditions for cycling in cities;
- a review of existing cycle paths with a view to modifying them and maintaining them for the benefit of cyclists;
- the provision of additional cycle parking spaces'

This, as the following paragraphs will show, has provided the framework for the provision of cycle facilities up to and including the present day.

In December 1978 the A45 Cambridge Northern Bypass was opened and in February 1980 the M11 Cambridge Western Bypass was completed. This provision of alternative routes for traffic, particularly through traffic, enabled the introduction of cycle facilities in Cambridge.

Table 7.2 Pedal cycle user casualties in Cambridgeshire.

Year	Cambridge <40 mph <64 km/h	Peter-borough <40 mph <64 km/h	Other urban areas <40 mph <64 km/h	Rural areas >40 mph >64 km/h	Total
1981	187	121	155	43	506
1982	246	136	180	79	641
1983	247	131	199	68	645
1984	297	157	193	78	725
1985	284	140	220	68	712
1986	322	139	181	93	735
1987	317	170	195	64	746
1988	294	179	208	77	758
1989	378	159	197	82	816
1990	398	180	212	87	877

Pedal cyclist accidents

Table 7.2 shows the number of pedal cycle user casualties in Cambridge-shire over a ten-year period. It also shows how vulnerable cyclists are, particularly in a historic university town (Cambridge) compared with a New Town (Peterborough) where there has been more opportunity to segregate cyclists from motor vehicles.

In 1981, 14 per cent of all casualties in the county were cyclists, and 37 per cent of county cycle casualties were injured in Cambridge city. In 1990 the corresponding figures were 17 per cent and 45 per cent respectively which shows little change. From 1981 to 1990 cyclist casualties in Cambridge have more than doubled (see Table 7.2) although the number of cyclists as measured across the River Cam screenline from 1982 to 1990 (see Table 7.3) shows very little change (−2 per cent). The corresponding figure for motorised vehicles is an increase of 9 per cent.

The relationship between cycle flow and cycle user casualties from 1982 to 1990 is shown in the graph (Fig. 7.1) and the similarity in the trends can be seen.

This background of increasing pedal cyclist accidents gave impetus to the introduction of new and innovative cycle facilities in the early 1980s and is just as relevant today when pedal cycle accidents account for half of all accidents in Cambridge city.

Table 7.3   River Cam bridge sites: pedal cycle growth (12 hour counts on a typical day in March).

Pedal cycle flow index – 1982 = 100

Location	1982	1985	1986	1987	1988	1989	1990
Green Dragon	100	79	93	104	87	73	106
Elizabeth Way	100	117	101	133	121	128	139
Pye's Bridge	100	120	141	111	122	97	–
Fort St. George	100	91	86	78	69	64	119
Victoria Avenue	100	92	103	75	64	73	84
Jesus Lock	100	101	105	106	99	111	119
Bridge Street	100	125	126	118	93	73	93
Garret Hostel Lane	100	191	141	127	146	202	140
Silver Street	100	123	133	91	91	106	116
Mill Lane Weir	100	134	112	158	166	181	192
Fen Causeway	100	89	87	72	77	93	–
Coe Fen	100	155	98	99	102	95	–
Total flow across bridges	100	117	113	104	95	97	98

Political background

In addition to the appropriate Highways Committees of the City and County Councils there are two other groups who have been instrumental in implementing the cycle schemes in Cambridge.

The Cambridge Traffic Management Joint Sub-committee

This Committee comprises six County Councillors and four City Councillors who direct the traffic management work which the City Council carry out as agents for the County Council who are the Highway Authority. This united direction is all the more important when the two Councils are controlled by two different political parties. It not only helps the County Council as Highway Authority to ensure that their priorities are implemented but also provides a forum for the City Council to persuade the County Council to include schemes in their budget.

The Cambridge City Council Cycle Working Party

This group reports to the City Council's Roads and Traffic Committee and is an informal Working Party consisting of City Councillors, City Officers, County Officers and representatives from Friends of the Earth, Cambridge University, Cambridge Constabulary and other interested

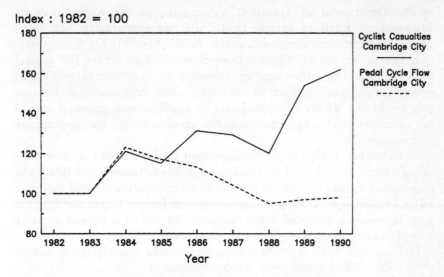

Index : 1982 = 100

Cyclist Casualties
Cambridge City

Pedal Cycle Flow
Cambridge City

Figure 7.1 Pedal cycle user casualties in Cambridge City.

parties. Being a Working Party it does not have any formal powers and its membership can be varied to suit its agendas. It does, however, have a budget allocated to it from the City Council currently in the region of £30,000. Each year a list of cycling schemes from various sources is presented by the City Engineer to the Working Party, with costs and recommendations for their selection and allocation of funds. The decisions of the Working Party are then submitted to the Cambridge Traffic Management Joint Sub-committee for approval. Some of these schemes have been additionally funded by the County Council from their traffic management or accident remedial funds, depending on the resources available.

This group forms a useful means of identifying, discussing and implementing cycle facilities in Cambridge and providing feedback on completed schemes. It forms an important focus and forum for people involved in cycling in Cambridge.

Thus, both the traffic conditions and the political climate are, and have been, conducive to the introduction of cycle facilities by the Councils. Many of these have been funded wholly or partly by the Department of Transport as demonstration projects in their national programme of innovatory cycle schemes.

Shared use cycle and pedestrian tracks

During the years 1980–83 several shared use schemes were introduced in Cambridge. One of the first experimental dual-use cycle tracks sponsored by the Department of Transport was created on the western side of Trumpington Road in March 1980. After an encouraging first year, further schemes were designed, and in September 1981 the Transportation Committee of the County Council resolved to accept the general principle that the conversion of footways to cycle tracks with joint pedestrian use was beneficial to road safety, but recognised that, because this would not always be appropriate or feasible, each proposal should be advertised and any representations considered by the appropriate committee.

In December 1982, the Cambridge Joint Sub-committee reviewed the initial shared use schemes in Trumpington Road, Huntingdon Road and Newmarket Road. It resolved to continue the experiments and mount a publicity campaign. During the following year further shared use schemes were introduced, some of which included the use of a pelican crossing at which cyclists were requested to dismount.

In December 1983, a study was carried out to investigate the use of these cycle facilities and their effect on accidents.

The effect of all the above shared use schemes had been to reduce the accidents involving cyclists on the corresponding lengths of road from 22 to 16 per year. There was no increase in other accidents. No injury accidents involving pedestrian/cyclist conflict on these tracks had been reported to the police. During the previous five-year period, one serious and four slight accidents had been reported on other footways or footpaths involving cyclist and pedestrian conflict.

Groups representing the blind and partially sighted did express concern about shared use, particularly when there was nothing physical to segregate cyclists and pedestrians. These groups should be consulted about proposals and their comments carefully considered before implementation.

Experience over the three-year period suggested that 60 per cent of cyclists were willing to transfer to the most popular shared use tracks if they did not have to cross a road to do so. Less than 20 per cent transferred from a wide carriageway to a narrow track which had many points of access with poor visibility. In these circumstances shared use proved not to be appropriate. Women and children particularly made good use of the facility where this met their needs. As can be seen in the next section a pelican crossing can be a useful complement to a shared use track.

Design standards can to a large extent be flexible. For example, a narrow kerbed footway can be converted to shared use to avoid a particularly hazardous site. Where the accident record on the carriageway is good, however, care needs to be exercised to ensure that the shared use does not create more problems than it solves in the form of conflict with pedestrians and vehicles emerging from accesses. Adequate consultation and advertising is essential as is signing, not only along the track but also at the ends. The general use of white lines to segregate pedestrians and cyclists is unlikely to be very effective. Lines are more efficiently used with discretion where there is a real need for care such as where visibility is restricted on a blind corner.

Several of the shared use schemes in Cambridge formed part of a larger study carried out on behalf of the Transport and Road Research Laboratory. The results of this study were presented in a paper which covered the use of converted footways, together with some conclusions on their capacity (Harland, Jacoby and Pickering, 1986).

The culmination of the Department of Transport's research is contained in Local Transport Note 2/86 (Department of Transport, 1986a) which gives advice on the design and procedures for implementing shared use by cyclists and pedestrians.

Pelican crossings

Several of the above dual-use schemes were complemented by pelican crossings. Generally, when carrying out a survey to justify new pelican crossings in Cambridge, cyclists crossing are counted as pedestrians. It is felt that pedestrians are willing to share a crossing with cyclists rather than possibly not have a crossing at all.

The increase in usage from 1982 to 1983 on the pelican crossing linked to a shared use scheme on Newmarket Road was thought to be the result of increased publicity. Several other standard pelican crossings in Cambridge (for example Queens Road) are on cycle routes and are used by large numbers of cyclists who, despite signs, bollards and chicane barriers do not dismount. Few problems occur, however, and this would appear to be confirmed in Transport and Road Research Laboratory Report CR173 (Trevelyan and Ginger, 1989).

Cycle lanes

In March 1980 Cambridge introduced its first experimental mandatory with-flow cycle lane on Huntingdon Road, at a cost of £2,100. This complemented the dual-use experiment on the other side of the road. The lane linked Girton College, which generated many student cycle trips, with the city centre. Other cyclists joined the route nearer the city.

The lane is 1.5m wide with a 3.5m vehicle lane which narrows to 3.0m over a short length. The mandatory lane runs for 1,400m from the College entrance and becomes advisory over a short length where, because of a junction with a heavy right-turn vehicle movement, there is a need for two vehicle lanes and this does not leave enough road space for a mandatory cycle lane. The lane then continues as mandatory for a further 600m.

Twelve side roads join Huntingdon Road along the length of the cycle lane. At the busiest side road a broken lane marking was continued across the mouth of the junction but at all the others the lane marking was discontinued. Although, in the former case, few drivers crept forward across the cycle lane and gave way at the second broken line the more usual discontinuity in the latter case gave no problems and was preferred. All the side roads were residential and carried local traffic and no signs were erected on the approaches to warn drivers of the lane. At the downstream side of each junction a cycle symbol was marked in the lane and a cycle lane sign was erected in accordance with advice contained in Local Transport Note 1/78 (Department of Transport, 1978) current at that time. Six of the side roads occurred within 430m and this resulted in a forest of signs over this length which led to the belief that some discretion should be allowed on the occurrence and spacing of these signs.

Infrequent loading, unloading and parking took place in the lane but caused few problems and was not prohibited in the Order. Buses were allowed to enter the lane to use the marked bus stops. In 1980 the lane was used in the morning peak hour by about 300 cyclists, with over 1,300 motor vehicles on the adjacent highway.

Injury accidents involving cyclists over the length of the lane averaged 4.1 per year before the lane was installed and 1.2 after. The lane is liked by users, cyclists are more disciplined and drivers give them more room. There were no objections when the draft Order to make the experimental lane permanent was advertised.

At the city end of this mandatory lane, on the approach to a busy junction, an advisory cycle lane has been created in the middle of the road between a left-turn vehicle lane and a straight and right-turn vehicle lane. This was done to ease the conflict at the junction between the large number of cyclists wishing to go ahead and the left-turning motor vehicles. The initial layout was slightly modified and later the junction was converted to traffic-signal control. This advisory cycle lane was retained throughout and is generally well used.

Several other lengths of advisory cycle lane were introduced early in 1983. One of these schemes involved an on-highway circumferential advisory cycle lane round the perimeter of a large roundabout at the junction of Brooks Road and Coldham's Lane. As can be seen, the accidents involving cyclists increased fairly dramatically after a short period and the scheme was taken out.

More recently concern has arisen in some locations over the increase in accidents involving cyclists turning right from cycle lanes. Further investigation is currently being carried out and solutions sought in the form of cycle crossings and central islands to protect waiting cyclists.

In 1975 two spine roads in the centre of Cambridge were closed to most classes of vehicles, allowing cyclists more freedom in the centre. As part of this scheme, all traffic was restricted to travelling eastbound only along Pembroke Street and Downing Street. Cyclists could no longer pass westbound through an area of the city 1,100m long by 400m wide. Several University premises lay within this area including colleges, lecture theatres and laboratories. A controversial contra-flow cycle lane was proposed in Pembroke Street and Downing Street to overcome this access problem. The carriageway in both these streets is only 5m wide in some places and when deliveries took place an overtaking vehicle would have to encroach into the contra-flow lane in the face of cyclists. The only entry and exit to a 650-space multi-storey car park was off Downing Street.

However, in the face of fierce opposition including the Police, the Cambridge Traffic Management Joint Sub-committee overruled the many objections and an experimental Order was introduced in 1980 with the Department of Transport providing the funds (£4,500). The lane is 1.5m wide but narrows to 1m alongside the islands which have been installed at both ends and opposite the exit from the multi-storey car park. Signs and markings were in accordance with the Advice Note (Department of Transport, 1978) current at that time except that additional arrows were marked in the lane to discourage cyclists from using the lane in the wrong direction. Loading and unloading was prohibited from the lane but, because the street was so narrow, the Order permitted vehicles to enter the lane when overtaking vehicles loading or unloading on the other side of the street. A refuge with a 'No Entry' sign was essential at the start of the lane to separate the cyclists from other vehicles. At the other end, the lane stops 10m short of the junction to enable large delivery vehicles to make the tight left turn into Pembroke Street and avoid hitting the island. Prior to the scheme almost 300 cyclists entered Downing Street illegally against the flow of traffic although over two-thirds of these pushed their cycles.

Within the first year about 1,900 cyclists (over 600 per cent increase) were recorded entering the contra-flow lane during the 12 hours between 7.00 a.m. and 7.00 p.m., with a maximum hourly flow of about 330. About 480 vehicles in the peak hour emerged from the two vehicle lanes at the start of the contra-flow lane. In the narrow part of Pembroke Street 150 cyclists were recorded in the lane in the peak hour, with 460 motor vehicles and 280 cyclists travelling in the other direction.

In the six months following the introduction of the scheme two cyclists had been slightly injured while using the lane but neither accident involved a motor vehicle. Throughout the area affected by the scheme there were 21 injury accidents per year involving cyclists before the scheme was introduced and initial indications afterwards showed a reduction in the rate and severity of accidents in the area. The scheme worked well and pre-scheme doubts did not materialise. As a result, the experimental Order was made permanent.

Other early innovatory cycle schemes

Two other experimental innovatory schemes in the early 1980s in Cambridge are worthy of note.

1   The traffic-signal-controlled combined pedestrian/cycle crossing of The Fen Causeway.
2   The dedicated cycle lane and phase at the traffic-signal-controlled junction of Hills Road and Brooklands Avenue.

The traffic-signal-controlled combined pedestrian/cycle crossing of The Fen Causeway

For many years cyclists and pedestrians had jointly used a footpath across Lammas Land towards the city centre. The continuation of this route involved crossing The Fen Causeway, part of the inner ring road. The mean peak flow of cyclists crossing the carriageway, including those pushing their cycles, was about 60 per hour. The scheme proposed was the installation of a parallel pedestrian/cycle crossing controlled by traffic signals in two stages. A detailed description of the scheme is contained in the Department of Transport's Traffic Advisory Leaflet 5/86 (Department of Transport, 1986b). The main elements of the scheme installed in September 1981 were:

– two stage signal operation, one for vehicles, one for pedestrians and cyclists who crossed at the same time on two almost parallel paths at a skew across the road;
– presence loop detectors at the cycle stop lines;
– experimental microwave cycle detection on the cycle approaches;
– banning of certain cycle turns by Traffic Regulation Order to avoid cycle/pedestrian conflict when both were given a green signal;
– the unsegregated approaches were widened in the vicinity of the crossing to provide segregation of cyclists from pedestrians by different colour of surfacing and a kerb. A broken white line delineated the two-way flow of cycles.

Extensive monitoring carried out by survey, observation and time lapse photography gave the following results:

– cycle movements increased except out of town in the morning peak;
– a diversion of cyclists from a nearby roundabout to the new crossing;
– drivers generally obeyed the signals and they were not deterred from using this route;
– occasional illegal cycle turning movements conflicted with pedestrians;

– 20 per cent of pedestrians used the cycle route rather than the pedestrian route over the crossing as this was the most direct route between the two approaches. Only 30 per cent used their route correctly.

The cost of the scheme was £13,000, mostly funded by the Department of Transport. The scheme was found to work well, including the experimental microwave cycle detection. In the four years after implementation there was no significant change in the accident rate at the site or in the surrounding area. In 1985, Cambridge City Council changed the input of cycle demands from the microwave detectors to push buttons. This was not because the microwave detectors did not function properly but it was felt that cyclists would be more inclined to stop and comply with the signals. Observation also showed that some cyclists were approaching the crossing along the paths, were detected by the microwave detectors and putting in a demand for the cycle/pedestrian stage and then cycling along the footways parallel to the road without crossing. The signals would change to red to the vehicles for no apparent reason as far as the drivers could see, which created frustration and a tendency to jump the red light. The push buttons gave a more definitive demand from a cyclist wishing to cross.

The dedicated cycle lane and phase at the traffic-signal-controlled junction of Hills Road and Brooklands Avenue

Hills Road is a main radial route into Cambridge from the south. Brooklands Avenue, which forms a T-junction with Hills Road just south of the city centre, has a large government complex along it which generates many trips particularly at peak times. At the time of the initiation of the scheme in 1979, an average 12-hour flow of motor vehicles through the junction was 24,000, with a cycle flow of around 5,400 (18 per cent).

The junction was signal-controlled, with a two-lane approach from the south, one lane for ahead and one for left turns. The signal sequence was:

1 Hills Road.
2 Early cut-off in favour of the right turn into Brooklands Avenue (with the left filter out of Brooklands Avenue).
3 Brooklands Avenue (with the left filter into Brooklands Avenue).

Conflict occurred between the left-turning vehicles into Brooklands Avenue (3,377 in 12 hours, 626 in the a.m. peak) and straight-ahead cyclists (1,990 in 12 hours, 357 in the a.m. peak). These cyclists tended

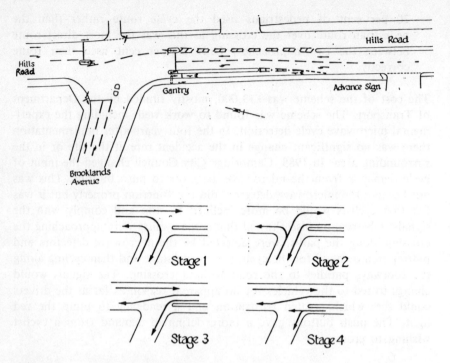

Figure 7.2 Hills Road/Brooklands Avenue junction cycle scheme,
          Cambridge.

to filter through to the front and wait between the two streams of traffic.
When the left filter turned to green they were caught between a stream
of moving traffic and a stream of stationary traffic made even more
hazardous by vehicles, particularly heavy goods vehicles, swinging out to
make what was a fairly tight left turn. Whilst these dangers were not
apparent in the personal injury accident record of the junction, the situation was exceedingly difficult and hazardous for many cyclists and could
be readily observed.

As a result, in 1980 the Cambridge Traffic Management Joint Sub-
committee determined to approach the Department of Transport for
financial assistance towards implementing a scheme to aid cyclists at the
junction. The revised junction layout and signal stages are shown in Fig.
7.2.

Physically the approach from the south was widened by reducing the
footway and altering the central reserve to allow for two traffic lanes as
before but also a 1.5m cycle lane segregated from the traffic by a 1.2m
wide, 32m long island. An additional stage was introduced into the
sequence (stage 4) which under normal circumstances ran instead of stage
3. The cycle stage was therefore introduced to the detriment of left-turning
vehicles. In order to compensate for this during the morning peak

when there is a very heavy left turn, an inductive queue loop was installed in the left-turn lane approximately 60m from the stop line. When a queue was detected by this loop, stage 3 was additionally included in the sequence.

The new cycle stage (stage 4) permitted cyclists to proceed straight ahead or left unopposed by other traffic and this was indicated to cyclists by their own dedicated signals. The conventional amber and green aspects were replaced by cycle symbol aspects and fibre optics were used experimentally to enhance their visibility. The amber cycle aspect was thought to be particularly important to ensure that left-turning motor vehicle drivers did not confuse the cycle red/amber aspect with their own. In addition the cycle aspects were louvred to cut down their visibility to motorists. Advance signing and road markings were used to indicate to cyclists how to use the facility, and Road Safety Officers circulated material and gave talks to local schools. The facility was completed and switched on in May 1982 at a total cost of £30,000, of which the Department of Transport contributed £20,000.

An experimental Traffic Regulation Order was introduced to ban motor vehicles from using the cycle lane which, after satisfactory operation of the installation for some time, was made permanent. Cycle detector loops were installed in the cycle lane at 8m and 20m from the stop line.

Details of the design, implementation and extensive monitoring are contained in a Department of Transport Report (Department of Transport, 1986c) and are summarised in the Traffic Advisory Unit Leaflet 6/86 (Department of Transport, 1986d).

Behavioural studies carried out before and after the scheme showed that hazardous lane changing by cyclists on the approach to the stop line had almost been eliminated and that nearly all cyclists used the lane provided.

During the 'after' study some vehicle conflicts were observed and a video tape recording was taken to investigate these further. As a result, two modifications were carried out:

1 Additional road markings within the junction for left-turning vehicles in the form of a swept arrow and broken line lane markings were laid and destinations were added to the advance direction signs. This alleviated the problem of vehicles arriving at the stop line in the wrong lane and moving off in the wrong direction at the wrong time.
2 Direction arrows (left and straight ahead) were erected above the double-headed secondary signal heads to northbound traffic to alleviate the problem of drivers moving off on a starting amber which did not relate to their lane and movement. Arrow symbols on the amber aspect were not approved for use by the Department of Transport and closely associated secondary signal heads would have meant moving the stop line

back, with a corresponding increase in inter-green time and reduction in capacity which was not acceptable at this junction in the morning peak.

Generally the amended junction was well received by users, compliance was good and the scheme deemed to be successful. No increase in flows was recorded as a result of the scheme. In relation to the scheme, there was one cycle injury accident in the three years before introduction. In the 18 months after, two accidents were recorded, one of which was not directly related to the scheme and one which may have been avoided had the modifications been carried out earlier.

Cycle route through south-east Cambridge

In 1986, an area of Cambridge bounded by two adjacent radial roads, the inner ring road and the outer ring, was identified as being the location of about 100 injury accidents involving cyclists per year, about one-third of the city's total. In this part of the city, where a large residential area is separated from the centre by the railway line, cyclists have no option but to use one of the congested bridges on the two radial roads, Mill Road and Hills Road. The 12-hour two-way flows on these bridges were:

	Motor Vehicles	*Cyclists*
Hills Road	19,500	4,600 (24 per cent)
Mill Road	11,800	5,100 (43 per cent)

In 1985, over 40 per cent of the cyclist accidents in this area occurred on Mill Road where attempts to reduce the flow of motor vehicles and conflicts at junctions had been unsuccessful. The only solution seemed to be to divert cyclists from the busy radial routes onto the quieter residential streets parallel to the radial roads and construct a new cycle/pedestrian bridge across the railway to complete the route.

The Department of Transport was approached regarding funding of the route. It was considered that there was a good chance of the scheme being accepted for a Transport Supplementary Grant as a demonstration project if more than 25 per cent of the 10,000 cyclists per day using the two existing bridges could be shown to be likely to transfer to the new bridge. A diversion of this order would be likely to achieve the 12 per cent reduction in accidents needed for a 10 per cent annual return on capital investment.

It was agreed that trips could be assigned to the new route if the extra distance in the cycle trip using the new route did not exceed 10 per cent.

The cyclists using the existing bridges were to be interviewed to find out their origins and destinations. The surveys took place on a weekday in March 1986 during University and school term times between 7.00 a.m. and 7.00 p.m. on the into-town direction.

Re-routing assignments were carried out which suggested that the diversion of cyclists to the new route from Hills Road would be similar to the 25 per cent target agreed with the Department of Transport and the diversion from Mill Road would be much higher.

The County Council allocated funds for 50 per cent of the cost of the scheme from its base budget which would allow the scheme to proceed if the Department of Transport were able to support the scheme as a demonstration project and with a Transport Supplementary Grant which would provide the remaining 50 per cent of the funds. This was agreed early in 1987.

The key element of the new route was a new cycle/pedestrian bridge over the railway just north of Cambridge station. The remainder of the route involved:

- traffic-signal-controlled pedestrian/cycle crossings to enable cyclists (and pedestrians) to cross busy roads safely;
- traffic-signal-controlled junctions with advanced stop lines to help cyclists negotiate the junctions and give them some priority;
- traffic-calming measures to reduce traffic speeds where motor vehicles joined the route;
- the use of quieter, safer residential streets to link these features together to create a safer, more attractive route for cyclists away from the busier roads.

Figure 7.3 shows the route and the location of these features, and a more detailed description is contained in Traffic Advisory Leaflet 9/89 (Department of Transport, 1989).

Public meetings were held and a consultation leaflet was produced containing a prepaid comments form, and many of the returned comments were incorporated into the detailed design of the route. The public's main concern related to security on the bridge, and as a result the bridge was constructed from a clear polycarbonate tube containing street lighting and closed-circuit television cameras.

The route was completed in November 1989 with a publicity campaign and the formal opening of the bridge (Fig. 7.4) at a total cost of about £2.8 million. Initial reaction to the route was very favourable, both from cyclists and pedestrians.

Repeat interview surveys were carried out in the same month as the previous ones and about five months after the opening of the route. At this time, over 2,000 cyclists and more than 600 pedestrians were using the bridge. Preliminary analysis of the survey data suggests that, over the

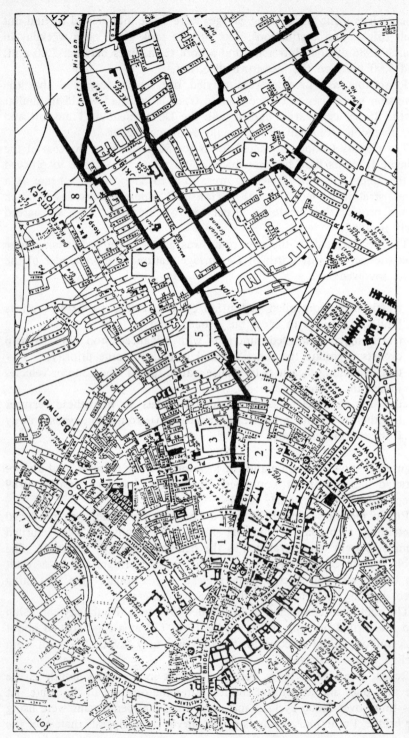

Figure 7.3 South-east Cambridge cycle route.

Figure 7.4 Carter cycle and pedestrian bridge, south Cambridge cycle route: aerial view.

12-hour period from 7.00 a.m. to 7.00 p.m., 38 per cent of cyclists have diverted from Mill Road and 4 per cent from Hills Road, lower than that estimated. In the morning peak, however, the corresponding figures are 53 per cent and 18 per cent in the into-town direction, and in the evening peak 40 per cent and 9 per cent, which are more in line with the estimated figures.

As part of the Research Contract between the County Council and the Department of Transport, further analysis is to be carried out to confirm these values and assess the following:

- the resulting reduction in accidents;
- the increase in journey distance cyclists will accept to use a safer route;
- how the diversion and extra journey varies with the age, sex and journey purpose of the cyclist.

More recent manual and automatic counts indicate that flows over the bridge have risen. Initial conclusions are that the route has achieved its aim of diverting cyclists from the busier roads but that there has not been an appreciable reduction in accidents.

Some operational aspects of the signal-controlled elements of the scheme have given rise to concern and possible improvements. The combined pedestrian and cycle crossing is cumbersome with respect to the signal timings, the space needed and the street furniture required. All these are at a premium, particularly on a busy urban road. A pelican crossing or a similar but legal dual-use crossing would be much more economical and environmentally acceptable. The advanced stop lines generally work well and provide a positive benefit for cyclists when the signals are on red. However, when the signals are on green and cyclists are on the approach, the benefits are not so obvious and depend very much on the volumes of conflicting turning movements of cyclists and motor vehicles.

Acknowledgements

The author of this chapter wishes to thank Brian Oldridge, former Director of Transportation of Cambridgeshire County Council, for permission to publish this chapter, and his staff for their help and contributions, especially John Edwards, now Assistant Director (Works – Client) but formerly Group Engineer (Traffic). Thanks also to Cambridge City Council staff.

References

Cambridge City Council, 1975, *Cambridge Cycleways Report.*

Department of Transport, 1978, *Ways of Helping Cyclists in Built-up Areas,* Department of Transport, London.

Department of Transport, 1986a, *Local Transport Note 2/86 – Shared Use by Cyclists and Pedestrians,* Department of Transport, London.

Department of Transport, 1986b, *Traffic Advisory Unit Leaflet 5/86 – Innovatory Cycle Scheme – Fen Causeway, Cambridge – Signalled Cycle/Pedestrian Crossing,* Department of Transport, London.

Department of Transport, 1986c, *A Segregated Cycle Lane at Traffic Signals. Hills Road, Cambridge – Design, Implementation and Monitoring,* Department of Transport, London.

Department of Transport, 1986d, *Traffic Advisory Unit Leaflet 6/86 Innovatory Cycle Scheme – Cambridge, Hills Road – Segregated Cycle Lane at Traffic Signals,* Department of Transport, London.

Department of Transport, 1989, *Traffic Advisory Unit Leaflet 9/89 The South East Cambridge Cycle Route,* Department of Transport, London.

Harland, D.G., Jacoby, R.G., and Pickering, D., 1986, Footways used by cyclists and pedestrians, *Traffic Engineering and Control,* May.

Travers Morgan and Partners, 1972, *Cambridge Transportation Plan.*

Trevelyan, P. and Ginger, M., 1989, *Transport and Road Research Laboratory Report CR 173 – Cyclists' Use of Pedestrian and Cycle/Pedestrian Crossings,* TRRL Crowthorne, Berkshire.

8 London

Nick Lester

Cycle use in London

At first sight, London does not seem promising ground for urban cyclists. Like most large cities – and London is the largest in Europe – average journey lengths are high and make many journeys too long for convenient or comfortable cycling by some people. At the same time, the pressure on road space is severe, with high levels of congestion leading to road accidents. Both the safety problems and the general unpleasantness of cycling in heavy traffic further discourage cycle use.

Unlike many major cities in Europe, London has not experienced much of the large-scale reconstruction and replanning that has followed devastation, such as from war, in recent times. Thus the opportunity given to cities such as Rotterdam (albeit in highly unpleasant circumstances) to rebuild with more space for movement generally, and for cyclists in particular, has not occurred in London. Nor has London experienced the massive roadbuilding programmes of the 1960s and 1970s which, on the one hand, encouraged more traffic and made roads less safe for cyclists but, on the other, also provided an opportunity to provide specific cycle facilities.

Despite these deterrents, the potential for cycling in what is a relatively flat city exists. And cycling has never disappeared in London. Indeed, much of the last 20 years has seen a growth in cycling, albeit varying in different parts of the capital. The 1981 Greater London Transportation Survey indicated that there were about 1.2 million cycles in Greater London, of which about 200,000 are used on an average weekday. About a third of all cycle trips are for journeys to work, with education and 'other' trips accounting for the next biggest proportions (Greater London Council, 1981a).

Cycle use varies both in scale and nature in different parts of London. The 1981 survey showed major variations. For example 5.1 per cent of trips to work made by residents of Richmond were by cycle, compared with only 1.5 per cent by residents of Haringey (Murray-Clark, 1985). In general there is much higher use in outer south-west London and, to a lesser extent, in inner south-west London, and relatively low usage in outer east London.

Cycle use is also heavily weighted towards those on lower incomes and in lower socio-economic classes in outer London, whereas in inner London cycling is much more an activity of the professional classes. In 1981, for example, 59 per cent of those cycling to work in inner London had non-manual jobs, compared to 29 per cent in 1971. (Greater London Council, 1981a).

About one-third of cyclists are women and the largest group of cyclists is in the 25–44 age range (Greater London Council, 1981b).

The 1970s saw a major growth in the use of cycling, particularly for journeys to central London, with a 300 per cent increase in cycle use in the a.m. peak period between 1971 and 1981 (Murray-Clark, 1985). This growth stemmed partly from an increasing environmental awareness, partly from the 1973 oil crisis and partly from a sustained deterioration in public transport, with fares increasing in real terms and service quality and quantity declining.

The growth of political pressure for cycling

The same period saw the growth of cycle activism in London. In 1974, Friends of the Earth published their early report 'Give Way' (Feilden, 1974) promoting the construction of safe cycle routes. The Greater London Council took up the issue and called a conference of the various activist groups that blossomed in the wake of 'Give Way'. This conference led to the publication by the GLC of the first modern guidelines for catering for cyclists in the capital (Greater London Council, 1976).

Looking back, these hardly seem ambitious. Among the more radical conclusions were that road closures for environmental reasons should 'normally' include gaps for cyclists, that new road schemes should be designed to take account of cyclists' needs, and that the GLC would consider whether cycling could be allowed in any of the parks that it managed (within many of which cycles were banned while cars were allowed).

The increasingly vocal activists felt that this was not enough and the GLC started to look at some specific schemes to help cyclists, notably at the Albert Gate entrance to Hyde Park, within which the Department of the Environment (predecessor super-ministry of what were in 1976 to become separate Departments of Transport and of the Environment) had already opened a convenient cycle route.

A new administration at County Hall in 1977 abandoned that scheme on the basis that too few cyclists carried out what was a dangerous and illegal manoeuvre at the time to justify any new construction, and effectively decided to ignore cyclists – a reversion to a long-standing policy. With further increases in cycling stemming from the 1979 fuel crisis and an accelerating decline in public transport quality (though fares increased), this attitude merely increased the vociferousness of the cycling groups.

In 1978 a number of small cycle groups merged to form the London Cycling Campaign (LCC), which quickly grew to about 3,000 members. It grew quickly, too, in its campaigning skills, embarrassing the GLC by 'implementing' the by now symbolic Albert Gate scheme with paper tape and cardboard signs. The Campaign's lobbying skill meant that, probably for the first time ever, cycling was mentioned in an election campaign, that for the 1981 GLC elections.

The Labour opposition promised to spend money on cycle schemes, while Councillors 'Sandy' Sandford, the Conservative Chairman of the Central Area Planning Committee, demanded that there should be one cycle route implemented in time for the election. Together with Kenneth Clarke, MP, then the Junior Transport Minister, he was pictured riding a bike and carrying a very large cut-out cycle symbol, as they launched the 'Ambassadors' cycle route (so called because it went past the French Embassy and other diplomatic premises) between Paddington and Chelsea Bridge. While an important first, the cycle route consisted of little more than a few white lines and signs at the time.

The GLC Cycle Project Team

It is now a matter of history that Labour won the 1981 election and Ken Livingstone became leader of the GLC. The annual LCC rally on the steps of County Hall, which took place a few weeks later, turned into a celebration as Ken Livingstone, wearing an LCC T-shirt, declared that he would implement his promises to cyclists quickly and aim to spend 1 per cent of the GLC's transport budget on cycling – a key LCC demand.

In fact, within four months of the elections, the GLC agreed three key policies:

- a target of 1 per cent of its transport capital budget to be spent on cycle facilities;
- the creation of a dedicated team of planners and engineers to work on cycle schemes; and
- the formation of a regular liaison group between the Council, the LCC and other cycling groups, the police and the Department of Transport. This was to be chaired by the Vice Chair of the GLC's Transport Committee, Paul Moore, whose enthusiasm quickly followed (Greater London Council, 1981c).

These three elements, in combination, were the key to the GLC's success in implementing cycle schemes over the following five years. This is obvious in the case of the budget, as this gave a clear aim on expenditure. At the time, the 1 per cent figure represented £1.7 million a year, which was significantly higher than any other authority in the country, to spend specifically on cycle matters and meant, in effect, that no worthwhile schemes would be turned down for lack of money. Liaison with the other interested parties also helped in a number of ways. The cycle liaison group was able to monitor and encourage progress, while ensuring that all the parties became committed to the success of the policy. On more than one occasion, the group was able to bring together boroughs or other agencies who were not keen on allowing cycle facilities to be developed to try and iron out the problems. The appointment of the Vice-Chair of the GLC's Transport Committee as the group's chair also gave the GLC's continued political commitment to the issue.

The creation of the team of officers, which became known as the Cycle Project Team (CPT), was a particularly important step. Not only did it harness the GLC's very considerable traffic management talents to design cycle facilities, but it also ensured that there would be a specific group of people who could examine other proposals by the Council to ensure that cyclists' needs really were properly considered.

Initially, the work of the CPT concentrated on design of facilities rather than on research into cyclists' needs. The overriding pressure – stemming mainly from cycle groups – was to see positive action on the ground. This meant that little work was put into devising a theoretical network on the basis of origin and destination surveys, computer models or the like, although there was a general commitment to the eventual completion of a network of 1,000 miles (1,600 km) of safe cycle routes. Instead, the emphasis was much more on seeing what schemes could be implemented quickly. While all these schemes were immediately worthwhile, it was assumed that they would become integral parts of the future network – and this was borne in mind during the design.

Research was needed, though, into the sorts of facilities and routes that cyclists would prefer and also into ways of assessing value for money of cycle schemes. Some considerable work was put into research by the GLC.

The issue of value for money was settled in a simple way based on the GLC's own criteria for assessing highway schemes. Any cycle scheme had to meet the formula that expenditure was no greater than £125 per cyclist per day per mile (£78 per cyclist per km) of route. Although produced fairly simply, this formula proved to be serviceable in general use. It was not possible to justify large-scale civil engineering works, such as new river bridges, except in very heavily used areas, and some other, more elaborate schemes were ruled out.

Other important research issues covered general questions such as data on cycle use, as well as detailed issues such as cyclists' perceived needs, the relative importance of back-street, as opposed to main road routes, and other changes cyclists felt to be essential.

The GLC was relatively well supplied with simple numerical data – cyclists had been included, for example, in the 1971 and 1981 Greater London Transportation Surveys, but even with this, more than 20 special surveys of cyclists, conducted using self-return questionnaires handed out on screen lines, took place. These helped to identify specific locations that were perceived as dangerous as well as identifying cyclists' preferred alternative modes and accident histories.

This research is still the only evidential base to suggest that back-street routes should be no more than 10 per cent longer than main road routes if they are to be popular alternatives, and to stress the importance of road maintenance (Greater London Council, 1984).

The issue of back streets or main roads proved to be of importance. Initially, the main objective for increasing cycling safety was seen as providing attractive back-street routes with safe main road crossings to encourage cycle use away from main roads. However, experience showed that for many cyclists the extra length of some back-street routes, combined with many extra stops and starts for junctions and corners and, in many cases, poor road surfaces and lighting, meant that they preferred the traditional, less safe main roads. By the time of the abolition of the GLC in 1986 the issue had not been fully researched and no policy conclusions had been reached, but it was significant that in some parts of London, notably in Hammersmith and Fulham, where a network of back-street routes had been implemented, attention was turning to providing facilities for cyclists on main roads. In Hammersmith, indeed, the decision was taken in principle to install advisory cycle lanes on all main roads.

While most relevant organisations and authorities were supportive of the GLC's approach, some boroughs were extremely hostile. This was partly due to political antagonism and partly due to a view amongst some borough engineers that catering for cyclists was somehow irrelevant, or, at best, unimportant. Thus the leader of Kensington and Chelsea Council, Nicholas Freeman, opined that there was no place for cycling in major cities. Kensington and Chelsea and some other Councils actively opposed the creation of cycle facilities in their boroughs, and while the GLC, with support from the LCC and others, could impose some schemes this was always difficult. As a result of this antagonism, cycle schemes which could have been of the greatest use in parts of inner and central London remained unimplemented.

The types of scheme considered by the CPT and subsequently implemented varied widely but fell, broadly, into the categories described in the following section.

Figure 8.1   The Albert Gate cycle scheme, London.

Examples of schemes

- schemes at particular locations which were dangerous for cyclists;
- specific routes to bypass dangerous junctions;
- schemes to overcome particularly circuitous or difficult spots;
- longer routes combining a range of features.

In addition, CPT promoted the provision of cycle parking facilities and monitored other schemes, such as pedestrianisation or town centre relief road schemes, to ensure that the needs of cyclists were fully included.

Examples of the range of schemes are very numerous, but some deserve a mention. The Albert Gate scheme (Fig. 8.1), which became such a symbol of the GLC's commitment to cycling was, in fact, a fairly simple scheme involving two signalised cycle crossings over parallel main roads, one of which was a conversion from a previous pelican crossing. A novel feature for the time was that a stretch of one-way street was replaced with what later became familiar as a 'plug' type of entry, providing a short section of one-way for motor vehicles with a short contra-flow cycle lane, while the remainder of the street reverted to two-way operation. The manner in which the Albert Gate scheme combined a number of fairly simple arrangements in a novel way became typical of many schemes within London. The only feature of the scheme which remained unique was the special arrangement to make sure that the

Figure 8.2 Cyclist 'weaving lane', Westminster Bridge Road, London.

French ambassador could continue to get his limousine right up to the front steps of the embassy!

Waterloo Bridge was another particular trouble spot for cyclists. The limited number of bridges across the Thames mean that all of them are busy and all are critical links for cyclists. In central London, in particular, the bridges are difficult for cyclists because tourist coaches and other vehicles driving slowly or stationary at the kerb-side add to the difficulties of cycling in heavy traffic. On Waterloo Bridge, with-flow cycle lanes were provided in each direction for the whole of the working day (7.00 a.m. to 7.00 p.m.). This resulted in the two general traffic lanes in each direction being reduced in width slightly.

This arrangement worked well generally for traffic (except for problems with illegally parked cars on the cycle lanes in the early evening) though a different traffic arrangement could have been tried. On neighbouring Westminster Bridge, where a similar cycle lane was installed inside a bus lane, the decision was made to replace what would have been two narrow traffic lanes with one very wide lane, an idea which worked very well in practice. Most of the time the traffic flowed reasonably freely and the lack of a formal second lane made no difference. When traffic was congested, though, the single wide lane was quite adequate for two cars to queue side by side, or even a car and a bus or lorry. Two wide vehicles would find difficulty but this combination was sufficiently rare for the disadvantages to be accepted.

At each end of Waterloo Bridge special arrangements were made to get cyclists on and off the bridge safely. At the south end, a physically segregated cycle lane in one direction, and a contra-flow cycle lane in the other, allowed cyclists to avoid the busy and fast-flowing roundabout and prevented motorists from executing fast, weaving movements. At the north end, a weaving lane for cyclists turning right was placed between lanes for left- and right-turning traffic. This was both safe and convenient for cyclists and had the side-effect of improving conditions for other traffic. Before the weaving lane was installed, cyclists would approach the traffic signals at red and spread out often along the whole width of the stop line. On the lights turning green, motor traffic would experience delays while the cyclists cleared the junction first. After the weaving lane was installed, cyclists queued down the length of the weaving lane rather than across the stop line – a substantial traffic improvement achieved, again, at the expense of slightly narrow traffic lanes.

A further 'plug' type road closure allowed cyclists direct access to the cycle lanes on the bridge from the north, while other traffic had to negotiate the whole of the Aldwych gyratory.

The scheme was considered a major success from the start with higher cycle flows, fewer accidents and better conditions for traffic generally. The only drawback was seen to be the cars which would park over the cycle lane illegally, pre-empting the 7.00 p.m. start of legal parking.

Mandatory cycle lanes were also introduced down the full length of the Fulham Road, a distance of about 2km. This scheme was introduced to cope with particularly high flows of cyclists in an area where convenient side road routes were not available. Despite the road being narrow in parts and including many shops which needed frontage access, it was possible to introduce cycle lanes without major increases in parking and loading regulations, although the lanes were narrow in places.

This scheme was strenuously opposed by the local Borough Council of Kensington and Chelsea, who claimed that businesses would suffer and that congestion would increase. Two years after its implementation, after the abolition of the GLC, Kensington and Chelsea Council were still so hostile to the scheme that they removed the cycle lanes at the earliest possible opportunity. This was despite analysis which showed no noticeable impact on businesses, but an improvement in conditions for both cyclists and traffic generally, with a reduction in congestion, and an overall reduction in accidents. Only substantial pressure on road safety grounds prevented them from leaving the end of the lanes right on their Borough boundary on the crown of a blind bridge!

A number of schemes introduced by CPT, while relatively small, allowed cyclists to avoid either major diversions or busy gyratories. A contra-flow cycle lane down Upper Ground in Southwark, where the one-way restriction for motor traffic had been introduced to prevent short-cuts by drivers, allowed cyclists to avoid two busy junctions, including a roundabout, and a length of main road. Instead they used a relatively quiet back street although illegal parking was a problem here as it was on Waterloo Bridge.

This scheme was completed with a cycle route through the car park of County Hall and a signalled junction onto Westminster Bridge at the other end. Put together, this series of schemes provided a safe and attractive route for cyclists of nearly 3km. Had the GLC lasted a further year, a cycle subway under Westminster Bridge would have resulted in this route being extended a further 1.5km.

Ironically, the County Hall car park scheme was bitterly opposed by some County Hall staff, mainly because a few car parking spaces were lost. It is, perhaps, indicative of the attitude of the GLC, that this opposition was allowed to delay the scheme for two years, although eventually the opposition was overruled. The scheme was also opposed by the Department of Transport on the grounds that the crossing of Westminster Bridge Road would cause congestion, and was implemented only with great difficulty (though the Department of Transport's fears did not materialise in practice).

A more typical route scheme was the Market Porters route, between Hackney and Shoreditch. This route, some 2.5km long, combined a variety of measures, starting with the conversion of a pedestrianised alley to shared cycle and pedestrian use, an advisory crossing of a main road, and a route through a park from where a signalled main road crossing led to a traffic-calmed shopping street. This road, previously a rat run, had a one-way section adjacent to another park, part of which was taken for a two-way cycle track before the route crossed Hackney Road at a signalled pedestrian and cycle crossing. A short section of newly constructed cycle track through an old bomb site led the route into more back streets before it ended at Shoreditch.

This was, perhaps, the best example of an implemented route which combined a number of measures to help cyclists while preventing other traffic. At the same time it provided a very direct route for cyclists, much shorter than that using conventional main roads. Despite a lack of signing it quickly became popular and extensions were planned for either end.

Elephant and Castle is a major junction in south London. Two large roundabouts control the traffic from seven major roads – three drawing traffic from all over south London and four distributing it to different parts of central London. Not surprisingly it is a very dangerous junction and one cyclists avoid as far as possible.

A three-stage project was implemented to provide a bypass for cyclists around this spot. The bypass relied on back streets, in the main, with signalled junctions over the major roads radiating out from the main junctions. A careful use of occasional road closures, contra-flow cycle lanes and shared cycle and pedestrian routes prevented the bypass from being used by rat-running cars. At the end of the process a bypass, linking all the seven main roads and nearly making a circuit around the junction, was provided.

By far the most developed scheme implemented by the GLC was at Shepherd's Bush. Here, five major roads meet at a large gyratory around the old triangular green. Instead of building a bypass, cycle tracks were constructed across the green with signal-led cycle and pedestrian crossings giving access to all but one of the main feeder roads. A bypass type scheme around the adjacent Holland Park roundabout provided access to the final main feeder. As a result, cyclists were able to avoid the gyratory, on a route which was safe, attractive and convenient.

Mention should be made of projects which were unsuccessful and others which failed to be implemented because of the abolition of the GLC. Among the former must be included the junction of Chelsea Bridge Road and Buckingham Palace Road. This was a scheme to allow cyclists a safe right turn from Chelsea Bridge Road into Buckingham Palace Road, on the Ambassadors Route. Instead of taking the crown of the road, right-turning cyclists were led to the left-hand side, then onto a short stretch of cycle track taken from the footway. A loop in the road triggered signals which allowed cyclists safe crossing into Buckingham Palace Road. At the same time, those cyclists going straight on could avoid the red light by taking the cycle track.

It was a failure – cyclists would not use the scheme, preferring a traditional right turn. The main reason was that the phasing of the lights and the traffic flows allowed a fairly easy right turn, in any case. And traffic signals, 100m further back, gave cyclists an opportunity to reach the crown of the road safely. Compared to this, the cycle scheme, which forced a stop in any circumstances, was bound to be unattractive.

Cycle lanes on Waterloo Bridge and Upper Ground were also not total successes as built because of illegal parking over them, as already mentioned.

One scheme which might have been a success deserves mention as an indication of the scale of thinking by the CPT. This was a scheme for a surface-level crossing of Park Lane. The cycle routes in Hyde Park were, and are, well used, providing safe and attractive alternatives to very busy radial main roads. But whereas cycle access was provided to these routes from the north and south, there was no convenient access from the east, which was the most popular direction for cyclists, leading into the heart of the West End. Between Hyde Park Corner, at the south-eastern corner of Hyde Park, and Marble Arch at the north-eastern corner lies Park Lane, a dual carriageway of three and sometimes more lanes in each direction. Pedestrian crossings of Park Lane are all by subway, while there is no need for traffic to cross Park Lane, only to join it from side roads on the east. Thus, while there are signals on the southbound carriageway of Park Lane, there are none on the northbound side.

Considerable thought was given to the possibility of a shared pedestrian and cycle subway under Park Lane. But all the existing subways were well used and none are particularly wide. While shared use might have been possible it would have to have been on the basis that cyclists should dismount. 'Cyclists must dismount' sections of route were disliked by CPT and strongly opposed by the cycle liaison group, particularly by the LCC. Not only are they unattractive for cyclists, but they are also widely flouted.

Instead, CPT put forward a proposal for surface-level signalled cycle crossings. This would have introduced traffic signals onto the northbound carriageway of Park Lane for the first time. It was hotly opposed by the police, the Department of Transport and Westminster City Council, who claimed it would cause congestion. This was not true, as the capacity of such a crossing for northbound traffic would, in any case, have been considerably greater than the capacity of the junction at Marble Arch, further north. Nor would the stop time for traffic be so great as to result in traffic blocking back over further upstream junctions.

In time, no doubt, the GLC would have had its way and introduced the scheme as an experiment, with the predicted traffic chaos failing to materialise (except, perhaps, for the initial few days). This sort of approach had, in fact, been a feature of many of the GLC's more innovative and successful traffic management schemes. However, abolition of the GLC intervened before it was possible to take this scheme forward. No alternative has been put forward in the meantime.

Abolition of the GLC also prevented a new pedestrian and cycle subway being built under the east end of Westminster Bridge which would, if built, have resulted in a riverside cycle and pedestrian route almost 4km long.

Other major issues

Other major issues were also on the horizon and these have yet to be addressed. These mainly concerned potential conflicts of interest, an obvious one being between cyclists and pedestrians. While the GLC adopted a policy that, in principle, space for cyclists was not to be found at the expense of pedestrians, the thorny problem of how cyclists fit (or do not fit) into pedestrianised streets was not properly tackled.

A similar, but wider, issue surrounds the needs of the emergency services, where general traffic-calming measures, and cycle facilities in particular, often raise difficulties for emergency access. This problem is now surfacing again with the widespread use of road humps but no resolution is in sight.

Abolition of the GLC, in fact, brought most activities connected with promoting cycle facilities in London to a stop. Although some effort was made to maintain the CPT as a free-standing unit able to help boroughs, this was unsuccessful – partly because the nature of the abolition process was so divisive between boroughs of different political complexions.

Most boroughs gave formal support to the continued promotion of cycling and the GLC's cycle liaison committee was maintained, in an informal way, as the London Cycling Forum, with many of the same groups of people represented. There were three main reasons why most activity stopped. First, the boroughs had little expertise in any form of traffic management, and the initial period after abolition was spent adapting to new responsibilities with many fewer practical achievements. One or two boroughs were actively antagonistic to cycling. As mentioned above, Kensington and Chelsea lost no time in taking out the Fulham Road cycle lanes, while Westminster and others dropped all cycle planning activity.

Second was the ambivalence of the Department of Transport. Although the Department formally supported the promotion of safer cycling it gave little priority to this and was, in any case as far as its London responsibilities were concerned, far more interested in initial ideas to set up a major roadbuilding programme for London stemming from the London Assessment Studies. Finally, and critically, was a shortage of money. For London boroughs the cash shortage became so severe that only the most urgent work on traffic management was carried out in many cases.

Changes since the end of the GLC

From a nadir in 1986 and 1987, perhaps the position for cyclists is now, again, on the way up. In many ways, this rise mirrors that of the late 1970s. By the late 1980s cycle use was rising again, after a period of decline stemming from cheaper and better public transport. The environment was becoming an important political issue again, while fares were on the way up and bus and tube quality on the way down.

At the same time, the LCC was recovering a pioneering and radical edge, a little of which it had lost during the early 1980s. In 1986 it formally launched a major campaign to implement a 1,000 mile (1,600km) strategic cycle route network. This network stemmed, in part, from a notional commitment in the GLC's report. But it was seen by the LCC as a rallying point which provided a target both achievable and measurable. It looked, also, to Dutch experience, where ideas were crystallising around a hierarchical approach to cycle route networks – the strategic level being the highest. (This Dutch link had been fostered by a Dutch cycle planner being seconded to the GLC for a few months.)

The LCC's timing was good. The launch coincided with the start of a major change in the Government's approach to transport planning in London generally. As part of strategic planning advice for London, the London Planning Advisory Committee, the statutory body set up in 1986 to consider strategic planning in the capital, was firming up on a strategy for London which relied on a mixture of traffic restraint and improved public transport. More cycling fitted into this scenario, ideally.

At the same time, the Department of Transport was finding that its roadbuilding proposals were running into trouble. In 1986 it had assumed that it was just an anti-car GLC and a few vocal but unrepresentative environmental groups that opposed roadbuilding in London and that there was an underlying groundswell in favour of its proposals. It was in this light that the London Assessment Studies put forward a £3.5 billion series of roadbuilding projects. By 1988 it was starting to find out the fallacy of its position as major opposition built up. An early commitment to the 1,000 mile network allowed it to claim that it was not just interested in roadbuilding.

By early 1990, the Government realised that it had to abandon all its roadbuilding plans or face major losses in the local elections. It chose the vote-winning option, clearly of a mind that the lack of a policy was easier to manage than the loss of power. As a result, promotion of the 1,000 mile network became a major part of its highway strategy. As part of strategic planning guidance for London it became official policy for all boroughs to follow, too.

LCC had been sensible, too, in putting forward only a diagrammatic network, rather than specific plans. This prevented arguments over detailed alignments from stopping support in principle. Detailed schemes are now being drawn up by boroughs individually and through the London Cycling Forum. Cash remains a problem although Government support through Transport Supplementary Grant was made available to all road safety schemes in 1990 – before then it was available only for schemes on main roads.

So by 1991, LCC had almost achieved the combination that secured so much success between 1981 and 1986. The political will is becoming increasingly firm, with a renewed perception that cycling is increasing and, what is more, must increase in the future. The passage of the Road Traffic Bill in Parliament during 1990 and 1991 was also marked with a stream of calls for more activities to promote cycling from MPs on both sides of the House. What is lacking is the establishment of technical expertise, and sufficient funds.

Lessons from the London experience

That combination of political will, technical support and funding must mark the key to the GLC's success. But two other lessons also need to be drawn. First, the continuing close coordination between the Council and the cycling groups encouraged positive achievements (even if officials found the campaigners irksome from time to time). Too often, elsewhere, political will has been translated by officials inadequately in touch with cyclists' needs into schemes without cyclists' support which are argued over and, if implemented, seen as failures. Second, and as just important, was an acceptance that to cater for cyclists, traffic flows can be adjusted and may be restricted, albeit to a limited extent. Many of the GLC's schemes could only be implemented on this basis.

I have said that the GLC's activities in cycling between 1981 and 1986 were a success. But it is hard to define by what measure they were a success. Certainly they did not engender an overall increase in cycling in London: indeed, during most of that period, cycle use was falling. Nor did they produce a measurable drop in accident rates. But it would not be reasonable to expect them to do so. Although a number of schemes were implemented they did not make a complete or large enough network to make a significant difference over the whole of London. It was clear, though, that the GLC's cycle schemes helped concentrate cycle flows onto safer routes and perhaps the Fulham Road scheme gave the clearest evidence of this. And in other locations specific accident records were improved.

But the most important way in which the GLC's activities were a success was in demonstrating that there were few, if any, locations where it was not possible to install safer and pleasanter facilities for cyclists. That is a lesson which will benefit cycle planners throughout the country in future.

References

Feilden, Richard, 1974, *Give Way*, Friends of the Earth, London.

Greater London Council, 1976, *Notes for Guidance in the Provision of Facilities for Pedal Cyclists*, Greater London Council.

Greater London Council, 1981a, *Greater London Transportation Survey*, Greater London Council.

Greater London Council, 1981b, *Greater London Transportation Survey*, Greater London Council.

Greater London Council, 1981c, *A Cycle Policy for London; Report T29*, Greater London Council.

Greater London Council, 1984, *The London Cyclist*, Greater London Council.

Murray-Clark, Malcolm, 1985, *Profile of London's Cyclists*, Greater London Council.

9 Groningen, Netherlands

Gerrit van Werven

Introduction

Groningen, a medium-sized city in the northern Netherlands, represents an extremely interesting position in the current discussion on traffic policy.

In nearly all developed countries, it is evident that the growth of motor traffic causes great environmental problems, especially air pollution and noise. Car use also creates a space problem, as cars take up a lot of space in terms of roads and parking space, both in the cities and in the countryside. In the Netherlands, these problems have induced the Government to change its traffic policy drastically.

Until the end of the 1980s policy was aimed at accommodating the growth of motor traffic by creating more and more infrastructure. In that same period, investments in ecologically sound means of transport were relatively modest.

Continuing to meet the demand for more roads proved a disastrous approach, however, as it led to a further growth of motor traffic. This meant that the elimination of one bottleneck caused a shift of problems to a place slightly further down the road. Tailbacks got longer and longer, which threatened to choke the major transport axes in the western part of the Netherlands. This gave rise to problems of economy as well as ecology.

In 1989, this old traffic policy was abandoned. The Dutch Government took another direction: public transport and also the bicycle received more attention than they had had for a long time. Investment programmes were modified, so that considerably less money will be invested in motor traffic infrastructure and far more funds will be available for alternative means of transport.

The goal now is to accommodate the growth of mobility with public transport and bicycles, so that car use will be stabilised. This political course was laid down in two policy notes that have been ratified by Parliament: 'Het Tweede Struktuurschema Verkeer en Vervoer' (The Second Structure Scheme for Traffic and Transport) and 'Het Nationaal Milieubeleidsplan' (The National Environment Policy Plan).

In the light of this development, Groningen is of interest, as it had already opted for the policy change 12 years earlier. From the introduction of the traffic circulation plan for the city centre from 1977 onwards, policy has been aimed at stimulating public transport and bicycle use. This has sometimes produced extremely encouraging results: the modal split for the population of Groningen is favourable compared with other European cities: bicycle, 57 per cent, car, 37 per cent, public transport, 6 per cent.

At the moment, the city of Groningen is still in the vanguard. In 1990, together with the surrounding municipalities, Groningen presented a traffic plan for the whole conurbation, the first of its kind in the Netherlands.

In this plan, the new policy of the national government is translated into concrete measures. Thus, the ecological traffic policy of the city itself is extended to a large number of surrounding municipalities.

In this chapter, the major components of the traffic policy of Groningen will be described. Three of its main elements are as follows:

- the need for city planning;
- traffic in the city centre;
- cycling in Groningen.

These elements involve different levels of planning: the cycling policy is part of a broader traffic policy, which itself is part of a city planning policy and the levels should be integrated.

What is Groningen?

First, some facts about the city. Groningen is situated in the north-east of the Netherlands, a little over 200km from both Amsterdam and Bremen. The city itself has a population of 170,000 inhabitants, 90,000 of which work there. Another 230,000 people, most of whom are economically dependent on Groningen, live within a radius of about 30km. So the conurbation as a whole has some 400,000 inhabitants. The plan area for the traffic policy roughly amounts to the same region.

Groningen is by far the most important economic centre in the north of the Netherlands. Main sources of employment are: services, the university, electronic engineering, telecommunications, and agriculture.

Because of the high number of students (well over 30,000), the average age of the city is low (33 years), which, together with the historic city centre and the presence of many cultural facilities, creates a cheerful and lively atmosphere. Outsiders therefore often describe the culture and way of life of Groningen as urban and dynamic.

Economic policy and transport

Before discussing the traffic policy itself, the framework within which it is executed should be briefly sketched. This is important as the traffic policy is often strongly determined by goals connected with city planning or the economy.

The basis for the total city planning and economic policy of the city is the Struktuurplan ('Structure plan'). In this plan, two main objectives have been formulated:

1   *The central position of Groningen in economy and culture should be strengthened.* To further this goal, a specific investment programme has been set up, in cooperation with trade and industry. In designated areas, new facilities are being built, such as commercial centres, museums, hotels, and so on.

In general, it must be said that good accessibility and an efficiently functioning traffic system are undoubtedly of great importance to a city's economy. This is certainly true for Groningen, because of the strongly regional support function of the city. In this respect, motor traffic also has a certain value. For many inhabitants of the countryside, the car is their only means of getting to the city.

To ensure good accessibility on the one hand, and to look after ecological interests on the other, the decision was made to choose locations for the new intensification zones near public transport junctions and cycle routes. This means that the majority of visitors to these facilities can reach them by train, bus or bicycle. For visitors from the hinterland, car parking spaces will still need to be made available, together with improvements in public transport. Some examples of this are given later.

2   *The quality of life in the city should be enhanced.* This second goal is linked with the environmental policy, in which special attention is given to the quality of living and housing conditions. The municipal system was decentralised, for example, and residents' organisations were allowed to participate in the decision-making about investments in their neighbourhood, which includes paying attention to traffic policies. From the quality of life perspective, it is important to reduce motor traffic and promote alternative means of transport, which also has a positive influence on road safety. Besides investing in the bus and cycling infrastructure, this also leads to the introduction of 30 km/h limits in residential areas.

The traffic policy of Groningen which results from these two principles can be characterised as follows: Groningen gives priority to promoting the use of the bicycle and public transport. Motor traffic, on the other hand, is to be restrained. The only exception is motor traffic that is economically necessary, for example, for delivering goods to businesses.

Unnecessary motor traffic, for example commuter traffic, should, however, be restricted.

The need for city planning

What measures are we taking to shape this traffic policy? These measures are not limited to the area of traffic management, but also concern city planning. This is necessary, as city planning determines the distances between the various buildings and their functions, and these distances partly determine the choice of a particular means of transport. The location with respect to the infrastructure is also of course very important. After all, the choice of a particular means of transport is also decided by the proximity of important motorways and public transport and cycling routes. This means that we should:

1 keep trip distances as small as possible; and
2 choose the locations of functions in such a way that cycling or public transport are good alternatives.

The urban development model which guides us here is the 'compact city model', which boils down to a relatively high building density that creates an urban quality. The built-up area is uninterrupted, and there are no 'satellites'. The main facilities are situated in the city centre.

The implications of this for actual planning practice are, among other things, that suburbanisation should be discouraged. In principle, people who work in the city should also live there. This means that living in the city should be made attractive to all groups of people. Fortunately, reasonable success has been achieved in this respect in Groningen, thanks to a balanced building of new houses and extensive urban renewal. The population of the city is growing, while it is declining in many rural areas. This is a reversal of the trend of the 1970s.

It is also important to plan carefully the locations for facilities and employment. These should, preferably, be near the main cycle and public transport routes. Large office buildings should therefore be situated near the stations or the city centre, which means that the establishment of 'office parks' near motorways or on the outskirts of the city is discouraged. This policy is being combined with a parking policy, which determines the maximum number of parking spaces, so that commuter traffic remains limited. In order to site a business at its appropriate location, as from 1991 three categories have been distinguished:

A – labour-intensive businesses near public transport and cycle route junctions. The maximum number of parking spaces is one for every ten employees.

B – less labour-intensive businesses in locations which can still be reached easily by public transport and bicycle, but are also accessible by car. Parking standard: one parking space for every five employees.

C – businesses that are not labour-intensive and have a high interest in good accessibility by car and lorry. These will usually be located on industrial sites. No parking standard.

The distribution of shopping facilities is designed in such a way that people can do their day-to-day shopping in the neighbourhood. The city centre functions as the main centre for shopping. No supermarkets are allowed near motorways or on industrial sites.

The station area

One concrete example of this approach is the area around the main station, immediately south of the city centre. This area has been designated as an intensification zone. This means that major investments will be made in this area in offices, cultural centres, shops, and also housing (Fig. 9.1).

The total investment in this project is 900 million guilders (£300 million), which will mainly be funded by trade and industry. Agreements have been made between these investors and the city about the responsibilities of the various parties and about phasing and infrastructure.

An important feature of the project is the emphasis on architecture. The architects Koolhaas and Kleihues have been asked to act as supervisors. Within the framework they have designed, many architects are working on the realisation of the individual buildings.

This area has been chosen for intensification for two main reasons. Firstly, because it is close to the city centre. We expect that the development of the station zone will have a positive influence on the city centre. Secondly, because it can be reached easily by various means of transport. Because of its central location, accessibility by bicycle is good, and there is both a train station and a bus terminal within the zone so that public transport accessibility is optimal. It can also be reached by car reasonably easily, because of the vicinity of the ring roads.

To help bring about some reduction in the use of private cars for commuting, the number of parking spaces near these offices is limited, for the time being, according to the standard of one space for every five employees. In the future, this standard will be lowered to one in ten.

In order at the same time to offer good transport facilities to workers who live outside the city, special shuttle services are being planned and a so-called transport coordinator will be responsible for car-pooling and coordinated arrivals and departures of public transport services.

Figure 9.1 Museum with cycle bridge, Groningen, Netherlands.

Traffic in the city centre

Besides applying city planning instruments, in a number of cases the traffic structure has also been deliberately altered in such a way that public transport and cycling benefited, while at the same time motor traffic was impeded. An important example of this is the city centre. In 1977, the first phase of this traffic policy was implemented by means of the traffic circulation plan. Since 1990 the City Council has been working on a second phase which builds on the first phase.

Before the implementation of the traffic circulation plan, motor traffic could move freely through the city centre. The central square, 'de Grote Markt', was essentially a traffic roundabout, along which the traffic moved from east to west and from north to south. Naturally, this caused much inconvenience in the often narrow streets of the medieval city centre.

The new plan divides the city centre into four sectors (Fig. 9.2). The boundaries of these sectors are not to be crossed by motor traffic. However, these boundary restrictions do not apply to public transport, cyclists, and pedestrians. In addition to these traffic measures, a set of accompanying measures was taken. The pedestrian area was extended, squares were cleared of cars, and several hundred trees were planted. Furthermore, the bus station was relocated in the city centre and the main goods market returned to it. At the same time, urban renewal was also intensified. Monuments were restored and new houses were built on the sites of demolished housing. An important characteristic of this phase

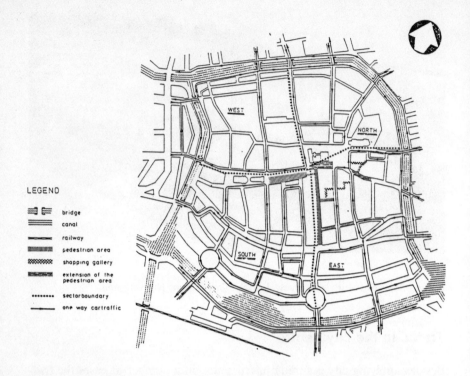

LEGEND

bridge	
canal	
railway	
pedestrian area	
shopping gallery	
extension of the pedestrian area	
sector boundary	
one way cartraffic	

Figure 9.2   City centre, Groningen, showing traffic sector boundaries.

of the traffic plan was that many streets remained accessible to motor traffic. It was still possible to enter them, and to park a car for a short while to do some shopping. However, it was no longer possible to get directly from one sector to another: to do so, one had to use a ring road, the so-called 'Diepenring'.

The citizens regarded these measures as drastic, and they resulted in intense debate. In most cases the public were opposed to the plan. Retailers were particularly hostile: they feared that their shops would become inaccessible, which would cause a drop in turnover. Because of the widespread publicity given to the plan, the turnover in some lines of business was indeed somewhat lower in the first two years after its implementation. But this trend had completely disappeared after two years.

Now, more than 13 years later, the retailers are on the whole satisfied. The number of visitors has risen sharply, and turnover and shop rents are high in comparison with other cities. There have also been positive effects on the traffic:

– the street climate improved because of the reduction in noise and pollution;

- bus travel increased (+18 per cent) and car traffic sharply declined;
- bicycle traffic increased slightly (+5 per cent), so that the bicycle became the predominant means of transport. This was also because of the reduction of motor traffic. In the city centre of Groningen some 100,000 bicycle trips are made every day.

In retrospect, it can be said that the traffic circulation plan has been a success. This does not mean that the plan is sacrosanct and that there have been no changes. Several small modifications have been introduced in the past few years, but the principles of the plan remain intact.

For some time now, there has been a new plan for the city centre, however, in which further incentives are given for strengthening the economic position of the city centre and the improvement of living conditions.

Naturally, part of this plan is a traffic policy. The intention is to uphold the principles of the old traffic plan, but gradually to extend the area without motor traffic and to reorganise the streets. This means a second phase in the traffic policy.

Not only will a large number of streets be cleared of motor traffic, but street parking will also be limited. This does mean, however, that we should provide new parking facilities for visitors. This will be done by building several multi-storey car parks on the outskirts of the city centre and by constructing park-and-ride facilities along the approach roads outside the city.

The City Council wishes to concentrate the bus traffic, so as to reduce the inconvenience caused by buses, and encourage cycle use by permitting cycling in all streets, with the exception of one busy shopping street. In addition, several guarded bicycle shelters will be built.

An important part of the traffic plan is the reorganisation of public space. The Mecano group of architects has drawn up a plan for this which comprises the complete rearrangement of the city centre paving. The current fragmented and tension-inducing use of the public space will be replaced by a much quieter picture, which radiates unity. Because parking for the most part will be banned from the streets, and the movements of motor traffic will be reduced to the necessary loading and unloading, the appearance of the city centre will be entirely dominated by pedestrians and cyclists.

Cycle traffic

Although bicycles are much in use all over the Netherlands, this means of transport is used more in Groningen than in other Dutch cities. I have said in the introduction that on average 57 per cent of the population travels by bicycle, as opposed to 37 per cent by car and 6 per cent by

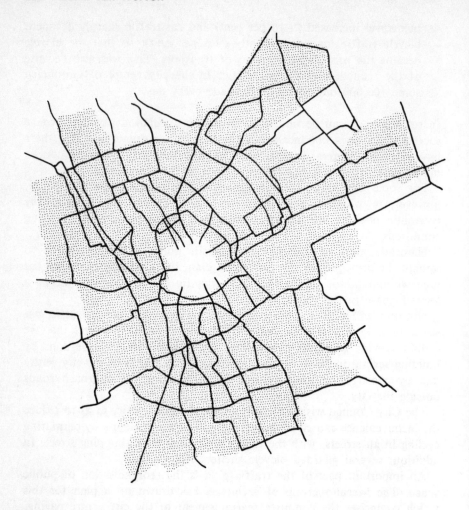

Figure 9.3 Main cycle network, Groningen.

public transport. This means that cycle use in Groningen is about 10–15 per cent higher than is the average for the Netherlands. There are several reasons for this.

First of all, Groningen is a compact city with relatively short distances, which can easily be covered by bicycle. From a suburb to the city centre takes at most 20 minutes by bicycle. Secondly, Groningen has a young population, for whom riding a bicycle does not pose problems. Finally, the implemented traffic policy has had a clearly positive influence on cycle use.

The City Council is pleased with this high number of cyclists, for several reasons:

Figure 9.4 Independent cycle path, Groningen.

- cycling is good for the environment;
- cycling is healthy;
- cycles do not take up a lot of space, which results in a large throughput capacity for a relatively modest amount of infrastructure. This is certainly important in a historic city such as Groningen;
- cycling is cheap for the citizens;
- cycling is cheap for the city, as the costs of creating and maintaining cycling facilities are much lower than the costs of motor traffic infrastructure. A high proportion of cyclists in the traffic therefore means considerable savings in road construction.

For these reasons, the City Council decided in 1987 to set up a special investment programme for bicycle traffic. Although there were already many facilities for cyclists, it was decided to bring the existing network to perfection. All the necessary short cuts will be constructed, and existing bicycle routes improved. This programme costs about 50 million guilders (£18 million), and will be completed in about 10 years. At first, the city itself was to fund it entirely, but since the change in national policy in 1989, the national government has agreed to pay 80 per cent of the costs.

A characteristic of the main cycling structure (Fig. 9.3) is that there are direct radial connections between the residential areas and the centre.

There are also tangential connections between city districts.

The following components of the cycling structure can be discerned by their form: independent cycle paths, (see Fig. 9.4), cycle paths along busy roads, and residential streets with few cars. In addition, there are separate facilities, such as road signs, bicycle stands and shelters.

In places where many visitors park their bicycles, guarded cycle parking facilities have been built. A facility for 3,000 bicycles was built near the station some years ago and in the city centre, there are at present five guarded shelters. A sixth, with room for about 1,600 bicycles, is being built.

Apart from the main network, there is a supplementary structure. This involves all other streets, separate small short cuts, etc. Special requirements have also been formulated for this supplementary structure. In principle, cyclists are permitted to go in both directions in one-way streets.

Although current bicycle use is very high, it is still growing. Annual counts indicate that cycle use in Groningen changes in accordance with the national trend, which shows a slight increase. The attitude of the City Council is that a decrease in bicycle use should be avoided. This is therefore the goal of the investment programme.

Conclusion

In this chapter, I have set out the outlines of the traffic policy of Groningen, a city that has gained a number of experiences in the past 13 years, which are now being followed all over the Netherlands.

An important feature of this policy is that there is now a complete integration with the policy concerning city planning. The first example (the station zone) shows the influence a good choice of location can have on mobility.

Moreover, it is important to make a clear choice for ecologically sound means of transport in the traffic policy itself. The second example (the city centre) illustrates how living conditions and the choice of a particular means of transport can be influenced by a comprehensive set of reorganisation measures for traffic space. Cycle traffic plays an important role here. It is important that we are not too modest when investing in this ecological means of transport. The bicycle has a huge potential in city areas: it is up to us to exploit that potential.

The examples given concern various levels of planning: city planning, traffic policy, and cycling policy. All three are important: however, they can only be really successful if they are implemented simultaneously.

A proper cycling policy presupposes good traffic planning, after all. And the latter can only succeed if the city planning is good. That is why the three planning levels should be integrated. In Groningen, the City Council has taken initiatives for such a policy on a number of fronts.

10 Odense, Denmark

Hans Jul Jacobsen and Leif Siboni

Odense is the third largest city in Denmark and is situated on the island of Funen, to the east of Jutland. It has a population of 175,000 and its boundaries cover an area of 300 sq. km. The city is an industrial, commercial, educational and administrative centre undergoing a steady process of development and change.

Most housing in Odense consists of single-family and semi-detached houses, except in the city centre and a few other areas where multi-family houses are mainly to be found. The rural area therefore is quite extensive, with some suburbs located up to 15km from the centre. Apart from the industry in and near the centre many industrial zones are located around the city. Furthermore, many green areas separate the housing areas from industrial zones and many of these green areas are directly connected to nearby farmland and woods.

Considering the population and the extent of the urban area there is a relatively large amount of travelling within the city. Part of this travelling is done by bicycle, as the area is flat and the distances are generally short.

In the 1960s a few cycle paths were constructed along some main roads on the outskirts of the city. In 1970 the city's area was enlarged, so neighbouring villages suddenly became suburbs of Odense and started expanding, with many new dwellings for families working in the city.

At this time motor traffic increased rapidly and many new roads were built, resulting in the demolition of old parts of Odense. Many old streets were not suitable for the fast-growing amount of traffic which had to use them.

The City Council decided that it was necessary to have a traffic plan for Odense so as to preserve the old town centre and to divert through-traffic. In 1974 the first municipal town and traffic plan was introduced. The main themes of the plan were:

- a quieter town centre with limited traffic;
- limited through traffic in residential areas;
- improving conditions for cyclists.

Two years later, in 1976, the City Council agreed on a general cycle path plan for the city of Odense. This plan consists of two types of cycle paths:

1 *Traffic paths* whose main function is to give direct access from housing areas to generating locations such as schools, sports grounds, institutions, shopping centres and the city centre. These paths are asphalted and equipped with lights and signs. During the winter they are kept clear of snow. The cycle paths are either built alongside main roads or as separate paths. Three of the separate paths have been built on disused railways.

2 *Recreational paths* which mainly connect residential areas with recreational areas such as parks, woods, green areas, allotment gardens and so on. These paths are normally narrow, gravelled and with no lighting. During the winter they are not cleared of snow.

The path system is planned to be an interconnected system, with safe crossings at all major roads i.e. tunnels, bridges, traffic lights and crossings with central refuges. The plan has been revised several times during the last 15 years, increasing the total number of paths.

By 1991 the length of cycle paths is as follows:

	Traffic paths	*Recreational paths*	*Total*
Completed by 1991	300km	150km	450km
Planned 1991-2000	175km	100km	275km
Total	475km	250km	725km

The total cost of the completed cycle paths is about Dkr. 25 million (£2.2 million) and the cost of the planned paths is estimated at Dkr. 15 million (£1.4 million).

As a result of the cycle path planning, 14 bridge/tunnel crossings were constructed for the future traffic paths in Odense, when the state motorway was built in 1985 close to the city. These crossings were totally financed by central government. Had the City Council not already approved the cycle path plans it would have had to pay for the crossings later.

Until 1984 all the traffic paths ended when they reached the edge of the city centre, an area of about 1km by 1.5km. Within this area the streets are narrow, often only 12–14m between the buildings and still with two-way traffic and pavements, there are buses, kerbside parking and usually a lot of traffic: motor vehicles, bicycles and pedestrians. In these narrow streets this mixture of traffic, together with high speeds, resulted in many road accidents and it became clear that if the conditions

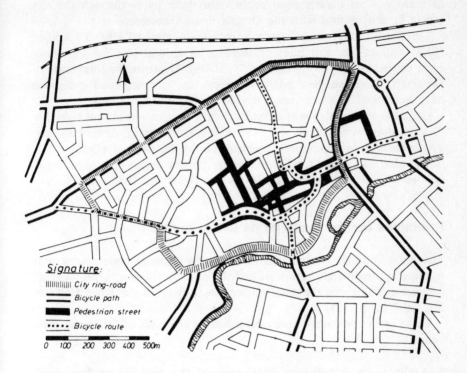

Figure 10.1 Traffic plan of Odense city centre, Denmark.

for cyclists were to be improved, the traffic pattern would have to be changed radically.

The transformation of the city centre

A comprehensive plan for all traffic categories using the city centre was approved unanimously by the City Council in 1984 (Fig. 10.1). The plan regulates changes and improvements in the road system, pedestrian areas, cycle paths, public transport and parking facilities. Through traffic is diverted from the city centre by means of a continuous ring road, which has been created by adding to existing roads. This ring road now marks the edge of the centre. The network of pedestrian streets has trebled in length, totalling now more than 2.4km. This makes it easier to walk around undisturbed by traffic and has proved beneficial to trade. City bus routes through the centre are now more direct and passengers can change buses at a central terminal.

It is interesting to note that this comprehensive plan for improvement of the traffic pattern in the city centre was triggered off by a decision to carry out an experimental project for cycle paths through the city centre in conjunction with the Danish Road Directorate.

The Danish Government made a special allocation of Dkr. 3.5 million (£0.31 million) for this pilot project out of a total cost for the whole cycle project of Dkr. 8 million (£0.7 million). However the total costs of the traffic diversion, new pedestrian areas, the city ring road and so on have amounted to more than Dkr. 30 million (£2.8 million).

Once the traffic plan was passed by the City Council several consultation meetings were held with shopkeepers, transport companies etc. These resulted in a number of alterations to the original plans.

The plan for a new traffic scheme in the city centre was fully implemented in time for Odense's 1,000th anniversary in 1988.

Principles for the cycle paths in the centre

The main solution chosen was to create two special cycle routes, one running approximately east–west and the other north–south, with a small connecting stretch on the main square just in front of the Town Hall (see Fig. 10.3 on p. 171).

These two cycle routes were established on the basis of four main principles:

1 Ordinary cycle paths on both sides of the road in the few places where this was possible.
2 A cycle path running in the opposite direction in one-way streets.
3 Cycle paths in pedestrian areas.
4 Cycle paths in areas reserved for buses.

Furthermore, different solutions were employed to protect cyclists at traffic signals.

Examples of special solutions

The establishment of the cycle routes through the city centre on the basis of these four main principles was only possible if unconventional solutions were employed. There were a number of considerations, especially in the pedestrian areas, to make the cycle route successful.

Buses, bicycles and pedestrians in one street

In one part of the pedestrian street Vestergade it was necessary to maintain three city bus routes in each direction as one of the main bus stops

Figure 10.2 Buses, cycles and pedestrians in Vestergade, Odense.

is located here and serves 10,000–15,000 passengers every day. In order
to make pedestrians aware of the buses and cyclists the concrete block
pavement of the pedestrian street changes colour, pattern and level
(40mm lower) in the 6.5m lane for buses and cyclists. The 'pavements'
are 2.5–5m wide and divided from the lane with trees and posts. The
difference in level is not vertical, but is a slope of 1:8, so as not to make
an obstacle for handicapped people (Fig. 10.2).

It has been necessary to have a speed limit of 20 km/h for the buses
as they have to travel at almost the same speed as the cyclists. At the
beginning the bus company was against driving in a pedestrianised street
full of people but later, after the speed limit was introduced, it was
accepted, and there have since been no problems. No accidents between
buses and pedestrians and cyclists have been reported.

In some parts of the pedestrian areas, bicycle lanes are constructed like
the above-mentioned bus lane, but with a width of 3.5m as a two-way
cycle lane. They are also constructed with a different colour, pattern and
level of pavement to mark the distinctive use of this lane only for
cyclists.

One-way traffic

Overgade, also a narrow street, was changed from being a two-way street without any cycle lanes to a one-way street with one narrow cycle lane, 1.5m, in the same direction and a combined contra-flow lane for buses and bikes.

In some other one-way streets contra-flow cycling is permitted, resulting in a more convenient route for cyclists, who will always try to take a short cut whenever possible.

Narrow cycle paths

In Klaregade, the cycle paths along the street were constructed with a width of 1.0m at the same level as the pavements by reducing these to the same width.

This solution appeared to go beyond the limits for mutual consideration from different road users and was abandoned after criticisms in the local newspapers following an accident between a pedestrian and a cyclist.

Construction of cycle paths

The cycle paths along the streets are constructed as:

1 Kerbstone and asphalt pavement approximately 100mm higher than the street level, but 30mm lower than the level of the pavement.
2 Same level as the street and separated with a narrow refuge or a white line.
3 Same level as the street, but with a different pavement of either concrete blocks, surface dressing with red stones or red thermoplastic.

Solutions at junctions

Junctions require particular solutions as many accidents happen there, especially when cars make a right turn (equivalent of left turns in the UK and Ireland) and are not aware of cyclists.

Some crossings are equipped with special traffic lights for cyclists. These lights turn green a few seconds before the traffic lights for cars and likewise with red, depending on the number of right-turning cars. In this way it has been possible to avoid some accidents between cyclists going straight ahead and right-turning motor vehicles.

At some crossings without cyclist signals the stop line for cyclists is

Figure 10.3 Cycle path in the Town Hall Square, Odense.

placed 2–4m in front of the stop line for cars so the cyclists are more visible and they can move off in front of the cars.

At crossroads with many right-turning cyclists (equivalent of left-turning cyclists in the UK and Ireland) the cycle path is continued around the corner behind the traffic signals avoiding obstruction of the cyclist flow. The cycle paths are continued through some junctions by marking the path either as a blue lane (thermoplastic) or with a white dotted line 300mm wide.

It is of great importance to safeguard cyclists crossing roads and streets. Several solutions have been adopted especially outside the city centre, where most of the junctions of separate paths with roads are to be found.

When a traffic path crosses a street with moderate traffic, the crossing is made at a higher level to slow down the speed of the vehicles. Other crossings are made by providing the street with a central refuge or narrowing the street to only one lane at the crosspoint. Streets with heavy traffic are crossed by traffic paths, either in a tunnel or on a bridge. In the city centre, however, there are no separate paths, and the cycle routes all follow the ordinary street areas.

The east–west and north–south cycle routes were constructed from 1984 to 1987 as a part of the comprehensive plan for the city centre. To safeguard cyclists, some crossings were made with traffic lights for bicycles. Since the completion of the routes some crossings have been improved by adding more traffic lights, cutting short the cycle path before the street crossing and adding some refuges to separate motor vehicles from bicycles.

Before and after studies

The before studies were conducted in 1984 prior to the establishment of the paths, and the after studies during 1986, when the cycle routes were almost completed.

Interviews with cyclists show that they use the routes almost daily. The most extensive use is transport between home and workplace or shopping area. A total of 49 per cent of the cyclists find that it has become easier to get from one place to another and only 20 per cent find it more difficult. With regard to safety, 42 per cent found it safer to use the routes and 15 per cent found it less safe.

The number of cyclists per day using the east–west cycle route in the city is as follows:

	Before (1984)	After (1989)	Increase
Eastern part of route:	5,500	9,300	+69 per cent
Middle part of route:	2,350	4,600	+95 per cent

Accidents involving cyclists have been reported by the police and the casualty department of the hospital. During the five years before construction of the two routes in the city centre a total of 279 accidents were reported. After construction, the reports show that the accident rate increased at the same rate as the increase in the number of cyclists. However, it has not been possible to make a complete comparison of accidents before and after. A five-year period has still not elapsed since the completion and some improvements on safety have been made in the last year.

Questionnaires

A questionnaire was given to cyclists before and after completion of the cycle routes. A total of 1,800 questionnares were distributed to cyclists before and 1,600 after, and the number of responses were respectively 1,111 (62 per cent) and 902 (57 per cent).

The main conclusions from the questionnaires after completion of the two cycle routes in the city centre are:

1 The rate of adults and children using the routes are the same.
2 Approximately 30 per cent fewer cyclists use a street parallel to the east–west route, but this is not reflected in an increase in the number of cyclists on this route.
3 Most cyclists feel safer when using the routes. The parallel street without any cycle paths is regarded as unsafe.
4 It is easier to use the cycle routes and they are more comfortable.

The reasons for choosing the routes are in general that the cyclists feel safer, the routes are easier and the travelling can be done more rapidly than before. 40 per cent to 60 per cent of the cyclists use the routes to travel from home to work, while approximately 20 per cent use them to get to school.

Shopkeepers and trade

One of the main problems in planning the cycle paths through the city centre was opposition from shopkeepers, who feared a fall in their trade. To construct the paths it was necessary to restrict car parking facilities. Kerbside car parking was prohibited and traffic was reduced on the streets. During the planning of the change in the city centre, many meetings were held with the trade organisations and the shop owners on the various streets, together with other street users. These meetings resulted in alterations in response to some of the demands from the shopkeepers. In this way, and as the cycle paths were only a part of the comprehensive plan, the cycle routes were agreed by the users, that is, shopkeepers, transport companies, refuse collection, residents' organisations, the police, taxi companies, goods delivery companies, etc.

A comparison of the turnover for the shopkeepers along the cycle routes has shown no significant fall in trade, partly because the cycle routes were part of the new comprehensive traffic plan. Many shops have, on the contrary, increased their turnover and improved their shops.

Cycle parking

After completion of the routes one major problem remains unsolved, cycle parking in the city centre. Parking areas are not available close to the pedestrian streets where cycling is prohibited. It has only been possible to establish small parking areas with cycle stands alongside buildings, at street corners and in adjoining streets. However, these are not sufficient, so bikes are parked everywhere, and become a nuisance for pedestrians and shopkeepers.

Cyclists want to park their bikes as close as possible to the shops, so the cycle stands in the streets adjoining the pedestrian areas are almost empty, while only 50–100m away the bicycles are parked untidily in the shopping area.

Costs

The cost of cycle paths varies according to location, pavement, width, light, etc. The price per square metre ranges from Dkr. 300 (£30) to Dkr. 1,000 (£100) with the most expensive cycle paths located in the city centre where pavements have to be removed, new drains have to be added and the paths are constructed with kerbstones, asphalt or concrete blocks.

Conclusions

The overall impression of the people of Odense is that the new traffic plan has proved to be a success and that the cycle routes are playing their vital part in this result. The unconventional solutions employed have, with the exceptions mentioned, proved satisfactory. However, it should be noted that very careful planning and the provision of a large amount of information to the public is necessary to obtain a satisfactory result.

The cyclists are satisfied with the convenience and safety they feel in using the routes. The extensive network of cycle paths in the municipality is of a high standard, with smooth surfaces, street lights and snow clearing. The paths are used daily by many cyclists, in total the bicycle traffic has gone up in the city area by 40 per cent during the last 10 years. The bicycle is being used by more people, which has influenced the use of private cars and public transportation. Car traffic in the city centre has gone down by 10 per cent since 1986 and statistics for the numbers of bus passengers also show a considerable decline.

To encourage the use of bicycles the City Council has produced a good deal of publicity material, maps and tour guides. The network of paths is still being enlarged and the safety of cyclists continues to be improved.

References

Municipality of Odense, 1989, *Safer Routes to Schools*, Status Report, Odense.
Transportokonomisk institutt, 1991, *Nordiske Storbyers trafik og miljø*, Rapp. 0076/1991, Oslo, Norway.

11 Germany

Tilman Bracher

Cycle policy and research

Many institutions have been involved in research and planning on cycling since the end of the 1970s, and a number of seminars and congresses have supported this development. The first international congress in the now well established 'Velocity' series took place in 1980 in Bremen. In 1982, the semi-official planning recommendations ('Empfehlungen für Planung, Bau und Betrieb von Radverkehrsanlagen') were published, with the participation of planners and cyclists. They included the first steps away from the classical 'Radweg' (cycle path) approach, which meant putting cyclists on the pavement with or without clear separation from pedestrians. This approach had been in practice since the unemployment programmes of the late 1920s and 1930s which promoted motorway and car schemes and bicycle-free roads.

Konrad Otto, an officer in the Federal Environment Office dedicated to cycling, initiated the first government note on cycle policy. This was a joint programme on cycling and the environment ('Fahrrad und Umwelt') from different departments of the Federal Government in 1983, but no measures to implement it were taken. Otto was also the initiator and manager of the project for bicycle-friendly cities ('Fahrrad-freundliche Stadt') which took place from 1981–87. At that time the bicycle was also included in the safety research programmes carried out by the Federal Transport Research Authority (Bundesanstalt für Strassen-wesen). A summary of those results was published in 1991 by the Federal Ministry of Transport (Bracher et al., 1991).

Aims of cycling policy

The Federal programme

While in many countries safety aspects have been the only concern of bicycle planning, the environmental movement, which started at the beginning of the 1970s in Germany, also saw the bicycle as a substitute means of transport to car use. The bicycle as a means of transport for sports, leisure and holidays has never been a major topic in transportation research and policy at the national level. Some holiday resorts, however, attract tourists by providing bicycle programmes and cycle tour networks.

Only a few cities actually adopted a bicycle-oriented transport policy. Most of the facilities from the 1970s and 1980s were planned in a context of continued car dominance. The classical 'Radweg' (cycle path on the pavement) has been popular among politicians and traditional transport planners since the 1920s, as it reserved road space for cars. Although its safety defects have become a problem to many of those concerned with cycling, classical 'Radweg' schemes are still commonly implemented. This may be due to the fact that segregation of different types of traffic has always been taught in Germany to be an appropriate strategy for improving safety, but has never been properly researched. This was despite the fact that safety always played a major role in discussions on cycling issues.

The Bicycle-friendly Towns Project (Modellvorhaben 'Fahrradfreundliche Stadt')

The original Federal scheme

Rosenheim in the north of Germany and Detmold in the south were chosen, in 1981, out of 131 towns who applied to become 'bicycle-friendly' towns. This was a research programme by the Federal Environment Office (Umweltbundesamt) which was involved in planning innovative cycling schemes and monitoring their performance. The two towns, however, were responsible for finance and implementation of their projects.

The scheme included a committee to monitor and support the programme. A wide range of interested people from nine further towns and cities, from Federal and State level Governments, from the bicycle industry, cyclists' clubs and campaign groups and other institutions met regularly with those who carried out the work to discuss the results.

When Detmold and Rosenheim began their schemes in 1981, they had no comprehensive provision for cyclists. The towns committed themselves to a town-and transport-planning policy aiming to promote bicycle traffic. An initial problem arose with both towns being unwilling to provide enough funds to implement all the schemes.

The research included more than 20 studies, on the following issues:

– the bicycle in the highway code and other laws;

- modal split;
- schemes for immediate implementation;
- the bicycle and public transport;
- foreign experience;
- potentials of cycle use;
- cycle theft;
- the schemes for Detmold and Rosenheim (planning and implementation);
- other non-motorised vehicles;
- consideration of handicapped people;
- facilities (infrastructure, service-stations, bicycle hire, bicycle trade and businesses);
- programme evaluation.

Many of the ideas suggested had been included in the local bicycle programmes of Detmold and Rosenheim. In the end, local public reaction and implementation problems became the major impediments to the speedy establishment of Rosenheim and Detmold as bicycle-friendly towns. It took a long time to reduce resistance to 'imported experts on bicycle planning'. Unconventional measures such as cycle lanes on the roads, cycle parking on the road, contra-flow cycling on one-way streets and shared use of pedestrian and cycling zones and paths in parks were not immediately adopted. The results were evaluated in terms of modal split. In Rosenheim, where even in 1981 23 per cent of trips were by bike, the implementation of a number of excellent measures led to an increase to 26 per cent by 1986. In Detmold, however, resistance had been greater, and at the same time major car parking and road construction schemes had also been carried out. In Detmold the level of trips by bicycle at the conclusion of the project in 1986, 14 per cent, was no different from that at the beginning, in 1981.

Experience of the project also shows that quick and cheap measures cannot persuade people to use bikes and to accept the project, and that efficient measures can only be realised years after they were first planned. The experiences of Rosenheim and Detmold did show, however, that only about DM400 (£140) per inhabitant would be needed to implement the full programme to make those cities 'bicycle-friendly'.

All the major results and the research papers were published by the Federal Environment Office in a series of research reports. At the end of the schemes the monitoring committee summarised the results and agreed a statement on the characteristics of bicycle-friendly towns ('Merkmale einer fahrradfreundlichen Stadt'). In its preliminary remarks it stated that walking, cycling and the public transport system together can provide a basic transportation system without the need for a car. The bicycle has a potential for about 30–40 per cent of all shorter trips in distances up to 15km.

In a bicycle-friendly city public bodies and private enterprises together should aim:

1 To improve bicycle availability by providing:
   – cycle hire stations;
   – office bikes for employees;
   – safe, long-term parking as well as sheltered cycle parking in houses, at shops, pubs, hotels, workplaces and other destinations.

2 To improve the ease and safety of access by introducing:
   – an area-wide and dense network of cycle facilities including cycle paths, pedestrian areas, cycle lanes (on the road), and over- and underpasses for cyclists;
   – a system for guiding cycle traffic including direction signing;
   – speed limits (e.g. 30 km/h) on all minor roads without segregated cycle facilities;
   – winter maintenance without spreading of salt.

3 To combine the joint use of the bicycle and public transport by providing:
   – safe and sheltered cycle parking stations at major bus stops;
   – cycle hire;
   – acceptance of bicycles carried on trains and buses;
   – easy access routes to public transport stations.

4 To improve attitudes towards cycling ('fahrradfreundliches Klima'):
   – campaign for cyclists to feel that they are always respected in planning and politics;
   – key personalities should use bikes;
   – car drivers should be educated to drive more cautiously.

5 To improve the implementation of schemes by:
   – adapting the organisation of local authorities to the demand for cyclists, e.g. by establishing appropriate working groups and officers in charge of bicycle issues;
   – establishing bicycle promotion schemes for the short, middle and long term;
   – allocating a specific budget for cycle planning and campaigning.

Many of the ideas of the original bicycle-friendly towns project have now been included in cycle schemes in other German cities.

The schemes of the State of North Rhine–Westphalia

A follow-up project of the national bicycle-friendly towns programme was set up in the State of North Rhine–Westphalia in 1989. Münster, Lünen and Troisdorf are among the cities now aiming to adopt higher modal shares for the bicycle and to reduce car use. In Münster a DM69 million (£24 million) investment programme for cycling has been adopted. Münster aims to reduce car traffic in its central area, and hopes to considerably increase its already high share of cycle use (29 per cent of all trips).

Münster plans seven combined parking places for cars and bicycles at bus stops at the edge of the city. This is to encourage park-and-ride and park-and-bike. Car drivers coming from the surrounding area of Münster into the city should park there and use bikes or public transport to continue their trip into the central area. Subsidies for public transport investment purposes are available for this project.

Some cycle path and other engineering programmes are included in car traffic schemes. A bypass-road for Münster, which is getting additional lanes, will also have two cycle bridges at appropriate crossing points. There is a programme for the optimisation of bicycle signalling. This includes the provision of green waves for cyclists at all signalled roads.

The area of the Münster main railway station has always been a place where hundreds of bicycles are parked day and night. Only a few of them can use official cycle parking facilities. On both sides of the main station two cycle parking areas for 600 and 1,200 bikes respectively, costing DM4.8 million (£1.7 million) and DM1.2 million (£0.4 million), are now being planned. They are intended to provide proper cycle parking and make the combined use of the bike and train more attractive.

For 1990 alone the programme included the expenditure of DM14 million (£4.9 million) which corresponds to about DM50 (£17) per inhabitant of Münster. The total plan will include projects for DM69 million (£24 million). More than two-thirds of that will be subsidised by the Federal or State level Governments.

Projects on area-wide traffic calming (Flächenhafte Verkehrsberuhigung)

In 1980 the joint area-wide traffic restraint projects by the Federal Environment Office, the Federal Road Authority and the Federal Research Office on Regional Planning (Umweltbundesamt, Bundesanstalt für Strassenwesen, Bundesforschungsanstalt für Landeskunde und Raumordnung) were set up. Schemes were implemented in six places (Berlin, the small village of Borgentreich, Buxtehude, Esslingen, Ingolstadt and Mainz), with traffic-calming programmes introduced in parts of the urban area. The schemes included engineering work and publicity campaigns.

The aims of the projects were to improve the traffic situation for pedestrians, cyclists and public transport, to reduce the number and severity of accidents, and to improve the environment of residential areas by reducing noise and pollution and by introducing more green and wider public spaces.

Measures to improve conditions for cycling included programmes for a more accessible and denser network, schemes at junctions to improve convenience and safety when crossing, and finally schemes on other stretches of road to improve safety when riding on these.

The implementation of the schemes started in 1983 and is, still continuing. However, first evaluations and before- and after-studies are available. The data show that cycle use has increased in all project areas, and car speeds have been reduced. The reduction has been greater in those places where the speed before was higher and where the design of the road was radically changed. Traffic safety was improved, but only the number of casualties fell, not the total number of accidents.

Considerable changes concerned the attitudes of road users, including the image of cyclists. In Esslingen, before the traffic-calming projects were introduced nearly half of the cyclists were regarded as reckless, after, only a quarter were so regarded. The image of car drivers, however, deteriorated, even though they drove at slower speeds.

Trade and commerce improved considerably after the introduction of traffic-calming measures. Turnover and the readiness to invest money increased in those places where the most extensive measures for area-wide traffic-calming were taken.

Surveys of public attitudes in Ingolstadt show that the speed of car drivers is more often judged as too high than previously and the risk of accidents is perceived as lower than before. Positive effects on pedestrians and the attractive image of the road-space give a positive image to traffic-calming.

Implementation problems with the improvement of cycle infrastructure

Both engineering and legal measures may be applied to improve the situation for cyclists. Many city administrators are reluctant to apply unconventional measures even if proved successful elsewhere. Most engineering handbooks in Germany have been written from the viewpoint of the car. This has caused problems in the implementation of:

- contra-flow cycling on one-way streets;
- cycling in pedestrian areas;

- a 30 km/h speed limit on urban roads used by cyclists;
- the voluntary use of classically designed cycle paths;
- cycle lanes and other on-road areas reserved for cyclists;
- bicycle streets ('Fahrradstrassen'), where cars are only allowed for access and at a low speed;
- cycle parking.

All of the above have been implemented in some places, but not nation-wide. Comprehensive evaluations of their effects encourage cycling organisations to campaign for a wider application while conservative transport engineers and lawyers largely oppose them. Some cities, however, changed their policies as a result of local research and pressure from campaign groups.

The Erlangen example on the 'classical' cycle path

In a number of German surveys Erlangen has been found to be the most cycle-friendly town in Germany. Erlangen has cycle paths on many urban roads. The classical German 'Radweg' is designed on the pavement next to the pedestrians. This type of facility has been criticised due to a lack of safety and comfort.

In the city of Erlangen regular analysis of the police data on cycle accidents shows that more than 60 per cent of all cycle accidents were collisions with cars. There is some variation from year to year, but half to three-quarters of all accidents occur at four-way junctions, T-junctions and approaches to junctions.

Particular accident black spots are places where cyclists have to travel on classical cycle paths. The most frequent cause of all accidents is the failure to stop at junctions, and this type of accident is most frequent where classical cycle paths exist. Collisions between cars turning left (right-hand traffic in Germany) and oncoming cyclists, who have the right of way, are very frequent. On private property drives, the number of accidents between cars and cyclists is three times higher when cyclists are forced to ride on the classical cycle paths.

The general prejudice that cyclists tend to be rude and cause more and more accidents themselves has no statistical basis. In two-thirds of all car/cycle accidents the police blamed the car drivers for having caused the accident. The most frequent cause of fatal accidents was speeding by cars.

Road design recommendations therefore suggest that safety schemes in Erlangen should include the abolition of classical cycle paths at junctions. Cyclists should be guided between 15m and 20m ahead of junctions to cycle lanes on the road. At junctions, special markings should guide the cyclists. In practice, however, implementation is progressing half-heartedly. Even in a cycle-friendly city much resistance has to be overcome!

Road-markings and cycle lanes in Bocholt and other places

Parts of the road allocated for cyclists by road markings are relatively safe and attractive. This is the major result of a study on 17 different cycle lanes on roads of differing widths, some with and some without car parking next to the cycle lane.

The majority of problems for cyclists on these lanes are caused by cars. Car speed and lateral distance seem to have a narrow statistical relationship. The higher the car speed, the more distance cars should allow when overtaking bikes. So it is not the type of road marking which is relevant, but the effective distance between cars and cyclists, which is influenced by the complete design of the road.

Cyclists judge all the different types of cycle lanes positively. Observations, however, show that the number of incidents between cars and cyclists has not been reduced by the introduction of these measures. There have been surveys on a cycle lane in Bocholt, where a 1.08m-wide cycle lane was marked firstly with a continuous wide line and afterwards with a double line. It could be shown that in the 'before' situation, without any road-marking, in cases of conflict only 20 per cent of car drivers didn't react in time, whereas with one continuous line 56 per cent, and a double line 64 per cent, of all drivers became negligent. The road-marking also had an effect on the speed of individual cyclists which was reduced from 21.7 km/h without markings, to 20.7 km/h with a single line and to 20.5 km/h with a double line.

The marking of a cycle path on the pavement in a shopping-street in Cologne also got poor results. The average speed of cyclists was rather low, 15.8 km/h. While a small majority of the cyclists approved of the cycle path, which was about 1.30m wide, 55 per cent of all pedestrians were against it. The observations showed many conflicts. Critical situations arose as pedestrians stepped onto the cycle path without looking and cyclists came into conflict with pedestrians when they had to overtake.

The new parking law in Berlin

A new law was adopted in Berlin in 1990 which considerably improved the conditions for parking bikes. One of its purposes is the potential to contribute to reducing car traffic by parking policy. The law therefore includes a differentiated strategy for restrictions and reductions of the number of car parking places to be provided at new buildings.

Figure 11.1 Carriage of bikes on the Berlin S-Bahn
(Urban Railway).

Any new and renewed building now must have a sufficient number of parking spaces for bicycles. While car parking spaces may be situated at some distance from the building, cycle parking areas must be on the site itself. In places with good access to public transport car parking may be restricted or excluded totally. In other places, developers have an option to provide car parking. Instead of providing car parking spaces, developers can pay into a pool a certain amount of money related to the number of flats or to the area of office space. This pool may be used for spending on public transport or on cycle or other parking facilities.

The bicycle and public transport

As the city of Berlin is expecting increasing transport problems, its public transport companies are making considerable efforts to improve the 'bicycle and public transport mode'. This is considered as an alternative to car ownership or use. Public transport alone is not a complete alternative to the car for many people. Therefore bikes and public transport complement each other for certain purposes or at certain times of the year. The bicycle should be seen as a means of transport which enables passengers not living close to stations to get easy access and use public transport as bike-and-ride customers. This market is mainly for journeys to work or education.

Since the 1920s the suburban rail network, 'S-Bahn', has been accepting cyclists on the train, and in 1990 even the peak-hour restrictions were withdrawn (Fig. 11.1).

Data from counts on weekdays and at weekends show that the number of customers with bikes may rise considerably. Big variations, however, exist between different lines and different areas. The main reason for taking bikes on trains is for casual leisure purposes. At weekends trains carry more than 100 bikes, but only 20–30 can be stored properly. All the other cyclists use other spaces. The low number of complaints shows, however, that this seems acceptable to other customers, and the public transport company does not enforce its regulations.

On weekdays only a small percentage of regular journeys to work and education is carried out by taking bicycles on trains. To improve the situation, all newly implemented S-Bahn trains, which usually have eight carriages, now have five places to store bikes in every carriage, so at least 40 machines can be carried properly. Peak numbers occur on fine summer Sundays when cycle trips are being made for leisure purposes; however, these can only be handled by improvisation.

A similar programme has been adopted for the underground trains (U-Bahn), but fewer cyclists use the U-Bahn since these trains do not extend to leisure destinations as much as the S-Bahn system.

Another programme includes lifts at all stations to provide easier access to the platforms. This programme had originally been set up for the handicapped, but it will now be adapted for the carriage of bicycles on lifts.

The implementation of some 40km of bus lanes in Berlin in 1989 led to a discussion as to whether cyclists should be allowed to ride on them or excluded. As no proper and comfortable alternatives for cyclists were available, access was granted. An evaluation study shows that no serious problems occurred. There have been no accidents according to the statistics, and the effect on the speeds of buses was not negative. Cyclists tended to ride attentively and sometimes gave priority to buses by keeping to the side. Bus drivers also drove more attentively than before and

Figure 11.2 Berlin: shared use by bikes of bus lane.

got used to judging the behaviour of cyclists when coming up from behind. The number of delays and interactions is so small that the implementation of these joint lanes can be judged to be very successful. The desired road width for a joint bus and cycle lane, however, is between 4m and 4.25m (up to 40km/h bus speed). Both cases allow over-taking of buses and bicycles in the same lane, as illustrated in Fig. 11.2.

Further programmes being discussed for the development of Berlin include avoiding park-and-ride facilities for cars. Instead, many more bike-and-ride facilities including locker-boxes and service-stations for cyclists are to be provided and these will include guarded cycle parking. Sites close to good rail connections, however, are not to be used for car parking but for shops and offices. This could minimise necessary average distances and maximise the share of the cycling and public transport mode together with walking.

As the rail network in Berlin is very dense, there are no plans to carry bikes on regular buses, which has become the practice during off-peak hours in more than 20 German cities.

Potential and approaches for stimulating cycle use

As the aim of substituting cycle use for car use has been of interest in

Germany for a long period, numerous studies on bicycle use and the potential of cycling have been carried out. Most of their results have been summarised in a study for the Federal Traffic Ministry (Bracher et al., 1991). Modal split data are available, as household surveys are carried out every six years at the national level and occasionally at regional and local levels. Local and regional cycle use show wide variations. Top levels with nearly 30 per cent cycle use are the towns of Dessau (Eastern Germany, with a population of 130,000), Erlangen (Western Germany, population 50,000), Münster (Western Germany, population 269,000), Rosenheim (Western Germany, population 50,000) and Landshut (Western Germany, population 55,000). In the big cities of Hamburg, Munich, Cologne and Frankfurt the bicycle has a share of about 10 per cent of all trips and comes close to the national average of 11 per cent. In Berlin (West and East) its share of 3–5 per cent is considerably lower.

Some objective factors have a strong influence on cycle use; the type of settlement and the distribution of distances are important. Big cities often have a distinct separation between the areas used for working, living and shopping. The functions of the city and the topography have an influence too. Flat, middle-sized and small-sized towns have the highest bicycle shares.

Children and young people use bicycles most frequently. Their participation rate has been calculated: the number of people who ride a bike on a certain day reaches a national average of 33 per cent in the 10–15-year age group.

Leisure trips are not the most important purpose of cycle use. The analysis of data on purposes of cycle trips by people aged more than 10 years shows that only 30 per cent of all cycle trips are leisure traffic, compared with 34 per cent for shopping and personal business, and 36 per cent for trips to work or school.

Seasonal variations lead to a peaking of cycle use between June and September. Lowest levels, about half the average levels, are between December and March.

Distances covered in cycle trips are relatively short. The national average modal share of the bicycle is 11 per cent. Its greatest use is for distances of between 1.1 and 2km. Not only shopping trips but also those for work, school and leisure have short average distances. The longest cycle tours are leisure trips. Important determinants of cycle use are attitudes towards cycling, and conditions. The most important reasons for not cycling are: 'Cycling is too much effort', fear of catching a cold, weather conditions, and image.

Cycle users themselves have different perspectives. Their main problems and reasons stated for occasionally not cycling are too few cycle paths, unsuitable clothing, car pollution, and recklessness of drivers.

Non-users and users perceive cycling conditions quite differently. Non-cyclists rate psychological problems higher. Therefore measures to improve attitudes to cycling seem to be appropriate for encouraging more cyclists. For cyclists themselves, improvements of the infrastructure and traffic conditions seem to play a bigger role.

Studies like those in the projects for 'bicycle-friendly cities' and 'area-wide traffic-calming' provide a list of measures to increase cycle use. The most appropriate are:

1 an increase of cycle availability by getting people to buy new or better bikes and by measures against cycle theft.
2 Weather, topographical conditions and distances show the limits of cycle use under certain conditions. However in dry weather, flat areas and for distances of up to 4–5km there is a considerable potential.
3 Traffic conditions and cycle paths must allow for quick and safe cycling. The cycle network includes all local roads, even those with high levels of car traffic. It has been observed that cyclists are prepared to avoid main roads only when cycling for leisure. That means that connections allowing lower speeds or involving detours are usually avoided.
4 As soon as parking becomes a problem for car users the readiness to use a bike increases. Strong factors for not using a bike remain as people tend to link trips together. Therefore total travel distances may be much longer than the return journey to work.

References

Alrutz, D., Fechtel, H., Krause J., 1989, *Dokumentation zur Sicherung des Fahrradverkehrs*, Reihe Unfall- und Sicherheitsforschung Strassenverkehr, Heft 74, Bergisch-Gladbach.

Apel, D., 1984, *Stadtverkehrsplanung Teil 3: Umverteilung des städtischen Personenverkehrs. Aus- und inlandische Erfahrungen mit einer stadtverträglicheren Verkehrsplanung*, Berlin.

Apel D., 1988, *Verkehrssicherheit im Städtevergleich (Stadtverkehrsplanung Teil 4)*, Deutschen Institut für Urbanistik (Ed.), Berlin.

Bundesforschungsanstalt für Landeskunde und Raumordnung (Ed.), 1988, *Tagungsband Forschungsvorhaben 'Flächenhafte Verkehrsberuhigung'. Ergebnisse aus drei Modellstädten. 4. Kolloqium in Buxtehude vom 26/27.05.1988.* Bonn.

Bundesminister des Innern (Ed.), 1983, *Fahrrad und Umwelt*, Umweltbrief 26, Bonn.

Bundesminister für Raumordnung, Bauwesen und Stadtebau (Hg.), 1988, *Stadtverkehr im Wandel*, Bonn.

Bundesministerium für Verkehr (Ed.), 1981, *Dokumentation 1. Internationaler Fahrradkongress Velo-City 10–12 April 1980. Verlauf und ausgewählte Beiträge.* Forschung Stadtverkehr. Sonderreihe Heft 9, BMV, Bonn.

Bracher, T., 1987a, *Konzepte für den Radverkehr. Fahrradpolitische Erfahrungen und Strategien*, Bielefeld.

Bracher, T., 1987b, Sicherheitsprobleme auf Radwegen – Verkehrspolitische Forderungen aus neuen Untersuchungen, *Internationales Verkehrswesen* 40, Heft 5/1987.

Bracher, T., Luda, H., Thiemann, H., 1991, *Zussamenfassende Auswertung von Forschungsergebnissen zum Radverkehr in der Stadt*, Forschung Stadtverkehr, Band A7, Bundesministerium für Verkehr, Bergisch Gladbach/Berlin, Bonn.

Forschungsgesellschaft für das Strassen- und Verkehrswesen, 1982: *Empfehlungen für Planung, Bau und Betrieb von Radverkehrsanlagen*, Hg. HUK-Verband, Koln.

Umweltbundesamt (Ed.), 1982–87, *Reihe Werkstattberichte des Modellvorhabens 'Fahrradfreundliche Stadt'*, Umweltbundesamt, Berlin:

Nr. 1D. Gersemann: *Sachexpertise Fahrradrecht*, 1982.

Nr. 2 *Tendenzen der Verkehrsbeteiligung in den Modellstädten*, 1982.

Nr. 3 *Sofortmassnahmen zur Förderung des Fahrradverkehrs*, 1982.

Nr. 4E. Muessener, V. Stillger: *Sachexpertise 'Fahrrad und Öffentlicher Verkehr'*, 1983.

Nr. 5A. *Das Fahrrad in den Niederlanden*, 1983.

Nr. 5B. *Fahrradverkehr in europäischen Ländern (ohne Niederlande)*, 1983.

Nr. 5C. *Fahrradverkehr in Übersee (Australien, Japan, USA)*, 1983.

Nr. 6. *Potentiale des Fahrradverkehrs in den Modellstädten*, 1983.

Nr. 7. W. Broeg, E. Erl, O. G. Foerg, *Konzeption und Methodik der verkehrs- und sozialwissenschaftlichen Begleituntersuchung*, 1984.

Nr. 8. J. Tebbe: *Sachexpertise 'Fahrraddiebstahl'*, 1984.

Nr. 9. F. J. Dammann u.a., *Bestandaufnahme und Analyse*, 1984.

Nr. 10 *Pressedokumentation*, 1984.

Nr. 11 *Bericht über die erste Projektphase 1981–1983*, 1984.

Nr. 12 F. J. Dammann, K. Hänel, J. Richard, *Planung und Ausbau des Radverkehrsnetzes in der Modellstadt Detmold 1981–1983*, 1984.

Nr. 13 M. Eichenhauer u.a., *Planungen zur Fahrradverkehrsinfrastruktur in der Modellstadt Rosenheim 1981–1983*, 1985.

Nr. 14 Angenendt/Grau, *Sachexpertisen Typenkatalog Nichtmotorisierte Verkehrsmittel und Zubehor – Berucksichtigung behinderter Menschen bei Planungen und Massnahmen zur Fahrradverkehrsförderung*, 1986.

Nr. 15 W. Brog, E. Erl, *Verkehrs- und sozialwissenschaftliche Begleituntersuchung – Zwischenbericht*, 1986.

Nr. 16 K. Hänel, *Sachexpertise Infrastruktur-Servicestationen-Fahrradverleih-Fahrradhandel*, 1986.

Nr. 17 M. Replogle, *Fahrradverkehr und Öffentlicher Personennahverkehr als integriertes städtisches Verkehrssystem*, 1987.

Nr. 18 W. Broeg, E. Erl, *Abschliessender Bericht zum Modellvorhaben 'Fahrradfreundliche Stadt', Teil A, Begleituntersuchung und übergreifende Aspekte*, 1987.

Nr. 19 F.-J. Dammann, K. Hänel, J. Richard, *Abschliessender Bericht zum Modellvorhaben 'Fahrradfreundliche Stadt', Teil B, Fahrradverkehrsplanung in der Modellstadt Detmold*, 1987.

Nr. 20 M. Eichenauer, H. H. von Winning, E. Streichert, *Abschliessender Bericht zum Modellvorhaben 'Fahrradfreundliche Stadt'*, Teil C, Fahr-radverkehrsplanung in der Modellstadt Rosenheim, 1987.

o. Nr. *Wegweiser zur fahrradfreundlichen Stadt. Erkenntnisse und Erfahrungen aus dem Modellvorhaben 'Fahrradfreundliche Stadt' des Um-weltbundesamtes.*

Hülsmann, W. und Umweltbundesamt (Hg.), *Wegweiser zur fahrradfreundlichen Stadt. Erkenntnisse und Erfahrungen aus den Modellvorhaben 'Fahrrad-freundliche Stadt' des Umweltbundesamtes. Reihe Texte*, Berlin 1987.

Wolf, J., 1988, *Zur Sicherheit innerortlicher Radwege,* Städte- und Gemeinde-bund 2/88.

12 The United States of America

Andrew Clarke

Introduction

Current cycling activity

Bicycle sales in the United States outstripped new car sales throughout the 1980s, running at an average of 10 million bicycles sold each year. There are more than 90 million cyclists in the US, with more adults riding than children. There has been a big growth in the popularity of cycling in recent years, a trend that shows no sign of turning around (Bicycle Federation of America, 1991).

It is equally clear that cycling remains primarily a recreational activity for most people. Interest in personal health and fitness has encouraged millions of US adults to start cycling again, after many years 'out of the saddle'. The popularity of mountain bikes, which now account for more than 65 per cent of bike shop sales, has also contributed to the growth. Mountain bikes have proved less daunting and more comfortable for new cyclists than more traditional 'sports' bikes.

Accidents

According to the National Highway and Traffic Safety Administration less than 2 per cent of all traffic deaths involve cyclists. Over the last decade the number of cyclist fatalities fluctuated between a 1989 low of 821 (840 in 1990) and a 1980 high of 965 – with no discernible trend emerging from the figures. More than 500,000 cyclist injuries are treated in hospital emergency rooms every year, based on figures compiled by the Consumer Product Safety Commission. Male cyclists account for 80 per cent of fatalities, and about one half are aged 16 or under.

The potential

In October 1990 the Louis Harris polling organisation conducted a nationwide bicycle commuting poll, on behalf of *Bicycling* magazine. They reported that nearly 3 million adults say they sometimes commute by bicycle, and that more than one in five, 35 million adults, would sometimes commute by bicycle if 'bike-friendly' transportation systems existed. Key findings from the Harris poll were:

- 20 per cent of adults, or 32.9 million people, say they would sometimes commute to work by bicycle if there were safe bike lanes on roads and highways.
- 18 per cent of adults, or 29.7 million people, say they would sometimes commute to work by bicycle if employers offered financial incentives.
- 17 per cent of adults, or 29 million people, say they would sometimes commute to work by bicycle if secure storage and showers awaited them.

Also in 1991, the Minnesota State Bicycle Committee adopted *Plan B: Letting bicycling work for Minnesota*. The report is a powerful justification for investing in bicycle provisions ranging from education and safety programmes to developing safe urban streets and highways. Current state expenditure on cycling of more than $4 million (£2.2 million) a year is planned to rise to $10 million (£5.5 million) a year by the end of the decade, by which time the investment will be more than offset by savings to individual cyclists and the state economy of more than $13 million (£7 million) per annum.

In a nation where urban congestion costs the top 29 metropolitan areas $41 billion dollars (£22,000 million) a year, where almost every metropolitan area has failed to attain clean air standards set in 1970, and where highways and parking lots take up half of most urban areas, cycling has a tremendous potential to flourish.

The role of cycling in urban transportation

The great potential for cycling has not been realised. Less than 1 per cent of journeys to work are made by bicycle, despite the fact that more than half of the population lives within 5 miles (8km) of their workplace. Other utilitarian trips are equally unlikely to be made by bicycle.

The major reason for this unfulfilled potential is that there are too few safe places to ride. Potential cyclists simply do not feel safe using the existing highway network and special provisions for cyclists are few and far between. Facilities such as bicycle-only traffic signals and advanced stop lines are unknown. Many explanations for this situation can be postulated.

1   *Predominance of the car.*   The car is truly king in the US. More than 15 per cent of GNP is directly related to automobile construction, operation, use and provision. While the US population grew by 0.89 per cent per annum during the 1980s, vehicle miles travelled grew by 3.5 per cent a year. Almost 200 million vehicles travelled a total of 2 trillion miles (3.2 billion km) in 1989. More than 84 per cent of journeys to work are made by private car.

Commuting now accounts for less than one-fifth of all trips. Social and recreational driving have become at least as important as commuter trips, and the overwhelming majority of these trips are also made by private car.

2   *Flight to the suburbs.*   Two-thirds of new jobs in the US are created in suburban areas, and almost all of the traditional urban centres are losing population and employment.

Ironically, the flight to the suburbs may have a positive influence on average commuting trip lengths. Suburb-to-suburb trips are about 50 per cent shorter than suburb-to-city centre trips. The problem for cyclists is that suburban development has been designed so exclusively for the car that bicycle access has actually been made more difficult. The centralisation of shopping facilities and other single-use development encourages more trip-making, in a more hostile highway environment.

3   *Highway design.*   Traffic engineers have stuck rigidly to a street hierarchy and classification system that is anathema to cyclists. Residential and collector roads feed inexorably into major, high-speed arterials, typically with four to six lanes of traffic moving at a minimum of 50 mph (80 km/h), connected by large intersections. Lane widths of only 12 feet (3.6m) do not provide the space necessary for cyclists to feel comfortable sharing the highway with fast-moving cars and trucks.

Alternative back-street routes simply do not exist in many places because of the street patterns. Access to buildings and services are only possible from the major arterials, and no special provision for cyclists is required.

4   *Mistakes of the 1970s.*   The oil crises of the 1970s prompted the development of state and local bicycle plans across the country. Few were implemented, and those that were often provided poorly conceived, constructed and maintained bicycle paths that were scorned by the cycling community. Special facilities for cyclists and cycle planning were given a bad name that persists to the present day.

5 *Defensive cyclists.* The cycling community, overawed by the ubiquitous power and influence of the motor car and its lobby, has been defensive, preferring to try and educate cyclists to behave more like cars rather than changing the infrastructure in which both must operate. This approach has failed, as surveys reveal only 1 per cent of the population is likely to be encouraged to ride a bicycle by the availability of bicycle education classes and programmes.

6 *Limited statistical information.* Cycling activity is routinely excluded from federal, state and local transportation data collection and use. Evaluation of bicycle projects is rarely carried out, and very little is known about the impact of different policies, practices and provisions for cyclists.

Bicycle-friendly communities – the exception to the rule

Despite the routine exclusion of cycling from the everyday operation of the transportation system by politicians, planners and engineers, some communities have done a considerable amount to encourage cycling.

These efforts are still modest compared to those of cities like Delft and Groningen in the Netherlands. In particular, even where bicycle planning has a long and successful tradition it has rarely been achieved at the expense of highway capacity or automobile convenience.

Seattle, Washington

The city of Seattle (metropolitan area population 1.6 million) was named the 'Best City for Bicycling' in 1988 and 1990, according to *Bicycling* magazine readers and other experts. The city has a bicycle and pedestrian programme comprising six people in the Engineering Department, and is developing an extensive network of both off-street trails and on-street facilities.

The backbone of the trail network is the 12-mile (20km) Burke Gilman trail, an 8–10 foot (2.4–3.0m) wide paved path along an abandoned railway line, used by more than one million people annually, 70 per cent of whom are cyclists. This is complemented by the Duwamish trail to the south of the city and the I–90 bike path to the east. The three trail systems are joined by a series of bike lanes and signed routes on the carriageway.

Land is at a premium in Seattle, as a growing population is constrained by water (Lake Washington and the Puget Sound) and hills (the foothills of the Cascades). As a result, facilities such as the Burke Gilman trail and the I–90 path are expensive. A feature of the city of

Seattle bicycle programme has been the way in which annual bicycle-related expenditures of more than $5 million (£2.7 million) are incorporated into ongoing projects.

For example, additions to the Burke Gilman trail can now cost up to $1 million per mile (£0.34 million per kilometre), including land acquisition and construction. However, sections of the trail have been built by fibre-optic cable-laying companies who are required by the City to finish their work by paving the trail.

Interstate 90 crosses Lake Washington from Bellevue to the heart of Seattle. Reconstruction of the freeway cost $1.5 billion (£830 million), and at a cost of $2 million per mile (£0.65 million per kilometre) the facility incorporates a 1,300-foot (400m) long, 15-foot (4.5m) wide bicycle and pedestrian tunnel and a 1.5-mile (2.4km) pontoon bridge carrying the cycle path parallel to six lanes of motor traffic.

The city also operates a highly successful 'Bike-Spot Improvement Program' to deal quickly with small-scale problems such as potholes, damaged signposts and lighting columns. The $100,000 (£53,000) a year programme also pays for the installation, upon request, of between 60 and 100 bicycle parking racks. A special report card is provided for bicyclists to inform the City of problems requiring attention.

Seattle is also one of the few cities practising some form of traffic-calming in residential areas. More than 200 'traffic circles' have been installed at four-way intersections of local roads, reducing vehicle speeds and conflicts. Installation is only at the request of residents.

In spite of these efforts, bicycle use remains relatively low in the city of Seattle, at no more than 2 per cent.

Eugene, Oregon

In 1970 the city of Eugene (metropolitan area population of 200,000) created a bicycle committee and embarked upon a programme that has resulted in national recognition. 5.5 per cent of journeys to work are made by bicycle in the metropolitan area and this rises to 8 per cent in the City.

Based on a 1974 Bikeways Master Plan the city now has more than 80 miles (130km) of separate bike paths, bike lanes and signposted routes, and cycle use between 1971 and 1978 increased by an average of 76 per cent at selected locations.

The key to the success of the Eugene network has been the construction of four bicycle and pedestrian bridges crossing the Willamette river. Three of the concrete bridges were built in the 1970s for a total of less than $1 million (£0.55 million), and are all more than 500 feet (150m) long and approximately 14 feet (4.3m) wide. A fourth structure, also carrying telephone, sewer and power lines across the river, was added in

1982 for a cost of $855,000 (£460,000). Counts indicate that more than half of the cycle trips across these bridges are for transportation rather than recreation.

In a 1981 report 'The Development of One Community's Successful Cycling Program', the use of various 'innovative' bikeway designs by the City is described. Among the techniques adopted have been:

- one-way road closures with exceptions for bicycles;
- narrowing car lane widths to 11 feet (3.3m) on some busy arterials to make more space for bike lanes;
- installing 4.5-feet (1.4m) wide concrete gutters instead of the usual 1-foot (0.3m), providing a smoother, more usable space for cyclists with contrasting surface colours;
- contra-flow bicycle lanes: 24-foot (7.3m) wide streets in the University area have been reconfigured to provide 6-foot (1.8m) bike lanes on either side of a one-way, 12-foot (3.7m) traffic lane.

The programme is backed up with education, promotion and enforcement efforts, the provision of cycle parking and a full-time bicycle coordinator.

To the north of Eugene is the larger city of Portland, (metropolitan area population 1 million). Efforts to encourage bicycle use here also began in the early 1970s, as a result of an aggressive state policy of bicycle promotion. In 1971 the Oregon State Legislature enacted legislation (ORS 366.514) mandating that not less than 1 per cent of the State Highway Fund be devoted to bikeway/footway improvements. Both Portland and Eugene have benefited from this regular source of income.

The city of Portland now has a 65-mile (105km) network of bicycle lanes, paths and routes based on a detailed local selection process involving a Citizens Advisory Committee, City staff, a special Task Force of Neighborhood and Business Associations and the City Council. Initial selection is based on 22 corridors (bicycle route planning areas) within which projects will be judged on their utility to existing, and new, riders; connection of existing facilities; directness; improvement in safety; cost; visibility; and ability to connect bicycle destinations.

Arlington County, Virginia

Part of the Washington D.C. metropolitan area (population 3 million), Arlington County has 85 miles (137km) of bikeways, comprising 37 miles (60km) of trails (primarily the Custis, Four Mile Run, Mount Vernon and Washington and Old Dominion (W & O D Trails) and a further 47 miles (76km) of signed bike routes. Over 90 per cent of Arlington residents live within a quarter of a mile (400m) of a bikeway.

Figure 12.1   Curtis Trail bridge over Lee Highway, Arlington, Virginia.

The Custis trail (Fig. 12.1) was built alongside Interstate 66 as part of the mitigation package for the highway (which also incorporated part of the D.C. Metrorail system). The trail was recently linked at its eastern end to the popular 17-mile (27km) Mount Vernon trail by way of a $1 million (£0.57 million), 12-foot (3.7m) wide bridge over the four-lane George Washington Parkway. To the west, the Custis trail feeds into the W & O D trail, a pioneering railway line conversion completed in the 1970s. The Custis trail is one of the few in the nation to be illuminated, 24 hours a day.

From March to October the trail system is maintained by a team of two, who work full-time on landscaping, sweeping, pothole repair, signpost replacement and other functions along the trail.

Despite this effort, the level of bicycle commuting into Arlington and the District of Columbia remains around the 1 per cent mark. Recreational use of the trail system is much higher.

Palo Alto, California

Another city renowned for its pro-bicycle policies is Palo Alto, California. In addition to having around 60 miles (97km) of signed routes, bike

Figure 12.2   Bicycle parking at Ballston Metro,
Arlington, Virginia.

lanes and off-highway facilities, the city has a number of specific
facilities and policies of note.

In 1981, the city installed an experimental 'Bicycle boulevard' along a
2-mile (3.2km) section of a residential street in between two major
arterials. Bryant Avenue, prior to the experiment, had numerous intersections where cyclists had to stop and give way to other traffic. After the
experiment, the stop signs and priorities were reversed to give cyclists
priority along the route. Barriers to prevent motor vehicle traffic using
the route were installed at two key locations.

During the demonstration project cycle use along the bicycle boulevard increased dramatically, and the rate of growth exceeded that of other routes in the city. The boulevard concentrated bicycle traffic in the corridor, and motor vehicle traffic declined by almost 50 per cent along Bryant Avenue itself.

With no increase in accidents, no adverse neighbourhood reaction, and no other traffic problems arising from the experiment, the bicycle boulevard was made permanent. Other such streets are being incorporated into the bike route network. The bicycle boulevard was recently extended to 3.5 miles (5.6km) by a vote of the Palo Alto City Council, and now passes through the heart of the downtown area.

The network also incorporates:

- Seven bicycle- and pedestrian-only bridges which bypass or underpass major highways.
- Straight-through bike lanes to the left of right-turn traffic lanes, with traffic signal detectors for cyclists.
- Bicycle-responsive, marked traffic signal detector loops are installed to enable cyclists to trip the lights. The 'green-time' at major intersections has been lengthened to allow cyclists time to cross the street in safety.
- Rubberised railway line crossing pads have been installed at three crossings, to reduce the likelihood of cyclists falling.
- Street repairs must meet stringent smoothness requirements, and are inspected regularly. Flaws developing within one year of repair must be replaced.

In addition, the City Police Department uses bicycles for patrols; drive-through facilities are required to serve cyclists (many banks and fast-food restaurants across the country do not); City employees are reimbursed 7 cents per mile (2 pence per km) for official cycle travel; a bicycle traffic school has been established for juvenile highway code offenders; and employers are required to provide showers and bicycle parking based on the size of the company and number of employees.

This extensive programme has helped to increase cycle use to over 11 per cent of journey-to-work/school trips in the city, one of the highest levels in the country.

Dallas, Texas

The Dallas–Fort Worth metropolitan area has more than 3 million inhabitants, almost 18,000 highway miles (29,000km), and total daily highway vehicle mileage of 76 million miles (122 million km). In the city of Dallas, there are 315 miles (507km) of signed bike routes based on a 1-mile (1.6km) grid pattern. The 1985 Bike Plan, on which the network is based, calls for a total of 480 miles (770km) of routes. A further 20 miles (32km) of wide kerb lanes have been added to the highway system since 1985. Bicycle use figures for the city are low.

San Diego, California

The San Diego metropolitan area comprises just over 2 million residents with a total of 5,500 highway miles (8,850km). In 1990 there were 64 miles (103km) of bike paths, 334 miles (537km) of bike lanes and 133 miles (214km) of bike routes available for use. The 1989 Regional Transportation Plan incorporates the goal of increasing average daily bicycle trips from 230,000 in 1988 to 500,000 in 2010. The bike network is expected to grow by around 30 miles (48km) a year, with an annual expenditure of some $750,000 (£400,000) by the City and a similar amount by the County of San Diego. If these targets are met, modal split will rise from 2.5 per cent currently to 3.5 per cent in 2010.

San Diego has also been at the forefront of developing bike-and-ride facilities in connection with their trolley system and bus services, and in promoting cycling through back-of-bus posters, maps and other materials.

Madison, Wisconsin

Home to the University of Wisconsin, and the state capital, Madison has 100 miles (160km) of bike routes, paths and lanes. More than 100,000 bike trips are made every day, including over 10 per cent of journeys to work. Features of the network include a contra-flow bike lane along University Avenue, a major thoroughfare in the downtown area; road closures with exemptions for cyclists; and abundant cycle parking.

In addition to the full-time bicycle coordinator, the City employs traffic monitors to enforce a licensing programme and bicycle traffic laws. The most common traffic violations are ignoring red lights and stop signs.

Davis, California

A challenger for the highest level of bicycle use in the United States, with 25 per cent of trips made by bike, Davis pioneered bike lanes and facilities in the US in the early 1970s. One-third of all city streets have bike lanes, and some busy intersections feature special left-turn lanes for cyclists.

Boulder, Colorado

Another city with a big university population, Boulder has 50 miles (80km) of bikeways. The centrepiece of the network is the 4.8-mile (7.7km) Boulder Creek Bikepath, used by more than 2,000 cyclists every day.

In the 1980 census, 3.8 per cent of journeys to work in the city were by bike. Other surveys carried out for the Boulder Transportation Master Plan and Denver Regional Council of Government's travel survey during the 1980s put the levels of cycling and walking at 1 per cent and 3 per cent respectively.

In 1990, the Boulder Citizens Transportation Advisory Committee commissioned a study of travel patterns in the Boulder valley in order to provide definitive baseline data for modal split upon which to base the cities' efforts to reduce single-occupant auto trips by 15 per cent. The results of the survey were surprising:

- 8.6 per cent of all trips are by bike, and 19.1 per cent are by foot. The two modes account for 4.5 per cent and 3.2 per cent of miles travelled.
- Cyclists accounted for 9.3 per cent of journeys to work and 20.4 per cent of journeys to school.
- The mean bicycle trip length was 2.1 miles (3.4km), and lasted 15 minutes, at an average speed of around 8mph (13 km/h).

By the year 2010 the City plans to complete a further 50 miles (80km) of bikeways to meet the needs of the cycling population, which is growing by approximately 20 per cent annually.

The role of the states

While much of the provision of bicycle facilities is in the hands of city and county governments, states play a crucial role in determining policies, setting standards and allocating transportation funds. California played a leading role in the 1970s, but in the 1980s other states have taken on the challenge of improving conditions for cyclists.

Florida

The Florida bicycle programme started in 1979 with the appointment of a state bicycle coordinator and a bicycle advisory council. The program was to include the development, implementation and coordination of policies, programs and facilities for the safe and effective integration of the bicycle into the Florida state transportation system.

Since then, between $8 and $12 million (£4 and £7 million) in bicycle-friendly highway improvements have been made to the urban and state highway system each year, mostly in the form of shoulders, wide kerb lanes and bike lanes on major highways. Improvements are based on bikeway design standards and criteria developed by the state. Most major metropolitan areas, including Orlando, Miami, Fort Lauderdale, Tampa, Jacksonville and Tallahassee have local bicycle coordinators part-funded by the state.

North Carolina

Set up in the early 1970s, the North Carolina bicycle programme has developed steadily over the years into one of the strongest in the nation. With a staff of six, the bicycle office has produced a wealth of promotional, safety and educational material, including one of the best series of state and local maps for cyclists.

Through the state's Transportation Improvement Program (1989–92), 40 independent bicycle projects – bike lanes, bike route signing, mapping, parking, shoulders and wide kerb lanes – will be funded at a cost of over $2 million (£1.1 million). In addition, more than 70 incidental projects (part of larger highway improvements and construction projects) will be completed.

Oregon

In 1971 the Oregon state legislature passed a bicycle bill requiring at least 1 per cent of the State Highway Fund distributed to city and county governments to be spent on bicycle and pedestrian facilities. This was the first legislation of its kind.

Non-motorised facilities are built in conjunction with all construction, reconstruction or relocation of roads, except where costs are excessive or if safety would be compromised. Rural highways now commonly include four- to six-feet (1.2–1.8m) wide paved shoulders signed as bikeways, while in urban areas bike lanes are more common.

In addition to facilities, the programme has also provided route maps, touring information, signed state routes and promoted bicycle commuting in urban areas.

Design standards and guides

In the late 1980s and early 1990s there has been a growing consensus in the United States over the value of different types of bicycle facility. This is reflected in the range of facilities provided in places such as Seattle, Arlington County, Eugene, and elsewhere.

This has not always been the case. As in Europe there have been opponents and proponents of special bicycle facilities such as bike lanes, segregated facilities and independent paths along railroad corridors. The arguments are just the same as in Europe. Throughout the 1970s and 1980s those who disliked these facilities – believing that cyclists should behave as much like vehicles as possible, in the traffic lane, having learned to become 'effective cyclists' – held sway.

To them, the important thing was that existing cyclists be trained to be like cars and the pleas of potential and novice cyclists who asked for more safe places to ride were largely ignored. Much of the fear of separate bicycle paths and other facilities were based on two perceptions.

First, during the bicycle boom (energy crisis) of the early 1970s almost every jurisdiction in the nation embarked on cycle plans and projects, with little or no experience or knowledge of what to do to help and encourage cyclists. The result was a plethora of badly designed, poorly maintained, isolated bicycle routes and paths that quickly fell into disrepute and low use. In many states this was compounded by laws requiring the use of such facilities.

Secondly, opponents of special bicycle facilities latched onto a study of experienced cyclists that showed them having more accidents on separate bicycle paths than on the street. Even though the study was flawed in many respects, its impact and influence has affected bicycle planning for many years.

Fortunately, the debate has lessened as people accept that different facilities serve different functions and different users, and that each has its place in the transportation system. The four most commonly used facilities are separate bicycle paths, shoulders, wide kerb lanes and cycle lanes.

In each case the premise is the same. Cyclists need space. The argument is over whether or not to demarcate that space, and if so, where on the highway should the space be marked?

As the bicycle boom was particularly pronounced in California, and California is considered a trendsetter in so many respects, it is not surprising that the California Department of Transportation was among the first to devise guidelines and standards for the development of bicycle facilities. Most current practice is based on their continuing work.

The State of California Highway Design Manual, section 1000, is on bikeway planning and design. In the chapter, bikeway refers to all facilities providing primarily for cycle travel. A bikeway classification system has been developed, and is widely followed throughout the country.

Class I Bikeway: provides for bicycle travel on a right of way completely separated from any street or highway.
Class II Bikeway: provides a striped bike lane for one-way bike travel on a street or highway.
Class III Bikeway: provides for shared use with pedestrian or motor vehicle traffic.

A more detailed analysis of the different categories discusses the appropriate selection criteria for each, stressing that it is not a hierarchy denoting that one type of facility is better or worse than the next.

For both Class I and Class III bikeways the manual emphasises that sidewalks are *not* bicycle facilities. Sidewalks are meant for pedestrians and do not share the same design characteristics as bikeways. Where pedestrian flows are high, separate bicycle and pedestrian trails are encouraged to prevent conflict.

The manual has extensive detail on the design criteria to be used in developing different facilities. For example:

Class I Bikeways: the minimum paved width for a two-way path or trail shall be 8 feet (2.4m). For a one-way path minimum width should be 5 feet (1.5m). For routes with heavy bicycle use, 12 feet (3.7m) is recommended for two-way paths.
Class II Bikeways: must always be one-way, and shall not be located between an on-street parking area and the kerb.
Class III Bikeways: are intended to provide continuity on a bikeway system, and are ordinary streets. Routes should only be signed if they provide for through and direct travel in bicycle-demand corridors; they connect discontinuous segments of bike lane; traffic control devices can be adjusted to give greater priority to cyclists; street parking has been removed or restricted in areas of critical width; surface imperfections have been corrected and maintenance of the route will be of a higher than normal standard.

Sidewalk bikepaths may be considered in special situations, according to the California manual, such as along high-speed or heavily travelled roads with inadequate space for cyclists and uninterrupted by driveways and intersections for long distances, or on long, narrow bridges.

As the United States has become more inclined to settle disputes in the court, so the need has grown for such guidelines and manuals of standard practice. In 1981, the American Association of State Highway and Transportation Officials (AASHTO) produced *A Guide to the Development of New Bicycle Facilities*. Based on the California manual, the

AASHTO Guide quickly became the standard reference work for bicycle planners and engineers, eager to base their designs on commonly accepted norms and principles.

In August, 1991 a new edition of the guide was published. The introduction states that:

To varying extents, bicycles will be ridden on all highways where they are permitted. All new highways, except those where bicyclists will be legally prohibited, should be designed and constructed under the assumption that they will be used by bicyclists. Bicycle safe design practises, as described in this guide, should be followed to avoid the necessity for costly subsequent improvements.

The guide provides a useful discussion of the criteria to take into account when developing different bicycle facilities, but most importantly offers design specifications for different treatments.

Shoulders

Shoulders are especially useful on rural roads and major arterials: 'Where it is intended that bicyclists ride on shoulders, smooth paved shoulder surfaces should be provided and maintained.' Shoulder widths are recommended to be a minimum of four feet (1.2m) when intended to accommodate cyclists. Shoulders with lesser widths should not be signed as bikeways. Where vehicle speeds are higher, i.e. 35 mph (57 km/h or more), and/or the percentage of trucks, buses and recreational vehicles is high, additional width is desirable.

Wide kerb lanes

'On highway sections without bike lanes, a right lane wider than 12 feet (3.7m) can better accommodate both bicycles and motor vehicles in the same lane . . .'. In general, a usable lane width of 14 feet (4.3m) is desired.

Cycle lanes

The guide stresses that bike lanes should always be one-way facilities, carrying cyclists in the same direction as adjacent motor vehicle traffic. Wrong-way riding, which two-way bike lanes would encourage, is a major cause of bicycle accidents in the US.

Bike lanes should be a minimum of 4 feet (1.2m) wide. In certain situations, 5-feet (1.5m) lanes are recommended, such as where a bike lane is next to a parking lane, or where conditions at the edge of the road are dangerous. A shared bicycle and parking lane should be a minimum of 12 feet (3.7m).

Cycle paths

Under most conditions the AASHTO guide recommends a width of 10 feet (3m) for two-way bike paths, but also offers 8 feet (2.4m) as a minimum adequate width where bike traffic is low, pedestrian traffic is occasional, there are safe passing places, and where maintenance can be carried out without vehicles damaging the edge of the trail surface. Where pedestrian or bicycle flows are especially high, 12 foot (3.7m) paths are recommended.

The AASHTO guide also covers maintenance issues, intersection design and many other technical details of facility development. In the ten years since its first publication the guide has served as a model to state design manuals and guides. New Jersey, Ohio and Florida (1982) and Arizona (1989), each have their own set of standards and North Carolina will soon publish a state-of-the-art design manual.

Areas of US expertise

The preceding review of bicycle facility programmes in the United States provides quite an encouraging picture. However, very few of the gains have been made at the expense of the speed, comfort and cost of cars and their drivers. Each year federal, state and local governments spend $75 billion (£40 million) on highway construction and maintenance. Traffic volumes increased by an average of 4.2 per cent annually throughout the 1980s, and are projected to continue to grow at 2.5 per cent per annum until 2009.

The cost of ever-increasing reliance on cars is starting to catch up. Congestion now costs the economy an estimated $120 billion (£64,000 million) in 1989, affecting 70 per cent of all urban peak-hour Interstate travel. Air quality costs the nation around $40–50 billion (£22–27 million) a year in health damage alone, and traffic crashes total more than $300 billion (£160,000 million) annually in injuries, deaths, property damage, pain, grief and suffering.

In urban and suburban areas across the United States, planners, politicians and private sector interests are starting to work to reduce this awful toll. New Clean Air Act mandates and a revamped national transportation programme have provided fresh impetus to these efforts. A primary target is the reduction of single-occupant car commuting.

This pressure has spawned many innovative and interesting efforts to promote cycling in the United States. Other well-developed and unique bicycle programmes in the US can also provide useful models for European governments.

The development of bicycle programmes

The Bicycle Federation of America has identified the three most important ingredients for success in making communities more bicycle-friendly. In all of the locations mentioned earlier in the chapter at least two of the three elements mentioned below are present.

1   A bicycle coordinator. Having a full-time staff member in the Highway Department makes it possible to review and influence the policies, practices and programmes of that agency to incorporate cycling as part of its normal routine. Coordinators are also able to initiate and design special bicycle facilities.
2   A bicycle advisory committee. The involvement and support of active citizens and groups is essential to the success of a bicycle programme. Such a committee can provide focus, continuity, volunteers and community input into developing and promoting the programme.
3   Responsive and supportive politicians, professionals and public. The goals of a bicycle programme will not be achieved by one coordinator and a few bicycle advisory committee members. Cycling needs to be 'institutionalised' within the community so that every agency, neighbourhood group and private concern is involved in making the programme work.

Thirty of the 50 states have full- or part-time bicycle coordinators, and there are more than 100 cities and counties with staff dedicated to bicycle programmes. New transportation legislation passed by Congress in late 1991 requires every state to have a bicycle and pedestrian coordinator. The City of Seattle has six staff working on bicycle and pedestrian projects, as does the state of North Carolina. Areas such as Boulder, Colorado; Portland, Oregon; and San Diego, California, have both city and county staff working together to promote cycling.

Bicycles and transit integration

Cyclists have limited access to most urban rail transit systems, usually in the off-peak hours and at weekends. Those such as the Washington D.C. (WMATA) and Miami systems require riders to pass a short test to demonstrate knowledge of handling bicycles in the system. These two systems also have comprehensive programmes to provide bicycle parking lockers and stands at stations. WMATA has over 600 lockers and more than half are usually rented out to long-term customers.

In San Diego, bicycle racks and almost 800 lockers have been installed at trolley and bus stops and park-and-ride sites. Lockers at the trolley stops have a waiting list for users. A 1988 survey of users found that each rider bikes 3.6 miles (5.8km) to the locker and rides on the trolley for a further 11 miles (18km), saving themselves an average of $750 a year (£410). Sixty-nine per cent reported they would drive alone to work if storage facilities were not available.

In recent years, however, more attention has been focused on cycle access to bus systems. AC Transit (Oakland, California) and the San Diego Transit agency have racks fitted to the front of buses on certain bus routes. In Phoenix, Arizona, the transit agency launched an experiment in March 1991 with racks on three bus lines. More than 900 riders travelled with their bikes during the first two months of the programme. The Dallas Area Rapid Transit Agency and the Santa Clara Valley County Transit Agency allow bicycles inside buses, and the Seattle metro system and Caltrans (San Francisco) operate buses with trailers to carry cyclists over particular obstacles.

Bicycle parking ordinances

Most city and county governments have, for many years, required certain levels of car parking in residential, commercial and retail developments, and the principle is being extended to cycle parking in more and more communities. For example:

- In Boulder, Colorado, at least 10 per cent of the number of car parking spaces must be provided for bicycles at commercial, retail, recreational and residential developments.
- Arlington County requires cycle parking spaces at employment centres to be dependent upon the number of employees, rather than the number of car parking spaces.
- In Tucson, Arizona, the local ordinance requiring minimum levels of cycle parking also specifies different types of parking facility depending on location and likely uses (i.e. short-term versus long-term parking).

Similar bicycle parking ordinances are in force in Palo Alto and Davis, California; Seattle, Washington; Portland and Eugene, Oregon; Austin, Texas; Gainesville, Florida; and Madison, Wisconsin. Federal legislation proposed in 1991 would require every federal government building to have a minimum level of cycle parking for employees.

Commuter encouragement programmes

Transportation demand management and congestion management by transportation control measures, ride-sharing programmes and trip reduction ordinances will be the feature of transportation agency activities in the 1990s. The cycling community has slowly been able to integrate bicycle promotion programmes into these activities.

Since 1989, Los Angeles area employers have been required to achieve average vehicle ridership targets among their workforce under Regulation XV, one of the nation's first Trip Reduction Ordinances. Similar regulations are being introduced in many areas failing to meet Clean Air Act air quality standards, and they are a considerable incentive for employers and government agencies to promote bicycling. Some of the programmes initiated as a result have been as follows:

Fleetwood Enterprises, Riverside, California: Cycling has been fully integrated into the company ride-sharing/car-pooling programme. Cyclists committed to riding to and from work two or three days a week can earn bonus points towards extra paid holidays or items in the company's 'Pool of Gifts' catalogue. Riders can also receive personalised bicycle storage lockers, may borrow a bike to try cycle commuting, and use the company cycle repair centre. A brochure promoting the company bike club, Mud Sweat and Gears, proclaims 'Fleetwood bicyclists are VERY SPECIAL! They don't bring cars into our parking lot!!!' Seventy-five of the 600 employees (12 per cent) now ride to work.

Bicycle Coalition of the Delaware Valley, Philadelphia: The coalition has produced a detailed employers handbook promoting bicycle commuting. Contents include a list of the benefits of cycling, commuter maps and tips, newsletters and profiles of existing bicycle commuters.

City of Glendale, Arizona: The city provides free bicycles (unclaimed stolen bikes obtained from the police) to employees committed to riding to work three or more days a week. Those who do so for 12 months are able to keep the bikes. Thirty-five of the 1,100 city employees are participating.

Bellevue, Washington: Four companies offer cyclists and pedestrians free car parking three or four days each month for the days when they cannot ride or walk.

Bike pools: Seattle and King County, Washington and Boulder, Colorado, are among the government agencies providing bikes for employees to use for site visits and other official business trips.

Many other companies and government agencies around the country provide maps for bicycle commuters, organise bike-to-work day events and commuter races between motorists and cyclists, produce fact sheets and brochures about bicycle commuting, and install cycle parking and shower facilities for employees.

Police on bikes

While the concept of having police patrol on bicycles is nothing new, the alacrity with which police departments across the United States have been adopting bike patrols is remarkable.

The Seattle police department is credited with starting the revival in 1988. By September, 1991, more than 130 police forces in 35 states had introduced patrols of between two and 26 riders. The City of Philadelphia was due to launch a patrol team of 32 riders in 1991.

Most cycle patrols carry out regular police work, concentrating on drug offences and other street crimes, but bicycles are also utilised by parks police, university campus police and security forces.

In 1990, the first 'Beat the Streets' competition between police departments was held in Seattle, and the League of American Wheelmen (LAW) sponsored the first 'Police on Bikes' conference for potential and existing bike patrols in Tucson, Arizona in May, 1991.

In their Police on Bikes Survey Report the LAW quote a Las Vegas bike patrol officer extolling the virtues of the programme.

The Department purchased and equipped 15 mountain bikes, completely outfitted the entire team, uniforms and equipment, for $18,000 (£10,000). This put ten officers on the Strip. The cost of one fully-equipped black and white patrol car without an officer is $23,000 (£13,000). Maintenance on a bicycle: $120 per year. Average maintenance cost for a patrol vehicle (including fuel): $6–8,000 (£3–4,500) per year.

Consider the following statistics. Between May 23 and September 8, 1990 the Bike Team handled 850 calls for service, took 941 reports, issued 1,058 misdemeanor citations, wrote 943 traffic violations, stopped 1,440 vehicles, stopped and spoke to 1,396 people, field interviewed 327 folks, made 49 felony arrests, 308 misdemeanor/gross misdemeanor arrests and recovered 16 stolen vehicles.

Almost every police department using bike patrols remarks on the tremendous public response to seeing police on bikes, and bicycle clubs and organisations have welcomed the sight of law enforcement officers riding bikes (with helmets, of course) as they lend legitimacy to the activity.

Conclusions

The popular perception of the United States as a society dominated by the car is still pretty accurate. While cycling is a phenomenally popular recreational activity and bicycle commuting is growing fast, it remains a poor alternative to the car in most communities for most trips. The United States offers very little choice in the transportation sector.

Gasoline remains at an absurdly low price compared to almost every other nation in the world. The real cost of gas has fallen since the 1970s and is still only $1.10 a gallon (18 pence per litre). More than 80 per cent of employees have free parking provided at their place of work, and the tax benefits for this free parking far outweigh those offered to transit users.

Federal Highway Administrator Dr. Thomas Larson stated at the 1990 Pro Bike Conference in Washington D.C. that 'bicycling and walking are two overlooked options in our national transportation mix'. The same could be said of almost every mode other than the private car.

Ten years prior to this statement a study completed for the Federal Highway Administration found that

a compact land use arrangement, combined with the provision of pedestrian and bicycle facilities, has the greatest potential for realizing a shift from the automobile to walking and bicycling.

The same report also put the promotion of cycling into perspective:

. . . it appears that in order to accomplish even modest increases in the levels of bicycling and walking, a family of measures of incentives must be implemented. This is precisely what motorized traffic enjoys and takes for granted. The infrastructure for automobile travel includes not only the street and highway system, but also safe levels of lighting, ubiquitous parking facilities, and a proliferation of signs, signals and controls aimed at a safer driving environment. . . . Assuming a need for travel exists, it is perhaps this type of commitment to a mode that is needed to insure its acceptability and success.

During the 1990s there is a real opportunity for that infrastructure for cycling to be developed. The Congress has shown more interest in cycling initiatives than ever before, and the federal agencies (including the Department of Transportation) are giving non-motorised modes more attention. In 1992 the Federal Highway Administration will complete a National Bicycling and Walking Study commissioned by the Congress.

With the added incentive of the Clean Air Act and new federal transportation legislation strengthening the planning process at the state and metropolitan area level, the opportunity to effect change at the local level will be present. Twenty years of experience in facility design and planning and programme development can now be put to good use. The United States will be the land of opportunity for cycling in the 1990s.

References

American Association of State Highways and Transportation Officials, 1991, *Guide to the Development of Bicycle Facilities*, AASHTO, Washington, D.C.

Bicycle Federation of America, 1991, *Nonmotorized Travel Facilities Integration Project*, Pierce Transit, Tacoma, Washington.

Bicycle Institute of America, 1991, *Bicycling Reference Book 1991-92*, BIA, Washington, D.C.

Bicycling, 1991, 'A trend on the move: commuting by bicycle', Rodale Press, Emmaus, Pennsylvania.

Bikeways Oregon, 1981, *Bicycles in Cities, The Eugene experience*, Eugene, Oregon.

Burden, D., 1989, *The Florida Bicycle Program: Aluminum Anniversary*, Florida Department of Transportation, Tallahassee, Florida.

Clarke, A., 1990, *Bicycle Program Specialist Survey*, Bicycle Federation of America, Washington, D.C.

League of American Wheelmen, 1991, *Police on Bikes Survey Report*, LAW, Baltimore, Maryland.

Martin, S., 1990, 'The 10 best cities for cycling', *Bicycling* magazine, April, Rodale Press, Emmaus, Pennsylvania.

Minnesota State Bicycle Committee, 1991, Plan B: *Letting Bicycling Work for Minnesota*, State of Minnesota, St. Paul, Minnesota.

Oregon Department of Transportation, 1988, *Bicycle Master Plan*, State of Oregon, Salem, Oregon.

US Department of Transportation, 1980, *Bicycle Transportation for Energy Conservation*, NTIS (National Technical Information Service), Springfield, Virginia.

US Department of Transportation, 1981, *Feasibility of Demand Incentives for Nonmotorized Travel*, NTIS (National Technical Information Service), Springfield, Virginia.

Wilkinson, W., 1986, *Selecting and Designating Bicycle Routes: A Handbook*, Bicycle Federation of America, Washington, D.C.

Index